INTERIOR
DESIGN
PRACTICE

EDITED BY
Cindy Coleman

ALLWORTH PRESS
NEW YORK

14   13   12   11   10   5   4   3   2   1

Published by Allworth Press
An imprint of Allworth Communications, Inc.
10 East 23rd Street, New York, NY 10010

Cover design by Geoff Bock, *Interior Design* magazine
Interior design by Mary Belibasakis
Page composition/typography by SR Desktop Services, Ridge, NY

ISBN: 978-1-58115-675-1

Library of Congress Cataloging-in-Publication Data
Interior design practice / edited by Cindy Coleman.
      p.   cm.
ISBN 978-1-58115-675-1
1. Interior decoration—Practice.   I. Coleman, Cindy.
NK2116.I59   2010
747.068—dc22   2009044555

Printed in the United States of America

Contents

I. BACKGROUND

1: Evolution of the Profession 1

2: Growing a Profession 17

3: Legislation Issues 33

4: The Regulatory Organization 47

5: The Legal Environment 57

II. THE WORK PROCESS

6: Scope of Service Matrix 79

7: Pre-Design Services 85

8: Programming for Change 93

9: Schematic Design: Communicating the Design Spirit 103

10: Design Development: Designing the Project 109

11: Contract Documents and Working Drawings 117

12: Contract Administration: Getting Started 129

III. MANAGEMENT ISSUES

13: Managing the Marketing Process 157

14: Financial Management 185

15: Goals of Project Management 195

16: Managing the Client Relationship 217

Contributor Bios 239

Index 245

SECTION

Background

1

Evolution of the Profession

BY CINDY COLEMAN

Introduction

Interior designers can trace their profession to many who preceded them, from the cave painters at Lascaux to the creators of the frescoed interiors at Pompeii to the holistic architecture, interiors, and furnishings of Robert Adam and Thomas Jefferson in the eighteenth century, and Frank Lloyd Wright in the twentieth.

In the mid-nineteenth century, during the Industrial Revolution, the farm economy, though still robust, was gradually supplanted by a new industrial economy centered in or near the great, developing American cities of New York, Boston, and Chicago. The transition from farm to industry allowed Americans to see their houses as more than shelter and a place to sleep when work outdoors was done. Industrial workers' days were not necessarily shorter than those of farmers. However, for industrial workers and city dwellers in particular, home became a refuge that provided physical comfort and even aesthetic pleasure in contrast to the noisy, gritty, and physically exhausting atmosphere of the factory.

As women had more time to spend on the comforts of home, the large department stores of England and America developed and included sections devoted to drapery and upholstery. Specialty retailers included Liberty of London for fabrics and Tiffany and Affiliated Artists in New York, which produced lamps, vases, and other finely crafted decorative items.

At the end of the nineteenth century in England and America, the arts and crafts movement developed as a direct response to the Industrial Revolution. Its members, including William Morris, Charles Voysey, and Gustav Stickley, celebrated handcraft and deplored the social conditions, as well as the machine-made designs, that the Industrial Revolution had created. The arts and crafts movement created small workshops devoted to woodworking, pottery, and weaving and brought together artists and architects to study the interiors as well as the exteriors of buildings. Design integrity within the contemporary cultural and social context was the concern not only of the arts and crafts movement but also of other groups, including the Wiener Werkstratte and the Bauhaus, which developed and flourished in the twentieth century.

Sensitivity to the role of design in society is as relevant in the twenty-first century as it was at the dawn of the twentieth. Some, in fact, have referred to the twenty-first century as "the design century." Today, design is relevant as never before, particularly to the world of work.

Following World War II, business theories and practices began to evolve and proceeded at a manageable pace; with the widespread use of computers in the 1980s, that evolution picked up speed and continues to do so today, when the only organizational constant is change. After World War II, the residential and corporate branches of the interior design profession began to move on separate tracks. Both have traveled rapidly, but each in a different direction. The interior designer's role as a professional consultant to business and organizations will be the focus of this chapter. It is important to emphasize, however, that design is a global language that transcends home, institution and workplace, geography, and culture. To be a designer is to understand what all men and women have in common—their humanity.

Interior Design Emerges as a Profession: 1900 to 1930

The formal study of interior design began in the United States at the end of the nineteenth century. Programs and curricula typically developed in art schools; at the great land-grant colleges of the Midwest, which were open to women and also boasted strong programs in home economics; and within academic programs in architecture, primarily at East Coast universities.

When interior design actually became recognized as a profession is a subject for debate. Some scholars believe that interior design was not acknowledged as an independent profession until 1897, when Edith Wharton and Ogden Codman, Jr., published *The Decoration of Houses*. The authors are considered the first to define the profession as it is viewed today by clarifying the difference between interior decoration, which deals with surface treatments, and interior design, which encompasses the design of interior spaces.

Elsie de Wolfe, a contemporary of Wharton's and a disciple of her approach, is considered to be one of America's first professional interior designers. Her expertise, however, was on the side of interior decoration, which she used with great skill in the creation of interiors for the industrialist Henry Clay Frick and other wealthy New York families. She also accepted commissions from the prominent Beaux-Arts architect Stanford White. Early-twentieth-century women who are also considered among the first design professionals are Nancy McClelland, who brought design services to the general public through the decorating department she established at Wanamaker's department store in Manhattan; and Eleanor McMillen, whose McMillen, Inc., is considered to be America's first interior decorating firm.

By the turn of the twentieth century, the Industrial Revolution had reached full maturity. Daily life in the developed world had become increasingly mechanized, and Thomas Edison's electric light bulb was adding time to the workday and changing the nature of work. At the same time, the seeds of the Information Age—a century in the future—were being planted with Bell's telephone in 1876 and Edison's subsequent inventions of the telephone transmitter, the stock ticker, the phonograph, and the movie camera. During the early part of the twentieth century, there was little if any distinction between residential and nonresidential interior design. It would not be until after World War II that North Americans would become open to the idea of hiring design professionals for their houses and offices as well. And as the century began, the archetype of the workplace was the assembly line that Henry Ford created to produce the Model T.

An early business theorist, Frederick W. Taylor, extended the assembly line from the product to the worker. Considered to be industry's first efficiency expert, Taylor conducted time-study experiments that he developed into the concept he called scientific management. In Taylor's view, human workers could—and should—function as mechanically as machines. If workers were discouraged from thinking creatively and independently and completely removed from decisionmaking, and if work was broken down into its simplest units, with all members of a single group of workers dedicated to identical tasks, efficiency was the result. Taylor's methods, developed for the factory, eventually found their way into offices, along with typewriters, calculators, and switchboards and the women and recently arrived European immigrants who were hired to operate them.

Ford's assembly line and Taylor's translation of it to human activity next found their way to business and the chart of organization. The hierarchical organization, with its mechanical, organizational, and psychological elements now delineated, was born and began to grow. Once a suitable interior was designed to contain it, it flourished.

In the corporate hierarchy, order ruled. To stay in control, however, the ruling order needed to keep an eye on the workers. Workplaces were designed for management, who typically constricted a large group of workers in a single, vast space. From the giant panopticon that was the top of the hierarchy, managers looked down over rows of workers at their typewriters or sewing machines or tables where they assembled the typewriters, sewing machines, Victrolas, and other machines that had become part of twentieth-century life.

At the turn of the twentieth century, the hierarchy was the metaphor for society in all its forms; the elevator, invented in 1857, suggested that, in a democratic American society, workers could aspire to access any level they chose. This was the era of the great retailers like Marshall Field, whose establishments were organized into departments, just like the Ford Motor Company. This was the era that saw the construction of the Eiffel Tower as a brand mark for Paris, along with the great railway hotels, large city apartment buildings, the modern hospital, and the first skyscraper office buildings.

In business, Taylor's scientific management prevailed, but he had his critics, who were concerned about issues that interior designers find themselves dealing with one-hundred years later. They included Mary Parker Follett of the Harvard Business School, whose humanist, behaviorist approach to the management of organizations represented the opposite side of Taylor's machine-tooled coin. In the 1910s, she championed such farsighted approaches to work and the workplace as "the law of situation" and cross-functional teams. She also insisted that individual workers, rather than being merely static units of work with a prescribed place on a linear assembly line, as Taylor would have it, contributed to the strength of the organization as a whole. She believed that within the organizational structure, men and women should be free to experiment until they found ways of working that were effective for the tasks at hand and for themselves, as individual human beings.

In the 1920s, Harvard was also the academic home of Elton Mayo and his colleague Fritz Roethlisberger, who are the acknowledged creators of the human relations movement and whose work also has contemporary implications. They conducted their famous Hawthorne experiments over a period of more than thirty years—from the 1920s to the 1950s—at the Western Electric Hawthorne Works in Cicero, Illinois. Their studies, which anticipated the current interest and advancements in ergonomics, focused on the physiological aspects of work, particularly the impact of various levels of illumination on workers' efficiency and the causes of fatigue. They also studied the psychological aspects of work and looked closely at employees' motivation, satisfaction, and personal wellbeing, particularly as these abstract states took form in workers' relationships with their supervisors.

The Harvard theorists, along with Chester Barnard at AT&T and other humanists, had created a groundswell against scientific management. It was now clear that not all work fit the model of Ford's assembly line. And simply because the assembly line itself depended on human beings but was, in fact, profoundly dehumanizing, it was time to step back and rethink the nature of work—and the workplace. The time had come for a paradigm shift in the way organizations were structured and in the way the physical spaces of organizations were designed. But then came World War II, and the hierarchy not only prevailed, but also joined the military.

The Bauhaus Arrives in America: 1940 to 1950

The end of World War II brought a period of prosperity to the United States that lasted almost twenty years. America had definitively won the war. By putting its own interests aside and contributing its physical and material resources to the war effort, corporate America was in large part responsible for the country's victory. Although American business quickly recovered from the war, the military mindset prevailed during the remainder of the 1940s. At the Ford Motor Company, decisionmaking was based on numbers; numbers and rigid control also defined management. This approach eventually led to systems analysis, a rational, mathematically rigorous method of decision making that was considered to be especially effective in situations of uncertainty.

The war effort had been American through and through, but now that peace had come, corporations wanted to reclaim their unique identities. They wanted new headquarters that would function like the great cathedrals of Europe—buildings that would announce the importance of these corporations to society, reflect their mission, embody their technological expertise, advertise their vision and confidence, and share their uniquely American exuberance. Corporate America looked to the architectural and design communities for its new image. It would be architects and designers associated with the Bauhaus in Germany who would make that image reality.

Founded by Walter Gropius at the end of World War I, the Bauhaus, or "building house," was conceived not only as a school but also as an artistic utopia that brought together artists, craftsmen, and workers. Its emphasis was on theory as well as application. Its goal, as Gropius stated in his 1919 prospectus, was "to unify all disciplines of practical arts as inseparable components of a new architecture." The Bauhaus, which could trace its roots to the arts and crafts movement in England and the Wiener Werkstatte in Austria, sought to humanize technology. Its curriculum taught the spectrum of arts and crafts, including planning and building; weaving; photography; the visual arts, including woodcarving, metalsmithing, and ceramics; and advertising and graphic design.

The members of the Bauhaus included the painters Paul Klee and Wassily Kandinsky; the architect Mies van der Rohe; the designers Josef Albers, Herbert Bayer, Marcel Breuer, and Laszlo Moholy-Nagy; and many others.

During little more than a decade, from 1919 to 1933, they produced works that have become icons of modernism. Bauhaus supporters included Albert Einstein, Arnold Schoenberg, and Marc Chagall.

After a post–World War I economic boom, the German economy deteriorated precipitously. One of the goals of the Bauhaus was to create an orderly worldview from the economic, social, and political chaos that prevailed in Germany between the two world wars. The Bauhaus was committed to giving its students "integrated personalities" and educating them in contemporary culture as well as artistic theory and technique. Bauhaus designs combined technological expertise with the school's philosophy of egalitarianism and dynamism.

The Bauhaus, however, existed in a climate of ascendant fascism. First located in Weimar, the school moved from there to Dessau, and finally, in 1932, to Berlin, where it stayed for less than a year. The Bauhaus closed voluntarily in 1933, unwilling to accede to the conditions of Hitler's Third Reich, now firmly in power. Many of the Bauhaus masters fled to America. In 1937 Walter Gropius took a position at Harvard, where Marcel Breuer later joined him. Mies van der Rohe settled in Chicago in 1938 and became the head of architecture at the Illinois Institute of Technology. Other "bauhauslers" soon joined him, forming the "new" Bauhaus that ultimately ushered the United States into the forefront of modern design.

Before World War II, the professionals who planned and designed office environments—known today as contract interior designers—were not identified with a discrete area of professional expertise. A doctor, lawyer, or corporation that wanted assistance in arranging an office interior space was referred to a furniture dealer, who provided desks, chairs, and credenzas, as well as sources for lighting, floor- and wallcoverings, and office equipment.

The selection of office furniture was primarily the domain of manufacturers' representatives, who were also responsible for delivery, installation, and customer service. There were exceptions to the rule, however—most notably, Frank Lloyd Wright. In his 1937 project for the Johnson Wax Company in Racine, Wisconsin, he designed not only the building but the interiors and furnishings as well.

Beginning in the 1930s, and especially with the prosperity that was to follow World War II, North Americans became open to hiring professionals to design their residences, especially with the growing celebrity and social cachet of decorators including John Fowler, Terence Herbert, Robsjohn-Gibbings, and Billy Baldwin. By definition, these residential interior decorators dealt with surface treatments, and their services were generally understood and valued. Films and popular magazines brought the idea of fine residential interiors to a broad audience. Eventually, women's magazines and particularly shelter magazines showed their audiences that, with the help of a professional, it was possible to turn the idea of a finely decorated residence into reality. Corporate clients, however, saw no need to call in a professional to design an office interior: in the business world, this service simply wasn't understood; or, if it was, it was considered to be the same as serious residential interior decoration—expensive and elitist.

In 1932, in connection with an exhibit at New York's Museum of Modern Art, Philip Johnson and John Russell Hitchcock had published *The International Style: Architecture Since 1922*, which clearly defined Mies van der Rohe's new building as a distinctive style. The international style had an immediate influence on corporate buildings, and later would influence residential architecture and interiors as well. Buildings in the international style have steel skeletons and eschew decoration. Their glass skins make them interactive, with the glass mediating between interior and exterior, between the buildings' users and the world outside.

These sleek new corporate buildings required interiors that were compatible with their exterior architecture. Recognizing the need for an innovative approach to the office environment, Florence and Hans Knoll established Knoll Associates in 1946 to design and manufacture furniture in the Bauhaus style. Florence Knoll, an architect who had trained under Eliel Saarinen and Mies van der Rohe, established the Knoll Planning Unit, a design studio that provided Knoll's furniture clients with interior architectural and planning services. The unit, which became a laboratory for interior spaces, experimented with the design, scale, and configuration of task-related furniture. One of Knoll's hallmarks was to insist on standardization of all of an office's design elements, with everything from furniture to stationery part of a coherent, seamless system. Although some corporate clients and their employees chafed at the Knoll approach and considered it too constricting, its rigor helped American businesses establish their identities firmly in the American mind. The Knoll approach was a precursor to the contemporary concept of branding.

Designers Learn to Study How Organizations Behave: 1950 to 1960

In the early 1950s, the New York office of Skidmore, Owings & Merrill (SOM) became one of the first major architecture and engineering firms to offer interior design as a professional service. SOM eventually became established as a world leader in contract interiors, providing design services for such major corporations as Pepsi-Cola, Chase Manhattan Bank, and Union Carbide. Under the direction of architect Davis Allen, SOM established its signature modern style.

By this time, Mies van der Rohe was established in America at the Illinois Institute of Technology (IIT) in Chicago. One of his colleagues at IIT was Herbert A. Simon, professor and head of the department of political and social sciences and a future Nobel laureate in economics. Simon's academic interest was the nature of organizations, which he viewed as not abstract and one-dimensional but concrete and complex, reflecting the individuals who comprised them. Simon maintained that, to understand how organizations make choices, it was first necessary to understand how people in organizations make decisions.

In the 1950s, the academy began to revive studies of human-centered work. At the Harvard Business School, the work of Malcolm P. McNair led to the development of organizational behavior as a new area of study. Conceived as a backlash against prewar concepts of human relations and the rigid systems analysis of the postwar years, organizational behavior was descriptive instead of prescriptive: it studied how organizations and workers actually did behave instead of recommending how they ought to behave.

Late in the decade, following the model of the Knoll Planning Unit, the larger furniture manufacturers established entities devoted to practical research. The Steelcase Corporate Development Center in Grand Rapids, Michigan, became a proving ground for the company's own designs. In 1958, another furniture manufacturer, Herman Miller, Inc., formed a research division to study the workplace. Herman Miller retained the artist-designer Robert Probst to direct the division and to convert his findings into design ideas. The result was Herman Miller's "Action Office," a system of free-standing panels, countertops, and file pedestals that were flexible and easy to configure, whatever the constraints or freedom of the interior space. This new "systems furniture" complemented Simon's theories and also echoed those of the prewar humanists who rejected the assembly line in favor of worker autonomy and flexibility. The modular elements of the Action Office could adapt to workers' changing needs and perform independently of a building's architecture.

Also in the late 1940s and 1950s, the husband-and-wife team of Charles and Ray Eames introduced their "recognition of need" philosophy of design, which insisted that interiors should be constructed primarily for the people who inhabited them and by the furniture and tools they needed to do their work effectively and efficiently. The Eameses believed that furniture should be appropriate, informal, egalitarian, ethical, and socially conscious. They used their talents to create furniture that was aesthetically pleasing, and by first studying human beings at work, they created furniture that actually improved the work process.

All of the Eameses work, from furniture to films, produced a deep, substantive reflection of America's technical ingenuity and particularly its postwar optimism. Their modular shelving and storage units, produced by Herman Miller, were the first products to combine the efficiency of mass production with integrity in design and materials. Previously, if corporate managers wanted custom furniture, the only sources were dealers who specialized in high-end furniture, or the architects of their buildings. The Eameses greatly influenced the product design industry, from furniture to lighting to general office equipment.

The Eameses' work was the genesis of the furniture and product design industry as it is known at the beginning of the twenty-first century. Their example, and their success, encouraged many designers and furniture manufacturers to establish productive, longstanding working relationships. Architects Mies van der Rohe and Eero Saarinen and designers Isamu Noguchi and Harry Bertoia produced chairs, tables, and lamps for Knoll International. In addition to work by Charles and Ray Eames, Herman Miller, Inc., produced designs by Isamu Noguchi and Alexander Girard, as well as the Comprehensive Storage System created by its design director, George Nelson.

Corporate Interior Design Finds Its Identity: 1960 to 1970

The 1960s in America saw widespread questioning and experimentation at all levels of society, from the personal to the institutional. Student protesters storming a university president's office and putting their feet up on his desk became one of the decade's many indelible visual metaphors. In a time that saw a U.S. president and other political leaders assassinated, civil rights marches proceeding peacefully alongside cities on fire and the Vietnam War back-to-back with TV commercials for toothpaste, the hierarchy was on shaky ground. Once the dust settled, it was clear that values had shifted and the time had come for the rigid hierarchy to relax and make room for individual talent and entrepreneurship.

The 1960s introduced the contract interior design profession as we know it today. While in the 1950s, architecture firms had begun to offer interior design services, the 1960s saw these interiors studios mature and develop into large, independent design firms that offered comprehensive interior design services.

One outstanding example is Gensler, Inc. In 1965, Arthur Gensler began his eponymous company in San Francisco with two colleagues and two hundred dollars. The company initially provided space-planning services to business clients. Since then, Gensler's focus has expanded from space planning and office interior design to comprehensive architectural services; the company has grown from one office to thirty around the world, with more than two-thousand employees.

The Interior Designer Joins the Management Team: 1970 to 1980

The volatile cultural climate of the 1960s and early 1970s may or may not have contributed directly to the ascendancy of the open office. Nevertheless, it was in the 1970s that major American corporations, including General Electric, began looking to Peter Drucker for management consulting expertise.

Drucker, who coined the term "management by objectives," was one of the first to see the information economy developing and with it a new type of employee—the "knowledge worker." Drucker also insisted that decentralization should be the model of a company's corporate structure, and many companies took Drucker at his word and extended decentralization to real estate.

Until the 1970s, office buildings and particularly corporate headquarters were primarily located in major cities. The obvious advantages were access to business services, workers, and transportation. But high rental costs, combined with the competitive advantage of new and rapidly changing technology, escalated the cost of new construction and maintaining existing structures. It became expensive, if not prohibitive, for a large company to relocate to another downtown building that offered up-to-date infrastructure, the required technology, and other amenities. Soon, companies began to move their headquarters from the city to the suburbs, with its abundant land and low-cost spaces. The workforce followed, continuing the boom in suburban and exurban housing developments and shopping malls that began after World War II.

These trends, in turn, led to the speculative office building. In response to the exodus of businesses from the city, real estate developers created an entirely new type of office complex. Suburban buildings were no longer created in the image of their corporate tenants, like the Seagram Building or the CBS headquarters in New York City. Instead, developers created anonymous groups of buildings on cheap and vast expanses of land, much of it unused farmland. The model of a low-profile, meticulously maintained corporate campus replaced the intense, vertical office tower. In keeping with its emphasis on cost control, the speculative office building was basically a shell that required the most efficient, most cost-effective use of space. This requirement demanded an entirely new type of professional: the space planner.

In the space-planning process, the first step is programming. The space planner interviews the client and, through questionnaires and face-to-face meetings with workers and their supervisors, determines the amount of space required for various functions. Projected growth or shrinkage is factored in, and the collected data help the planner determine the amount of space needed for each function or employee. The end result establishes the square footage the client requires. Armed with this information, the real estate broker can shop the various spaces or buildings on the market, looking for the most favorable lease option. If the client is considering more than one building, the design firm rejoins the team to organize the program information into a space plan showing locations of partitions, doors, and furnishings. This allows the client to visualize how the organization will fit into space in one or more buildings.

Many large interior design firms were formed during this time, with several created for the sole purpose of offering space-planning services. Between 1974 and 1984, the number of jobs in the United States, many of them occupied for the first time by women, increased by approximately 24 percent. Commercial interior designers became increasingly competitive, positioning real estate brokers as intermediaries between their firms and their clients.

For the industry, this situation was a double-edged sword. Interior design professionals entered the decisionmaking process earlier than ever before, which gave them an opportunity to expand their role and increase their influence. Many interior design firms became experts at analyzing building options and expanded their services to include a full range of pre-lease services. This ultimately positioned designers as consultants who offered valuable advice that would have a strategic and economic impact on their clients' businesses.

The downside, however, was that, interior design firms that provided only space-planning services contributed to the confusion about what a professional interior designer actually does. Traditionally, a new tenant's landlord had paid for space planning. The fee for this service was extremely low, averaging five cents per square foot. Full-service interior design fees, meanwhile, averaged three dollars per square foot. Many clients did not understand the differences between space planning and comprehensive interior design services that include an expanded scope of services. A contract interior designer has expertise in conceptual design, design development, contract documentation and furniture specification, and contract administration. In addition, qualified interior designers have the technical knowledge to integrate architecture and construction and the ability to create interiors that not only are efficient, cost-effective, comfortable, and aesthetically pleasing, but also make workers more productive.

On a parallel track during the 1970s, as large interior design firms grew to accommodate the increasingly specialized needs of their corporate clients, residential interiors were created by practitioners associated with small or frequently solo design firms that offered a much more abstract product—good taste. Beginning in the late 1950s, Mies van der Rohe created landmark apartment buildings in Chicago whose interiors were in spirit, if not in fact, made for Bauhaus furniture. In the 1970s, European and especially Italian furniture design, notably from the Memphis group, contributed to the creation of innovative residences. For the most part, however, especially in America, homes that were professionally decorated recalled scaled-down versions of traditional British or Continental interiors. Following their training, as well as public perception, residential specialists were recognized experts at furniture, finishes, and overall visual presentation. They were not considered—nor did they consider themselves to be—strategists or planners. The public perception of "interior design" had solidified early in the twentieth century. In the intervening century, particularly in corporate America during the decades following World War II, the definition changed but the perception did not.

The widespread misunderstanding about their expertise put interior designers on the defensive. Since clients who were knowledgeable about design were the exception rather than the rule, designers were forced to explain and justify the value of design. The situation was exacerbated for designers in the late 1970s with the beginning of the country's first post-World War II recession.

The 1970s were a wake-up call for corporate America. Not only was the economy shaky, but Japan, Inc., also offered formidable competition. The corporate hierarchy was by now on the endangered list. W. Edwards Deming, an independent business consultant, had been an advisor to the Japanese after World War II. His concept of the learning organization, which he developed in the 1950s, had helped Japan achieve its own postwar business recovery. Deming believed that insights into the system and useful ideas for changing it should find their way upward from the bottom of the organization, not be handed down from above. He encouraged companies to foster their employees' intrinsic motivation and insisted that no one is better equipped to resolve systemic problems than the people who work with the system daily and know it best. A true visionary, Deming foresaw the transformation of the American economy from goods to services and steered companies toward an emphasis on quality and customer satisfaction. He is popularly known for his concepts of "total quality management (TQM)" and "quality circles."

Globalization signaled the beginning of the end for the bureaucratic mindset, particularly when it came to corporate design. The days of rigid design standardization were clearly over. As they acknowledged global influence and competition, corporations knew that developing new business approaches was part of the deal.

The Computer Joins the Workforce: 1980 to 1990

By the early 1980s, global competition had forced America to completely rethink the way it did business; in addition, advances in computer technology had reached critical mass. The resulting profound change for organizations, the workplace, and individual workers created a host of euphemisms for the word lay-off—reengineer, downsize, and rightsize among them. Just as the early 1980s brought profound change to the structure of business, it also changed the way corporate leaders thought about their companies' real estate holdings, offices, and equipment. The 1980s brought radical change to the profession of interior design as well.

In the 1980s, companies continued the workplace economies that they had introduced during the heyday of reengineering. Because workers spent a greater amount of time at the office, they became attached to their computers and their workspaces. For the first time, interior designers needed to understand the concept of social dislocation as it applied to the workplace. Ergonomic and health issues came up as well. Workers complained that computers produced eye strain. The repetitive keystroking used during word and information processing created something entirely new: carpal tunnel syndrome. Long hours sitting in one place produced back problems and made choosing a well-designed office chair not only a matter of aesthetics but a health and insurance issue as well. Interior designers began to take a holistic approach to their work and explore new areas of knowledge, such as management and the social sciences, that their education may not have included.

The furniture systems that had been designed in the 1960s and 1970s, though an ideal solution for their time, were not able to address the technologically and physiologically based problems of the new workplace. Now, interior designers were called upon to do no less than integrate furniture, technology, ergonomics, building systems, and the environment. Design professionals not only had to expand their skills and knowledge, but they also needed to change their work style. Specifically, they had to learn to work quickly and collaboratively with their clients and to see office design from the perspective of every position on the organizational chart.

For a time, the speculative office building and its emphasis on first-time costs had relegated interior designers and furniture manufacturers to the periphery of the business decisionmaking loop. The new client-designer collaboration brought designers and manufacturers together for the first time in decades. Designers had gained a deep, fundamental understanding of workplace issues. Manufacturers realized that they could intensify the partnership if they listened to what designers had to say and learned from it. In addition, they could add the critical component of research to their knowledge base. Manufacturers began behavioral and observational research to study different solutions to workplace problems; that research continues to the present.

The economy was moving rapidly, too, with the high-risk economic climate creating great fortunes almost overnight. Talented residential designers, including Peter Marino, Sister Parish, and Mark Hampton, saw their once small firms burgeon during the 1980s. Their clients became more significant as well. In addition to increasingly high-end residential work in New York and cities around the world, many received commissions to restore landmark residences and public buildings in the United States and abroad; others created and licensed their own lines of furniture or home accessories. At the same time, shelter magazines hit their stride. Computerized printing techniques made color reproduction beautiful but relatively inexpensive, and magazines like *Architectural Digest* had influence to match their circulation. On the residential side of the street, interior design was becoming big business and remains so as we draw near the end of the first decade of the twenty-first century.

Global competition, coupled with a recession in the late 1980s through the early 1990s, lured many American interior design firms—corporate and residential alike—into the global market. These firms, particularly those specializing in corporate interiors, were lauded for their understanding of the building process. Some corporate design professionals, however, were criticized for bringing large but efficient buildings to countries where they were culturally problematic. Many European workers, for example, consider direct sunlight and fresh air to be standard office equipment and found it hard to adjust to permanently closed windows, closed-off interior cubicles, and air conditioning.

As an outcome, a new breed of interior design professional had emerged. The weak economy of the early 1990s required many design firms that had been successful in the previous two decades to redefine their own businesses. In addition, the design profession became capital-intensive rather than labor-intensive. To rationalize the expense of capital expenditures for new technology, design firms began expanding the scope of services they provided. Many followed corporate America's lead and downsized, reengineered, or even closed their doors. Those left standing were stronger and better qualified to work in partnership with their clients and found themselves equal to their clients not only in business sophistication, but often also in taking the leadership role.

The Societal Implications of Design: 1990 to 2000

By the mid-nineties, as the media was doing its job exposing the many corporations and their executives' unethical behaviors, people like William McDonough and Michael Braungart (*Cradle to Cradle*) and later, Al Gore (*An Inconvenient Truth*), were busy educating the world about social and environmentally responsible design.

In 1993, the U.S. Green Building Council (USGBC) was founded as a not-for-profit organization to promote sustainably designed buildings. To assist educating the design and client community, the USGBC developed the Leadership in Energy and Environmental Design (LEED) rating system and exam as a framework for meeting and assessing sustainable goals. In response, designers embraced this system as being good, but also good for business—a source of competitive advantage.

Competition among the interior design profession, tougher than ever before, no longer comes from within the built environment—architects, contractors, manufacturers, or other interior design professionals. For this decade and the future, competition is much more diverse: industrial designers creating "experiences" for clients, management consultants assessing business and real estate goals, and marketing consultants creating appropriate images and branding. All are being called in to do the work of interior design.

As an outcome, the work of design is much more strategic; it's consultative, interdisciplinary, and focused on positive performance. Knowledge of business, behavior, sociology, technology, and environmental factors is critical.

To design spaces well, interior designers have developed methodologies to study the users of the spaces they design, and they must continuously cross back and forth among many different terrains of knowledge. Successful outcomes are those solutions that reflect the way people actually live, work, study, and play.

Conclusion

Since the early twentieth century, American designers have primarily been concerned with visual symbols and artifacts. The current information revolution, however, has shifted the designer's focus away from the exclusively visual toward the interaction of people with each other, the spaces they jointly occupy, and the environment they reside in. A new definition of symbol and artifact acquires meaning only in the relationships people create with the things and the spaces around them.

The relevance of Frederick Taylor's theories ended with the last century. As the third millennium continues, the machine and the linear assembly line no longer work as metaphors for the social organization. The accurate metaphor now—fragile, robust, and continually changing all at once—is the human brain itself.

Today, successful design firms are embracing the brain-as-metaphor and taking a holistic and nonlinear approach to the process of providing design services. Now, more than ever, effective design demands widespread collaboration and the integration of ideas from diverse sets of participants. To design spaces well, interior designers must continuously cross back and forth among many different cultures and terrains of knowledge. In this sense, like the brain, design connects discrete areas of knowledge to all other elements of culture.

Interior designers' professional competence today, and in the future, depends on their full participation in the information revolution. Designers must consider learning a lifelong enterprise and transform what they know into a deep understanding of the role of the designer—the professional who makes it possible for human beings to accomplish their goals individually and as participants in whatever organization or situation they are part of. The journey will no doubt be difficult, but in undertaking it, designers will continue to enhance their role and their importance to society.

2

Growing a Profession

BY EDWARD C. FRIEDRICHS

Introduction

Some historians of interior design believe that the profession really started in 1965, when a Cornell-educated architect named Art Gensler opened a small firm in San Francisco focused on corporate office design. An entrepreneur by nature, Gensler saw that the demand for interior design services among corporate clients (and those catering to them, like the owners of office buildings) vastly outstripped the supply of firms prepared to provide these services competently. While there were others, like SOM's Davis Allen, specializing in corporate office interiors, Gensler went beyond them in organizing his small architecture and design firm around this market.

In doing so, he helped to separate interior design from architecture and interior decoration and establish its identity among the design professions. As this new book on interior design practice demonstrates, the process that Art Gensler helped set in motion succeeded in creating a new profession, yet even now, interior designers are struggling to gain official sanction for its title and practice and to define their boundaries. This struggle pits them against architects and residential interior decorators, both of which claim—with some legitimacy—to practice interior design.

To put this in perspective, consider that it took centuries for the architecture profession to define itself, secure its boundaries, and finally obtain public sanction for its title and practice. Even today, the American Institute of Architects and its state and local offshoots battle with building designers, contractors, engineers, interior designers, and others over the question of who is entitled to design what in the built environment.

One reason for the struggle is that interior design is a hybrid profession whose roots can be traced back to architecture, the fine and decorative arts, graphic design, and even home economics. Especially at a larger scale, designing building interiors is a collaborative process. Interior designers are routinely part of teams that include architects, engineers, and other professionals and specialists. In this context, these "border wars" are meaningless. The interior designer's specific contributions are what matter.

Interior Design as a Profession

Until recently, interior design has been a self-certifying profession, similar to urban and regional planning (with its professional appellation, "certified planner"). In many states, individuals are still free to call themselves interior designers, regardless of their qualifications, and to offer interior design services. Only a business license is required.

This is beginning to change. Regional chapters of both the American Society of Interior Designers (ASID) and the International Interior Design Association (IIDA) are pushing hard now to secure for interior designers the same protections—of title and practice—that architects now enjoy in the United States. Architects are licensed on a state-by-state basis, and their activities are overseen by registration boards that administer licensing examinations, issue licenses, and discipline their licensees for malpractice and other practice act infractions. To advocate change in the interest of their profession and their clients, design professionals should understand the nature of the arguments currently made for and against professional protections and the factors that justify protecting interior design as a profession.

Arguments and Counter-Arguments

Historically, professions and trades have sought to limit entry to their ranks and guard their traditional privileges by eliminating potential competitors. When possible, they have used the law to support this gatekeeping. California Governor Jerry Brown, in the late 1970s, proposed to "sunset" the practice and title acts of a wide range of trades and professions, including architecture and landscape architecture. They all resisted him by arguing that public health, safety, and welfare would suffer if registration ended. That was their only possible argument; in America, anything else would be restraint of trade.

In seeking to license the title and practice of interior design, ASID and IIDA are also making a public health, safety, and welfare argument. Opposing them, understandably, are architects and interior decorators, their main competitors among design professionals, who question whether such public health considerations apply. Some architects question the need for state sanction of interior design practice, given its focus on non-load-bearing structures. Some interior decorators and residential interior designers argue that the requirements put forward by the proponents of interior designer licensing go beyond what is actually needed to protect public health, safety, and welfare. That would make those requirements exclusionary and therefore in restraint of trade.

The arguments for and against licensure have a political component as well. A dispute in the early 1980s in California pitted licensed architects against registered building designers—a category created as a compromise to preserve the traditional rights of draftsmen, carpenters, and others who design houses and small buildings. Similarly, the AIA and its civil, professional, and structural engineering counterparts regularly bicker over what their respective practice acts allow them to design or engineer. Similar compromises can be expected for interior design in relation to architecture, interior decoration, and residential interior design.

The legal and political possibilities available to both sides in arguments for professional protections will continue to cloud rather than resolve the issue of what constitutes a profession, so let's consider other factors that justify interior design as a profession.

PROFESSIONALISM

Traditionally, professionals have pointed to their credentials as evidence of their professionalism. This is what separates them from lay people, paraprofessionals, and "mere technicians." However, David Maister—a well-known consultant to professional service firms—argues that while these things may point to competence, true professionalism depends on attitude. A professional, in Maister's view, is a "technician who cares"—and that entails caring about the client.

In defining professionalism, Maister lists the following distinguishing traits:

- Taking pride in your work (and being committed to its quality)
- Taking responsibility and showing initiative
- Being eager to learn
- Listening to and anticipating the needs of others
- Being a team player
- Being trustworthy, honest, loyal
- Welcoming constructive criticism.[1]

His point is that professionalism is not just education, training, a certificate or license, and other credentials. In saying that these things are *not* the *sine qua non* of professionalism, Maister is really arguing for a client-responsive professionalism—as opposed to one that uses its credentials and presumed expertise as an excuse for ignoring or even bullying the client.

Arrogance is an issue in the design professions. Too many designers regard their clients as patrons, not partners. Design commissions become opportunities to further personal ambition rather than meet the client's goals and needs. The implication is that design is self-expression, that the creative process is largely, if not exclusively, the province of the designer alone.

Although there is inevitably an aspect of self-expression in the design process, its creative power is enhanced, not diminished, by collaboration. In collaboration, we become partners in a larger enterprise, and that gives our work its energy and spark. In arguing for "professionals who care," Maister is drawing attention to the collaborative nature of their relationships with their clients. It's a partnership to which both parties contribute their expertise. Formally, professionals act as the agents of their clients. As professionals, they have other obligations that impact this relationship—obligations that are intended, among other things, to protect clients from themselves. However, designers who assume they "know better" than their clients miss the opportunity to get into their heads and understand their world. They need that knowledge to connect their work to the client's larger goals and strategies, the real starting points of innovation in the design process.

What Makes Interior Design a Profession?

Interior design is a profession in part because of designers' special skills and education, but also because of designers' special relationship with their clients. According to *Webster's*, a profession is "a calling requiring specialized knowledge and often long and intensive academic preparation."[2] An art is a "skill acquired by experience, study, or observation, an occupation requiring knowledge and skill, and the conscious use of skill and creative imagination especially in the production of aesthetic objects."[3] A craft is "an occupation or trade requiring manual dexterity or artistic skill."[4] These definitions stress a difference in training, suggesting that professions alone require university study. That difference doesn't precisely hold anymore, since both arts and crafts are taught at the university level. Recalling David Maister's definition of a professional as a "technician who cares," we might ask, "Who benefits from the care that interior designers exercise in the course of their practice?" Clearly, the beneficiaries are those who use the settings that they design.

In defining the professional practice of interior design, the National Council for Interior Design Qualification (NCIDQ) provides the following description of its scope:

Interior design is a multifaceted profession in which creative and technical solutions are applied within a structure to achieve a built interior environment. These solutions are functional, enhance the quality of life and culture of the occupants, and are aesthetically attractive. Designs are created in response to and coordinated with the building shell, and acknowledge the physical location and social context of the project. Designs must adhere to code and regulatory requirements, and encourage the principles of environmental sustainability. The interior design process follows a systematic and coordinated methodology, including research, analysis and integration of knowledge into the creative process, whereby the needs and resources of the client are satisfied to produce an interior space that fulfills the project goals.

While accurate as far as it goes, this definition misses the heart of the matter. The real subject of interior design is enclosed space—that is, the *settings* within buildings that house human activity. First and foremost, interior designers are concerned with how people experience these settings and how design supports their different activities. These concerns form the core of the interior design profession's specialized knowledge.

Educating Interior Designers

Like architecture, interior design is taught through a combination of studio work and coursework—the former a remnant of the old apprenticeship system that characterized architecture and the arts and crafts. In addition to studio training in design and visualization, professional interior design programs typically provide a foundation in:

- Human factors
- Materials and systems
- Codes and regulations
- Contracts and business practices

Unlike architecture, most interior design programs do not address the engineering side of building construction—e.g., coursework in the static and dynamic analysis of structure. Interior design also differs from architecture (and interior decoration) in its concern for every aspect of the interior environments that people use every day.

The human experience in these settings is a broad topic that takes in history and culture, human psychology and physiology, organization theory, and benchmark data drawn from practice—along with lighting, color theory, acoustics, and environmental concerns, universal access, and ergonomics. These subjects need to be part of the professional interior designer's education and training.

How do interior designers gain an understanding of client and user needs? "By asking them" is a reasonable answer for smaller projects, but larger ones make use of social science research methods such as participant observation, network analysis, and surveys. Exposure to these methods through coursework in anthropology and sociology is helpful, especially as strategic consulting emerges as a specialty within the profession. (Strategic consulting seeks to align a client's real estate and facilities strategies with its business plan. Typically, it helps the client define its real estate and facilities program and establish the quantitative and qualitative measures of its performance.)

Business clients expect their design teams to understand the strategic context of their projects. Coursework in business and economics can begin that process; immersion in the industry, by reading its journals and participating in its organizations, is the next step. Once designers reach a certain level of responsibility, management becomes part of their job description. Coursework in business and management can make this transition easier.

A KNOWLEDGE OF SUSTAINABLE DESIGN PRINCIPLES

Building ecology, as the Europeans call it, needs to be part of the interior designer's knowledge. They should know how to design to conserve nonrenewable resources, minimize waste, reduce CO_2/SO_2 levels, and support human health and performance.

INTERIOR DESIGN'S CULTURAL IMPACT

Settings, the designed spaces within buildings, are "where the action is." When human or organizational change occurs, settings are where it takes place first. As my colleague Antony Harbour points out, the U.S. workplace has been dramatically transformed over the last forty years, but U.S. commercial office buildings still have the same floor plan. The settings have changed much more than their containers. Although settings are more ephemeral than buildings, they have equal if not greater cultural impact.

Interior Designers and the Workplace Revolution

Because of the economic pressures of recession and globalization and technological developments such as bandwidth, the workplace has undergone profound change in the last decade. While technology is given credit for the productivity gains that have swept the U.S. economy in this period, interior designers who specialize in the workplace have had a major role in helping U.S. companies integrate new technologies and work processes. Alone of the design professions, they understood that these settings are the "connective tissue" that could make this happen.

Interior design professionals understand that design fuels organizational change, regardless of the scale of its application. Think about where we work today. Behind the modern city, whether it's London, Tokyo, or New York, are nineteenth-century assumptions about work—that it occurs at specific times and in specific places, for example. Now people work "anywhere, anytime," and there are compelling reasons, such as the problems of commuting, to distribute work geographically.

Not only has the locus of work changed in our culture, but the mode of work has changed as well. In the last century the workforce moved from Frederick Taylor's "scientific management" to ways of working that are increasingly open-ended, democratic, and individual- or team-tailored. Along the way, the workplace changed, too. Taylorism was about efficiency (and uniformity). What followed shifted the focus to effectiveness (and diversity). What's the difference? As Peter Drucker explains, "Efficiency is doing things right; effectiveness is doing the right thing."

The Modern movement, aping Taylor, took "Form follows function" as its credo. Today, though, we might amend this to "Form follows strategy." If design firms are now involved in strategic consulting, it's because interior designers paved the way. Their ability to give form to strategy gave them an advantage over competing consultants because they knew how to make strategy actionable.

Yet this focus on strategy does not entirely explain the impact that interior designers have had on the workplace. More than people in any other profession involved in the design of these settings, they have been able to use their knowledge of workplace culture to design work settings that genuinely support the people who use them. Interior designers make it their business to know how people actually inhabit and experience the built environment. The best of their work consistently reflects this understanding. The licensing controversy notwithstanding, interior designers today are valued members of building design teams precisely because they bring this knowledge to the table.

Interior designers who specialize in work settings for corporate, financial, and professional service clients have done some of the most valuable research on the workplace in recent years. Former Gensler colleagues Margo Grant and Chris Murray, for example, have done pioneering work documenting the changing strategic goals of these companies and how they play out in spatial terms. Their benchmarking studies give Gensler and its clients a wealth of comparative data about facilities trends across the developed world's economy. Needless to say, this is a competitive advantage in the global marketplace.

An Evolving Profession

As Peter Drucker points out, it used to be the case that the skills needed in business changed very slowly:

> My ancestors were printers in Amsterdam from 1510 or so until 1750 and during that entire time they didn't have to learn anything new. All of the basic innovations in printing had been done . . . by the early sixteenth century. Socrates was a stone mason. If he came back to life and went to work in stone yard, it would take him about six hours to catch on. Neither the tools nor the products have changed.[10]

Today, though, we are in the midst of a period of remarkable technological innovation, equivalent in its impact to the cluster of spectacular breakthroughs that occurred in the last quarter of the nineteenth century. Technological innovation is one reason that professions evolve. Social change—the evolution of "everyday life" and its values—is another. "Faster, cheaper, better!" is the catch phrase of the new economy. Every shaper of the built environment faces these related changes, as clients demand a new responsiveness. Design professionals should rethink linear and segmented processes, reflecting nineteenth-century practices, and begin to envision how everyone engaged in designing and constructing the built environment should approach their practice to achieve the speed, responsiveness, and innovation that clients require.

Bandwidth's Implications: New Tools, Processes, and Practices

The bandwidth revolution has given interior designers an entirely new set of tools—not just for design, but also for collaboration. As is true for most innovations, their early applications were focused on existing practices. Today, though, there is a new generation of designers at work who grew up with these tools. As they move into the mainstream of practice, they will start to use them to reshape practice.

Bandwidth is transforming the production process: how furniture, furnishings, and equipment get from designer to manufacturer to end-user. It makes it possible to both speed the production process by tying it more directly to purchasing and to consolidate orders to secure bigger production runs and better prices, and it creates a world market for these products that should increase their variety.

Bandwidth also makes it steadily easier for virtual teams to work collaboratively to "construct" a virtual setting in three dimensions. This collaboration is not just between people but computers, too, so that in time fabrication will follow design without the need for detailed working drawings. As this becomes more seamless (and more common), it will extend to other aspects of construction. At some point, "design/build" may really be a single process. Currently, we are only halfway there. We have a lot of the infrastructure in place, but the interface is still maddeningly primitive. At the same time, we are trying to use the infrastructure to support traditional practice models. It may take a "push" from the outside, like another oil shock that makes the price of airline tickets less affordable, to force designers to change their ways and embrace virtual collaboration wholeheartedly.

Thanks to bandwidth, manufacturing has gone from Henry Ford's assembly line, with its uniform products, to Dell's (and now Ford's) "mass customization." It's the same now with services, too. Across the economy, customers want the cost advantages of mass-market mass production, along with the quality and performance of custom design.

Designing in Four Dimensions

At the same time that clients demand an increased level of responsiveness, their knowledge workers demand "consonance" in the workplace. They approach potential employers looking for a "fit" with their values and lifestyle. In a buoyant economy, they can afford to be selective—and intolerant of "dissonance." The built environment gives form to consonance and provides its framework. To keep pace with social and technological changes, design professionals must learn to see that framework as one that changes with time—and design in four dimensions.

The current rate of technological change suggests that designers will face considerable pressure to practice with time in mind. Both the container and the contained—"structure and stuff," as Stewart Brand put it in *How Buildings Learn*[5]—change over time, but at different rates of speed. The trends of mass customization and congruence suggest that settings will change frequently, which puts pressure on the rest to facilitate the change. This brings us back to *sustainability*, which also demands of "stuff" that its residual value be salvaged through recycling and reuse.

Designing in four dimensions means rethinking our conceptions of buildings. "There isn't such a thing as a building," Frank Duffy asserts. Buildings are just "layers of longevity of built components"—they exist in time. What matters for their designers is their "use through time." Duffy finds the whole notion of timelessness to be "sterile" because it ignores time as the building's fourth dimension[6]—they exist in time, so they have to evolve to meet its changing demands.

Also working from a "time-layered" perspective,[7] Brand proposes a holistic approach to time-sensitive design. He identifies six components of buildings: site, structure, skin, services, space plan, and stuff. While interior designers are focused on the last two, they have good reason to want to influence the rest: they all impact the building's use through time. To exercise this influence effectively, of course, they have to understand their characteristics and possibilities of the other elements of the built environment. An interior designer doesn't need to be an engineer, or *vice versa*, but both need to know enough about the other's business that they can approach the building in a holistic or time-layered way. As Brand says,

> *Thinking about buildings in this time-laden way is very practical. As a designer you avoid such classic mistakes as solving a five-minute problem with a fifty-year solution. It legitimizes the existence of different design skills, all with their different agendas defined by this time scale.*[8]

To be responsive to the user in the building design process, interior designers need to have this broader knowledge of the building and its components. In the end, their ability to sway others in the design/delivery process will rest primarily on issues of use over time—issues that are primarily functional and strategic and that constantly require new skills.

Looking Ahead

Interior designers face resistance in their quest to have their profession recognized as a separate one. In 1999, the American Institute of Architects put a task force together to review the question of licensing interior designers. As *Architectural Record's* Robert Ivy reported,

> *They found that interior designers seek to distinguish themselves from less-qualified decorators, protect the right to practice, establish gender equity in a field dominated by men, and earn the respect of their fellow professionals.*[9]

"The designers' viewpoint is consistent," Ivy added, citing his magazine's April 1998 roundtable discussion with interior designers. "Despite their gains in the industry, they feel slighted or disparaged by architects." Yet, he says, "there are unavoidable differences between architects and interior designers":

> *Architectural education is more rigorously focused on life safety, as well as structure, building science, and codes. By contrast, the AIA task force reported that in the 125 interior design programs currently available, education can vary from two to four years, and current testing for certification focused more on aesthetics than safety. The differences do not stop with pedagogy. Architects tend to engage the entire design problem, considering not only the contents of the interior, but the interior's relation to the exterior envelope, its construction and building systems, and the natural and human-made surroundings. A healthy building— light-filled, safe, and promoting human habitation—should be architects'*

professional norm. When we are operating at a high level of accomplishment, our work is holistic, integrating complex technical systems and social require- ments into structures that engage the landscape, sustain their inhabitants inside and out, and enrich the community.

Should interior designers be licensed? Here is Ivy's answer:

Our own professional status reflects a public trust we have earned at high cost, and it should not be diluted. . . . Practice legislation may not be the panacea that interior designers seek, if it is achieved without commensurate, funda- mental changes in [their] education and experience.

But interior designers can make a strong case that they should be afforded the distinctions and protections that are a part of other design professions such as architecture. No less than architects, interior designers are engaged in "the entire design problem." As advocates of the user, and as designers who are "fourth-dimension sensitive," they are often the first ones in the building design process to point out how one or another of the building's components make it harder for its settings to evolve easily to meet new needs. As their interest in indoor air quality demonstrated early on, they are concerned with quality of life, too—with user performance, not just building performance.

Interior design came into its own in the 1990s as settings came to be seen as a strategic resource. The catchphrase, "Place matters!"—so emblematic of the second half of this decade—turns out to be literally true. When people have real choice about when and where they spend their time, the quality of these settings—their ability to support them in their desired activities— becomes crucial, often the deciding point. A "place" can be part of the land- scape or cityscape, a building or building complex, or an enclosed indoor or outdoor setting. The word implies a richness and wholeness that mocks the design profession's efforts to carve it into parts.

The built environment today has immense range and diversity. So much development embraces multiple uses. The time dimension of buildings is changing, too, with more of the components wanting (or needing) to be ephemeral rather than "permanent." Already, many projects today feature hybrid teams that are organized around each project's particular blend of uses and timeframes. These interdisciplinary teams are the future. They expose each profession to the others and give all of them a shared perspective about "place" that transcends each one's necessarily narrower view.

This shared viewpoint may eventually give rise to entirely new profes- sions, which we may no longer be willing to categorize as "architecture" or "interior design." In time, the division between design and construction may prove to be an artificial boundary, no longer justified by practice. Professions are conservative forces in society, constantly resisting pressures to change, yet constantly placed in situations where the need to change is obvious and imperative. New professions arise in part because old ones fail to adapt.

Compared to architecture, interior design is still in its infancy—a profession that is just now marshalling its forces to secure the recognition to which it feels entitled. All this is taking place against the background of our entrepreneurial and bandwidth-driven era. How important is it, in this context, to secure the profession's boundaries or win state sanction for its practice? If it helps strengthen the education and training of interior designers and encourage them to meet their responsibilities as professionals, then it is probably well worthwhile.

Especially today, it's hard to predict the future of the interior design profession. One clear way to prepare for it, though, is to make the education of interior design professionals much more rigorous. This argues for a more comprehensive curriculum, as I have outlined previously, and for a four-year professional degree program at the undergraduate level.

It also argues for learning, as Peter Senge calls it—not just maintaining skills, but actively learning from practice. Senge's point, admirably made in his book *The Fifth Discipline*,[10] is that work itself is a learning experience of the first order. Our interactions with clients, colleagues, and other collaborators provide constant glimpses into an unfolding future. If we are attentive, we can understand some of what the future demands and take steps to meet it appropriately. People who care about their careers and take their responsibilities as professionals seriously need to make learning a constant priority.

ARCHITECTURE'S STRUGGLE TO BECOME A PROFESSION[11]

Interior designers who anguish about the time it's taking to secure state sanction for their profession's title and practice should bear in mind that it took architects a lot longer. Arguments over who is and is not qualified to design buildings punctuate the history of the profession.

In the Middle Ages in Europe, the master masons were the building architects. During the Renaissance in Italy, artist-architects supplanted them. They were considered to be qualified as architects owing to their training in *design*. Architects like Brunelleschi and Michelangelo took a strong interest in engineering and technology, too, as they strove to realize their ambitious building projects. With Vitruvius, they believed that architecture was a liberal art that combined theory and practice. Master masons who apprenticed in the building trades were disparaged because their training was purely practical.

Yet the Italian Renaissance also saw the emergence of the professional in Europe's first true architect, Antonio Sangallo the Younger. Apprenticed to the artist-architect Bramante, Sangallo helped implement many of his later buildings. In time, he established a studio that is recognizably the prototype for today's architecture and design firms. The architectural historian James Ackerman has described him as "one of the few architects of his time who never wanted to be anything else."

Four diverging traditions emerge from the Renaissance: artist-architects trained in design; humanist-architects trained in theory; architect-architects focused on buildings and striving for a balance between theory and practice; and builder-architects focused on construction but still interested in designing buildings.

Artist-architects looked for patrons; architect-architects looked for clients. In the seventeenth and eighteenth centuries, we see this distinction played out between "gentleman" architects and the emerging profession. Thomas Jefferson counted architecture among his gentlemanly pursuits, a trait he shared with others of his class. Lord Burlington, who did much to establish the architectural profession in England, was widely criticized by his peers for his "unwonted" interest in the pragmatics of building construction. When the Institute of British Architects was established in 1834, noblemen could become honorary members for a fee. (Significantly, all connection with the building trades was forbidden.)

In the eighteenth and nineteenth centuries, English architects also faced competition from surveyors. In his *Dictionary* of 1755, Dr. Johnson gave essentially the same definition to the words "surveyor" and "architect." In England, the two professions were closely aligned over much of the nineteenth century, with both designing buildings. Engineers designed buildings, too. In 1854, one of them even won the Institute of British Architects' Gold Medal.

Professional Ethics

Like other professionals, interior designers must contend with ethical issues. Indeed, the issues can be quite similar to those of allied and other learned professions. Like architects, lawyers, and doctors, interior designers can also do bodily harm and financial damage if they practice incompetently or unethically. They can put people at risk by failing to be effective advocates of their interests, too. Here are some examples of these issues as they arise in interior design practice:

Life Safety

Designers often bemoan codes and regulations, but they exist to provide a minimum standard of health and safety. Failure to meet code can delay a project, which damages the owner, and can also cause bodily harm.

Confidentiality

Interior designers often have access to confidential business information—a planned acquisition, for example, or a new business plans or strategy. This knowledge is shared with interior designers only because it has a direct bearing on their work, and it is shared with them in confidence. Ethically, and often by contract, that confidence must be respected.

Conflict of Interest

Interior designers are their clients' agents, so they have an obligation to avoid or disclose to them any potential conflicts of interest. (Disclosure means that you are prepared to end the conflict if the client so requests.) The *appearance* of conflict can be as problematic as the reality. Just as voters worry when politicians get too cozy with special interests, clients start to wonder when interior designers accept gifts and junkets from contractors and vendors. The occasional lunch, party, box of candy, or bottle of wine is no problem, but all-expenses-paid vacation trips and other costly "perks" cross the line. They create the appearance if not the reality that design decisions—specifying a product, for example—are being made to repay favors rather than protect the interests of the client.

User Advocacy

Interior designers have a responsibility to users. If, in their judgement, a project's requirements—although legal—compromise user comfort and performance unacceptably, they have an obligation to try to change them, and to resign from the project if the client is unwilling to make the changes. Design professionals have a broader obligation to educate their clients on the value of design features that improve user quality-of-life and performance.

Competency

Professional competence reflects ongoing mastery of the skills and knowledge demanded by professional practice. Professional certification or licensing formally requires a level of mastery that necessarily lags behind what design professionals actually need (for example, FIDER's requirements do not yet specify that interior designers know the principles of sustainable design). That lag does not excuse professional interior designers from having to master these principles, though, or any new skills that are required to maintain their professional competence.

Interior Designers and Sustainable Design

In tackling the problem of indoor air pollution in the 1980s, the interior design profession led the way in raising public awareness of the value of sustainable design. As advocates for the user, interior designers have a special responsibility to understand sustainable design principles and evaluate their appropriateness for projects. Sustainability offers many opportunities to deliver added value for clients, too. As case studies by the Rocky Mountain Institute[12] have shown, the resulting gains in building and human performance provide a reasonable (and even rapid) payback on the client's investment, especially when these measures are used in combination. Here are some examples:

- Lockheed Martin Building 157, Sunnyvale, California: Lockheed Martin spent $2 million to add sustainable design features to this 600,000-square-foot office building that reduced its energy consumption and provided a higher quality work environment. Control of ambient noise was also achieved. Lower energy costs alone would repay Lockheed's investment in four years. Because the improved quality of the workplace reduced absenteeism by 15 percent, the investment was actually repaid in less than a year.

- West Bend Mutual Insurance Headquarters, West Bend, Wisconsin: West Bend gave the building a series of sustainable design features, including energy-efficient lighting and HVAC systems; roof, wall, and window insulation; and thermal storage. Utility rebates kept its cost within a "conventional" budget. The building is 40 percent more efficient than the one it replaced. It provides an "energy-responsive workplace" that gives users direct control of thermal comfort at their workstations. A study showed that the building achieved a 16 percent productivity gain over the old one. A productivity gain of 5 percent (worth $650,000 in 1992 dollars) is attributable to the energy-responsive workplace feature alone.

- NMB Headquarters, Amsterdam, Netherlands: this 538,000-square-foot project exemplifies what the Europeans call "integral planning": designing the building and its systems holistically to reduce operating costs and increase quality and performance. About $700,000 in extra costs was incurred to optimize the building and its systems, but this provided $2.6 million a year in energy savings—a payback of only three months. Employee absenteeism is down by 15 percent, too.

Gensler's experience reinforces the Rocky Mountain Institute's findings. On office campus projects, we've found that providing under-floor air supply and ambient lighting can reduce the cost of workplace "churn" (the need to shift workstations to accommodate changes in occupancy) from as much as $5 per square foot to less than $1. For an office campus in Northern California, these same features allowed us to redesign the entire workplace to accommodate a different set of users just six weeks before its opening—with no delays. By avoiding the cost of delay, the client essentially paid for the 10 percent higher cost of these features before the campus had even opened.

ENDNOTES

1. David H. Maister: *True Professionalism*, The Free Press, 1997, pp. 15–16.

2. *Webster's New Collegiate Dictionary*, G. & C. Merriam Co., 1977, p. 919.

3. *Webster's*, p. 63.

4. *Webster's*, p. 265.

5. Stewart Brand: *How Buildings Learn*, Viking, 1994, p. 13.

6. Quoted in Brand, pp. 12–13. The quotes are from Francis Duffy, "Measuring Building Performance," *Facilities*, May 1990, p. 17.

7. John Habraken took a similar position, initially in relation to housing, in the 1960s. See for example his *Variations: The Systematic Design of Supports*, MIT Press, 1976, and *The Structure of the Ordinary: Form and Control in the Built Environment*, MIT Press, 1998.

8. Brand, p. 17.

9. Robert Ivy, FAIA: "The keys to the kingdom," *Architectural Record*, September 2000, p. 17.

10. Peter Senge: *The Fifth Discipline*, Currency/Doubleday, 1994.

11. This brief account is drawn from Spiro Kostof, ed.: *The Architect*, Oxford University Press, 1977, pp. 98–194.

12. Joseph J. Romm and William D. Browning: *Greening the Building and the Bottom Line*, Rocky Mountain Institute, 1994.

3

Legislation Issues

BY DERRELL PARKER

Legislative History

The history of legislation regulating interior design in America began with the attempt to pass the first interior design regulation legislation in California in 1951. This attempt was not successful in creating new, groundbreaking legislation. It was, however, successful in bringing forward a perceived idea that the profession was changing and becoming more complex. It also forewarned practitioners of the need for legislation that would not only protect the health and safety of the public utilizing interior design services, but would also protect the practice of interior design.

Since that time, the face of interior design has changed dramatically, and through this evolution, the responsibilities of design professionals have become more complex. Today, interior designers are responsible for a variety of life safety issues that have, in the past, only been in the purview of other design professionals, such as architects and engineers. In many states and jurisdictions today, the designer is responsible for planning ingress and egress from interior spaces, many of them in large, complex high-rise projects. In many cases, the interior designer serves as the project programmer, planner, and lead design professional. Because of this evolution of responsibilities, one of the most important factors facing interior designers today is their right to practice the profession for which they are educated, experienced, and examined.

Designers may wonder why they should know the history of legislation in their field. They may believe that professional self-regulation is sufficient to ensure that the design profession fulfills its responsibilities. Like other professions that impact public welfare, there is a strong case for legal regulation of interior design. The professional interior design community, bolstered by advances in education and experience, has taken custodial responsibility for interior design in today's society. It has developed and promoted a scientific core of knowledge; formal education requirements, including a college-level accreditation system; and a professional examination to focus specifically on interior design. With this professionalization comes regulation—not only title acts (allowing designers to call themselves interior designers), but also practice acts (establishing standards for professional conduct), and ethical codes as well.

Conceived in the late 1960s and incorporated in 1974, the National Council for Interior Design Qualification (NCIDQ) seeks to create a universal standard by which to measure the competency of interior designers to practice as professionals. The birth of this examination came as a result of the growing complexity of the interior design profession and serves to identify to the public those interior designers who have met the minimum standards for professional practice. NCIDQ has become the hallmark examination for interior design legislation. In all states with interior design legislation, the NCIDQ is a requirement.

In 1982, Alabama became the first state to enact legislation for the regulation of Interior Design. This enactment became the catalyst for other states to pursue legislative actions. Interior Design professional organizations began to establish state-to-state coalitions for the sole purpose of gaining Interior Design Legislation. Today there are twenty-four states (Alabama, Arkansas, California, Connecticut, Florida, Georgia, Illinois, Indiana, Louisiana, Maine, Maryland, Minnesota, Missouri, Nevada, New Mexico, New York, Tennessee, Texas, Virginia, and Wisconsin), plus the District of Columbia and the territory of Puerto Rico, that have interior design regulation. Colorado is unique in that it has a Permitting Statute for Interior Design, which was passed in 2006. This Permitting Statute did not create new interior design regulation. It gives qualified interior designers permitting privileges. While regulation in some of the states is only for title, in others it regulates both title and practice.

In 1989, the National Legislative Coalition of Interior Design (NLCID) was formed. This coalition was established to aid those state coalitions. NLCID strived to aid state coalitions by becoming a clearinghouse for information about local and national legislative activities. In 1989, the AIA Interior Design Accord was signed. This accord was an agreement entered into by several design organizations; namely The American Institute of Architects (AIA), the American Society of Interior Designers (ASID), The Institute of Business Designers (IBD), and the International Society of Interior Designers (ISID). The purpose of the accord was to establish guidelines for states seeking to implement interior design legislation. The general scope of this accord was that the AIA would not oppose attempts by interior designers to gain legislation at state levels so long as those attempts were only for title acts and did not include any regulations that pertained to definition of scope of practice, sealing of construction documentation, or performance of any design that affected health or life safety.

While the accord was looked on by some to be an instrument to aid interior designers in obtaining title act legislation for their states, many people on both sides of the accord perceived the document to be nothing more than a way for the AIA to control how, and if, interior designers would gain legislation. The accord was abandoned by interior design participants in the spring of 2000, primarily because of a lack of participation by both interior designers and architects. What had been written as a living evolving document had been allowed to wither and was no longer viable.

Today there are twenty-four states, as well as the territory of Puerto Rico and the District of Columbia, with varying forms of interior design legislation. There are now active coalitions in all fifty states, of which some are seeking to enact legislation acknowledging interior design as a profession, while others are actively pursuing modifications of existing legislation.

Practice Acts vs Title Acts

In some states, interior designers may not be able to practice until they meet the requirements of a title act, which establishes the qualifications they must meet before they can practice. Once they qualify to practice, they may be subject to legal requirements that limit the scope of and set the standard of professional conduct for their practice. The differences between the two types of legislation deserve some elaboration.

Practice Acts

Practice Acts define a particular scope of practice, as well as regulate the actual performance of such practice, by any individual registered to perform those services. Persons wishing to engage in the practice must demonstrate their ability to meet certain standards as set forth by practice legislation. These acts usually require aspects of education, experience, and examination. Practice acts are usually reserved for those professions dealing with health, safety, and welfare issues, such as architecture, engineering, and medicine. Professions are regulated by the state. This regulation is usually done by a state board made up of a group of peers appointed by the state's governor.

In states where interior design is legislated, government regulators have concluded that interior designers, especially those working in the commercial or contract arena, have a great deal of influence over the health, safety, and welfare of the public. Therefore, law-makers have insisted, in some cases, on practice legislation for their interior design laws. All practice acts require that the professional register with a state regulatory board. In most cases where practice legislation is enacted, professionals are also usually restricted from using a particular title until they have met specific qualifications outlined in the law.

Title Acts

Title acts are less restrictive than practice acts because practice acts are based upon the performance and ability of the registrant. Title acts define what professionals may call themselves. The most important reason for title acts is to enable the public to more readily identify those individuals who are qualified by law to use a certain title. This qualification ensures that the person has met the minimum standards required to provide competent services. These standards may or may not be set by education, experience, and examination. In states with title legislation, it is unlawful to use a title without first having met the qualifications as outlined in the state's laws. Title acts do not necessarily regulate who may partake or act in said profession; rather, they limit what practitioners may call themselves and how professional services are offered to the public. Any person who has not met the requirements for title registration set by the state may not represent or identify him- or herself by title. Title acts require registration with the appropriate state regulatory board.

Advocacy

The interior design profession is represented by a number of professional organizations. This discussion will be limited to those who are the most actively involved in the legislative arena: the American Society of Interior Design (ASID) and International Interior Design Association (IIDA). These organizations have played major roles in state-to-state coalitions seeking legislation for interior design. Both organizations have Government and Regulatory Affairs Departments that dispense information to their members. Legislative activities in state-to-state and national legislation may affect the associations' membership and the way they practice and pursue legislative agendas.

It is the mission of professional organizations, not only interior design but also architecture, engineering, etc., to assure that their members retain the right to practice and receive their fair share of the marketplace. Even so, the primary reason both ASID and the IIDA support legislative regulation of the interior design profession is to protect the health and safety of the public.

Along with the professional organizations, there are other collateral organizations who contribute to the efforts of interior designers to shape legislation passed to regulate the profession. These organizations do not operate in such a direct manner, but certainly their efforts are of no less importance.

One such organization is the Council for Interior Design Accreditation (CIDA). CIDA accredits undergraduate programs of interior design for the sole purpose of ensuring the highest quality of interior design education. A CIDA-accredited degree is not a requirement for registration in all states regulating the practice of interior design; however, it is recognized as the definitive accreditation in many states with regulatory legislation. The original accreditation body was FIDER, the Foundation for Interior Design Education and Research, founded in 1970. The name was changed in 2006 to CIDA, the Council for Interior Design Accreditation. It was felt that the new name more accurately described the mission of the organization.

Another collateral organization not involved in the actual legislative process is the National Council for Interior Design Qualification (NCIDQ). NCIDQ is involved in the examination process. Its membership is composed of the state and provincial agencies that regulate interior design. In all of the states and jurisdictions with legislation, interior designers must successfully pass the NCIDQ examination if they are to be registered as interior designers by the state. NCIDQ is also responsible for and maintains the model language available for states to use when they draft new legislation.

Model Language for Legislation Regulating the Interior Design Profession

Interior Design Model Language is, as the title indicates, a model that states may or may not choose to follow when they decide to draft legislation regulating the interior design profession. The model language is a living document, meaning that it is constantly changing and evolving along with the profession itself. The model language is domiciled at the headquarters of NCIDQ in Washington, D.C., and pertains only to the registration of interior designers. The model language is helpful in the effort to create a more uniform profession nationwide and can be used as a guideline to develop more standard and consistent laws from state to state. This standardization would allow for reciprocity between states that recognize interior design as a profession and would make it easier for design professionals to receive certification as interior designers in more than one state.

This model language, like that of other professions, outlines a definition of the profession of interior design and describes services that may be offered by the registrant. In addition, it outlines the education interior designers must achieve, the examination they must pass, and the experience they must accumulate before they can perform the tasks specified in the legislative definition of services. Model Language for Interior Designers requires that interior designers use a seal and obtain sealing powers to certify technical documentation. Without those powers, interior designers would not be able to submit their documents to building authorities or other governmental agencies for issuance of building permits. The Model Language also addresses the structure and duties of a state regulatory board. In the case of Interior Design Model Language, where health, life, and safety concerns are paramount, the regulatory board must address registrants who may cause harm to the public through neglect or error. Therefore, the model language contains provisions giving the state regulatory board enforcement and disciplinary powers. As in most laws, the model language offers an exemption clause. Exemptions are usually offered to members of other professions, who, by virtue of their education, examination, and experience, are also deemed qualified to practice in the interior design profession.

Coalitions

There are now interior design coalitions in nearly all states, working to enact legislation or revise existing legislation. These coalitions are supported by both the ASID and the IIDA through their government and regulatory departments. Each coalition focuses on its state and works to establish grassroots connections in that state. Who better than residents of a state to talk to legislators about why their home state needs legislation? State coalitions were originally formed so that legislation could be approached on a local level to give state lawmakers and local constituencies a face and a name.

Education

At this time, states that regulate the interior design profession require varying amounts of education from design professionals. One state has no educational requirement, while others require four- or five-year degrees. Most states do, however, require at least a two-year degree. Since 1998, NCIDQ has required that interior designers have at least a two-year degree to be eligible to sit for the examination. While some States recognize other examinations, the NCIDQ exam is the only one that has been adopted by all states and jurisdictions that have interior design legislation.

In 1968, the Interior Design Educators Council (IDEC) was founded with the primary purpose of advancing the needs of the educators of interior design professionals. In 1970, FIDER (now CIDA) was established. CIDA's primary purpose is to review and evaluate accreditation programs of interior design. CIDA accredits only undergraduate programs of interior design education. The accreditation is based on CIDA's Twelve Standards of Excellence for the Interior Design Profession. CIDA is in the review process for new standards at this time. These standards will be adopted in July of 2009.

- Standard 1. Curriculum Structure (The curriculum is structured to facilitate and advance student learning.)

- Standard 2. Design Fundamentals (Students have a foundation in the fundamentals of art and design, theories of design and human behavior, and discipline-related history.)

- Standard 3. Interior Design (Students understand and apply the knowledge, skills, processes, and theories of interior design.)

- Standard 4. Communication (Students communicate effectively.)

- Standard 5. Building Systems and Interior Materials (Students design within the context of building systems. Students use appropriate materials and products.)

- Standard 6. Regulations (Students apply the laws, codes, regulations, standards, and practices that protect the health, safety, and welfare of the public.)

- Standard 7. Business and Professional Practice (Students have a foundation in business and professional practice.)

- Standard 8. Professional Values (The program leads students to develop the attitudes, traits, and values of professional responsibility, accountability, and effectiveness.)

- Standard 9. Faculty (Faculty members and other instructional personnel are qualified and adequate in number to implement program objectives.)

- Standard 10. Facilities (Program facilities and resources provide an environment to stimulate thought, motivate students, and promote the exchange of ideas.)

- Standard 11. Administration (The administration of the program is clearly defined, provides appropriate program leadership, and supports the program. The program demonstrates accountability to the public through its published documents.)

- Standard 12. Assessment (Systematic and comprehensive assessment methods contribute to the program's ongoing development and improvement.)

Experience

For many years, in interior design as in many other professions, practical experience has been an important item for a professional's résumé. Indeed, most designers considered the value of experience only when they were trying to secure employment. Today, now that more states regulate design, design professionals are learning that the length and nature of their experience matters for obtaining certification to practice.

In many areas, the interior designer is realizing the value not only of the length of their employment-related experience in the design field, but also of the diversity in the type and quality of that experience. Because of the rapid changes in the field, it is of great importance that today's interior designer get broad-based experience in the profession. This experience becomes crucial when interior designers are required to meet demands for technical accuracy in documentation, in planning and programming, and in health and life safety issues. Just as the profession is evolving and responsibilities are becoming more complex, the value of diverse experience is increasing.

Along with the need for diverse experience, design professionals also need a monitored process to accurately document that experience. Until 1999, interior design had no program that monitored interior design experience. Now, however, NCIDQ is tracking experience for those persons who wish to take the NCIDQ examination. The Interior Design Experience Program (IDEP) is a monitored experience program that ensures that a design professional is exposed to and gains the appropriate experience in all areas of interior design, including those that will be a part of the examination. Up to the present time, the NCIDQ has measured experience for those candidates who wish to sit for the exam based upon the candidate's merit and letters of recommendation. When the new IDEP experience program goes into effect, all experience will be tracked and verified by NCIDQ. In states that rely heavily on experience, education, and examination as evaluative criteria for certification, this verification element becomes a very important component of a candidate's application for state registration.

Examination

In 1974, NCIDQ was founded with the goal that it would protect the public by identifying interior design practitioners competent to practice by administering a minimum competency examination for interior designers. It is the major credentialing agency for the interior design profession in the United States and Canada. NCIDQ offers a comprehensive examination that states use for licensure and professional certification of interior designers.

NCIDQ requires that candidates who sit for their examination meet an education requirement of at least two years in a formal interior design program of study and that they have at least four years of full-time work experience in the field of interior design practice. The NCIDQ examination measures minimum competency in the practice of interior design. It is the only interior design examination developed and administered in the United States and Canada by an agency that is independent from other interior design organizations. Since this examination is used by regulatory boards as a criterion for registration, and since regulation is based on protection of health, safety, and welfare, it is vital that this examination not be influenced by organizations within the profession. Within professional organizations, the primary agenda may be right to practice and market share for members, and not safety and welfare issues for the public. Without outside voices, the examination may become biased. NCIDQ continually changes and updates its examination and its procedure for administering the examination.

Regulatory Boards

Another goal of NCIDQ has been to establish a council of regulatory boards of interior design. This council is known as the Council of Delegates and, today, there are sixteen regulatory boards represented on the Council. Anytime state legislatures pass legislation that regulates a profession, there must be a state regulatory board to oversee the profession. In some states where interior design regulations are in effect, there are independent regulatory boards to oversee interior designers, while in other states, the regulatory board may be composed of many design disciplines, such as architects, engineers, and interior designers. Regardless of the structure, the duties, and the responsibilities of regulatory boards, they are much the same.

According to the state statute, boards register, license, or certify interior designers, and they maintain rosters of the persons who are registered, licensed, or certified for the purpose of identifying them. Regulatory boards have the power to discipline those registrants, licensees, or certified professionals who do not protect the health and safety of the public or who fail to adhere to the performance standards required of their profession. Regulatory boards may set and adopt rules of conduct for practitioners. Most regulatory boards are composed of practitioners of the represented profession or professions and one or more public members. The regulatory board is the venue through which the public can register complaints that a registrant, licensee, or certified professional has harmed someone's health and safety. The members of a state regulatory board are responsible to uphold the statutes governing the profession for which the board is formed.

Regulation in Light of the Way Design Professionals Practice

In 1904, Elsie de Wolfe began a career in what we now refer to as interior design in America. Nearly a century later, it is doubtful if Ms. de Wolfe would recognize the profession that she created. It was not until after World War II that the face of the building landscape began to dramatically change in the United States. The changes occurred with the onset of curtain wall construction, suspended ceilings, and central building systems, which allowed for environmental control and changes in construction methods. The changes to construction methods led to larger contiguous areas of interior real estate and the introduction of open office planning concepts. These events, along with the formation of large-scale corporations brought on by the post-war boom, all laid the groundwork for the interior design field and its responsibilities.

Today, interior designers are hired to complete tasks as varied as programming new or reused facilities and planning spatial layouts for large and small interior spaces. Interior designers develop programs for clients based on the varied needs of the end user. Design professionals provide project management and execute technical documents for construction, such as drawings and specifications. The interior designers of today must be able to perform multitasking in which they must exercise a high level of independent judgment and know local, state, and national codes. They must be able to negotiate contracts, schedule and budget projects, and coordinate work in progress. No matter what the project, they must be capable of identifying problems, analyzing requirements, and making realistic assessments, all within the confines of code, budget, and time constraints. Interior designers may work as independent consultants or as a part of a design team with other design professionals.

Whatever the role of the interior designer today, it is paramount to the profession that the health and safety of the public be protected at all times. Interior designers protect the health and safety of the public by being aware of the consequences of each of their choices and maintaining a direct knowledge of local, state, and national codes. For instance, when interior designers plan an exit route from an interior core space to a building exit system and design it in compliance with code, they are protecting the health and safety of the public who occupy or use the space. When interior designers demonstrate their ability to know where and how to place grab bars in handicap toilet rooms, or design an accessible counter where reach and approach are correct, they are protecting the health and safety of the public who uses those facilities. These components are not design elements that the designer can guess about or leave to chance. Before designers can approach them properly, they must possess a base of knowledge that they can access and apply.

In the last *Analysis for the Interior Design Profession* (1998), conducted for NCIDQ, commercial designers expressed their conclusion that some of the most important health and safety issues facing interior designers in the commercial field today were field survey skills, specification writing skills, knowledge of building codes, the Americans with Disabilities Act, and flammability and testing standards. When asked how interior designers create a safe and effective design solution, they responded that design professionals needed to have a knowledge base in the following areas:

- Verbal communication and basic language skills
- Working drawings
- Space planning principles
- Human factors (ergonomics)
- Professional ethics
- Barrier-free design
- Building codes
- Project management
- Interior construction
- Contract specifications

Self-Regulation: Ethics

The profession of interior design is like any other. No matter how much legislation regulates the field, a profession must still police its own practitioners. Most interior design professional associations have codes of ethics. Most regulatory boards have adopted these or their own codes of ethics for their registrants. While these codes of ethics are different for each group or organization, they are usually written to protect the welfare of the public the profession serves. Codes of ethics may deal with disclosure to a client; for instance, a code of ethics may require that the interior designer disclose a financial interest in a company that may be bidding on the client's project. Codes of ethics may cover truth in advertising. For example, they may provide that interior designers are subject to sanctions when they tell a client that they are capable of working on projects that require special knowledge, even though they have never done work in that particular area.

Codes of ethics adopted by the design profession play a key role in ensuring the honesty or integrity of the market place. In addition, regulatory boards use them as an additional method of protecting the public from unscrupulous practitioners, those who live up to the letter of the law as set out in the statutory regulatory scheme, but who may otherwise, through dishonest activities, put the welfare of the public in jeopardy. And while ethics are important to any profession, they cannot be legislated. Although regulatory boards may adopt a profession's ethics code or establish a code of its own, it remains up to the profession to establish and maintain its own standards of ethical conduct.

Team Assembly

Interior designers work with a variety of different professionals, from architects and engineers to contractors and art consultants. In the built environment, interior designers most likely deal with the largest amount of differing consultants. For instance, on a large architectural project, an architect's team may consist of the architect; structural, civil, electrical and mechanical engineers; an interior designer; and landscape architect. Similarly, depending on the size and complexity of the project, and interior designer's team may be composed of the interior designer and the lighting, acoustics, furniture, art, interior plantscaping, window covering, and furniture consultants. Regardless of the numbers or types of professionals on a project team, the interior designer must possess the ability to communicate with each one on a knowledgeable level and guide the project to conclusion. With the complexity of interior design today, no designer can effectively be a one-person show. Design professionals must rely on the expertise of other professionals, yet all of them must function as integral parts of the team.

Because of the onset of interior design legislation, it has become even more critical that interior designers be aware of how best to assemble a project team. Interior designers are now called upon more and more, not only to participate in the design team, but also to convene, control, and lead the team. In states with interior design legislation that allows for collaboration with other design professionals, the interior designer may serve as lead professional or professional of record. In some instances, the interior designer may be the lead, with the architect as consultant.

Understanding the Designer's Influence in a Regulated Field

Today's interior designer is a blend of technician, artist, sociologist, and psychologist. Interior designers must master the ability to bring facets of all of these elements to their work. They must have detailed technical knowledge of construction and codes, as well as a thorough understanding of health and safety issues as they pertain to the built environment. In addition, the interior designer must be capable of recognizing cultural changes and how they relate to the welfare of society.

To date, interior design has not been adequately acknowledged as a profession that requires a distinct set of core competencies that extend well beyond simple decoration; nor have the broad social and economic impact of the profession been recognized. Yet the increase in product testing, codes, ergonomics issues, environmental issues, civil rights legislation, and other government mandates testify to the increased level of knowledge and implementation skill required of the interior design professional. The prominence of these issues in laws, in regulations, and among the public underscores the need for legal regulation of the interior design profession.

Driven by cultural and societal changes, economic developments, and technological advances, the practice of interior design has become more cognizant of, and responsible for, public health, safety, and welfare. Even the most fundamental design service, such as space planning, which requires attention to corridor and aisle width in addition to reach dimensions, is critically concerned with the health and safety of the public

Today, we are living longer and enjoying better health than at any other time in history. Along with this longer life comes the need for more specialized interior environments. The graying Baby Boomers of today are more demanding and expectant of interior environments that not only provide for their healthcare services but also fulfill their cultural and social needs. To provide a viable professional service to these clients, today's interior designer must specialize, diversify, and develop more breadth in both education and experience.

Now that workers use the computer more and more, they also perform more work tasks in office environments. Those office interiors create very specialized environments. The interior designer must be cognizant of the nature of these environments and have a familiar working knowledge of such things as illumination, acoustics, ergonomics, and indoor air quality, along with the ability to properly plan space, interpret code, and plan for barrier-free design.

Design professionals can address these tasks only by developing knowledge bases through education, examination, and experience, and they must address these tasks, for their application is paramount to the protection of the health and safety of the public.

4

The Regulatory Organization

BY BETH HARMON-VAUGHAN

Modern Profession

THE OCCUPATION WHICH ONE PROFESSES TO BE SKILLED IN
AND TO FOLLOW, APPLIED SPECIFICALLY TO THREE LEARNED
PROFESSIONS OF DIVINITY, LAW, AND MEDICINE.
—*The Oxford English Dictionary (definition from 1541).*

Modern professions have emerged as occupations, which offer a unique value to the society in which they exist. By these definitions, interior design has developed into a true, modern profession over the past thirty years. It has experienced growing demand for sophisticated services, which enhance the client's quality of life as well as their bottom line. Through this growth, interior design has defined itself as a true profession, sharing characteristics of most other professions with a unique body of knowledge and theoretical foundation, standards for formal education, testing candidates for basic knowledge and skills as entrée into the profession, ethical standards, and legal recognition. Professions begin to define themselves through an institutional infrastructure, which develops and monitors standards of practice for the profession.

For interior design, two key aspects of the professional infrastructure are the Council for Interior Design Accreditation (CIDA) and the National Council for Interior Design Qualifications (NCIDQ). The Council for Interior Design Accreditation is a specialized accreditor whose mission is to establish standards for postsecondary education and then evaluate and accredit programs on the basis of those standards. NCIDQ develops and administers an examination for qualified, entry-level designers seeking professional status. The examination tests minimum competence in the theory, knowledge, and skills necessary to enter the professional practice of interior design and protect the public health, safety, and welfare. The exam is required for professional status in the North American interior design associations as well as license in the American states or Canadian provinces where interior design licensing is available.

Both CIDA and NCIDQ subscribe to the definition of interior design that has been endorsed by the International Interior Design Association, American Society of Interior Designers, Interior Designers of Canada, and the Interior Design Educators Council. CIDA and NCIDQ consider this definition as they address their missions of accreditation and testing. The definition states that the professional interior designer is qualified by education, experience, and examination to enhance the function and quality of interior spaces for the purpose of improving the quality of life, increasing productivity, and protecting the health, safety, and welfare of the public.

The professional interior designer:

- analyzes client's needs, goals, and life safety requirements

- integrates findings with knowledge of interior design

- formulates preliminary design concepts that are aesthetic, appropriate, functional, and in accordance with codes and standards

- develops and presents final design recommendations through appropriate presentation media

- prepares working drawings and specifications for non-load-bearing interior construction, reflected ceiling plans, lighting, interior detailing, materials, finishes, space planning, furnishings, fixtures, and equipment in compliance with universal accessibility guidelines and all applicable codes

- collaborates with professional services of other licensed practitioners in the technical areas of mechanical, electrical, and load-bearing design as required for regulatory approval

- prepares and administers bids and contract documents as the client's agent

- reviews and evaluates design solutions during implementation and upon completion

CIDA

The Council for Interior Design Education Accreditation is a specialized accrediting agency, accrediting interior design programs at colleges and universities in North America. Its mission is to ensure a high level of quality through 1) establishing standards for postsecondary interior design education in interior design education, 2) evaluating and accredit college and university interior design programs, and 3) facilitating outreach and collaboration with all stakeholders in the interior design community.

CIDA is recognized internationally by design professionals and is acknowledged as an information source for excellence in interior design education. As a specialized accreditor, the Council for Interior Design Accreditation is a member of the Association of Specialized and Professional Accreditors (ASPA) and recognized as a reliable authority on interior design education by the Council for Higher Education Accreditation (CHEA). CHEA is an association whose mission is to ensure good practices in accreditation by reviewing processes used by accrediting agencies.

Accreditation is a process unique to the United States and Canada that replaces government regulation of education found in most other countries. It is a process of self-evaluation and peer review that promotes achievement of high academic standards, making education more responsive to students' and society's needs. Standards developed by interior design practitioners and educators with concern for continued growth and development of the profession are central to effective accreditation. Graduates of CIDA-accredited programs receive an education that is recognized by the interior design profession as meeting requirements for entry into the profession. In the future, this factor may impact the right to practice in states with licensing or registration acts.

Though graduation from a CIDA-accredited program is not required to practice interior design, students can be confident that these programs voluntarily placed themselves under the scrutiny of the profession. Accredited programs have invested time, energy, and money to ensure that their graduates receive an education that meets the standards of the profession, which will serve them immediately after graduation and into the future.

History

The CIDA was originally established as the Foundation for Interior Design Education and Research (FIDER), a specialized accreditor of postsecondary education programs in interior design, in 1970. The founding organizations were the Interior Design Educators Council (IDEC), the American Institute of Interior Designers (AID), and the National Society of Interior Designers (NSID). AID and NSID merged in 1975 to form the American Society of Interior Designers (ASID). The intent of the founders was to promote excellence by developing standards for interior design education, acknowledging the increasing demands of an emerging profession.

In 1997, the professional societies' leaders joined FIDER trustees in developing plans to address the future of interior design accreditation. FIDER's governance structure was identified as a significant strategic concern. With the support of the founding organizations, FIDER was restructured in 1999 from a trust into a nonprofit corporation and in 2006 changed its name to the Council for Interior Design Accreditation to be more consistent with its mission. The new structure was designed to maintain productive connections with all "communities of interest" to ensure continued collaboration between interior design educators and practitioners. Today, CIDA maintains strategic relationships with those organizations.

The CIDA Board of Directors is responsible for ensuring that the organization fulfills its mission. The Board sets standards, determines the process through which accreditation occurs, maintains relationships with the design community, and secures funds and other resources. The Board of Directors is responsible for maintaining the legal, fiscal, and ethical integrity of the Council. Financial support for the Council comes from fees paid by institutions for accreditation; annual fees paid by programs to maintain their accreditation; and contributions from the profession, industry, and interior design press. There are nine directors on the Council Board, each serving a maximum of two three-year terms. A director represents each of the five constituent groups. Those five directors appoint four other directors who represent all other stakeholders in the profession. The executive director is an ex-officio member of the Board.

The mission of the Council of Interior Design Accreditation is further achieved through the work of additional commissions and committees. The Accreditation Commission and Board of Visitors are the hands-on volunteers, trained in the standards and evaluation process that are responsible for implementing the process of program accreditation. The Standards Council monitors the standards through periodic surveys. Standards are revised when significant or cumulative developments in the interior design profession occur, which must be addressed through education.

Because postsecondary interior design programs exist in different types of institutions, in 1999 the Council adopted a single set of standards for professional degree programs. These standards were developed through research with practitioners and educators to determine appropriate levels of preparation necessary to successfully enter the practice of interior design. The standards are structured around a series of educational outcomes rather than a prescribed length of time or number of credit hours. The panel of visitors assigned to conduct the on-site program review is responsible for evaluating evidence of these outcomes against the standards. The single set of standards focuses on theory, method, technical foundation, and skills necessary to practice interior design, as well as thirty credit hours of general education.

Beginning January 2000, new programs and programs applying for reaccreditation will be evaluated using the Council for Interior Design Accreditation 2000 standards. By 2002 all Council-accredited programs must comply with the standards including those programs currently accredited as preprofessional, two-year programs.

THE ACCREDITATION PROCESS

Accreditation is initiated when a program applies to the Council and meets the minimum standards for application. Once the application is accepted, the program prepares and submits a standardized self-study. When the self-study is received, the Council assigns an evaluation team composed of a three-person panel of qualified educators and practitioners and schedules the site visit. Program evaluation occurs through a site visit conducted by the evaluation team. Site visits are usually three days in length. During this time, the panel of visitors evaluates samples of student work and meets with faculty, students, administrators, and an advisory board. Specific program outcomes are reviewed against the Council standards. At the conclusion of the visit, the team prepares its written evaluation. The team report, with comments and recommendations, is sent to the Council Evaluation Committee and is then forwarded on to the Accreditation Commission for a final accreditation decision. The Commission may grant a maximum six-year accreditation or deny accreditation, depending on the program's level of compliance with the standards. The timeframe for the initial accrediting process can be twelve to eighteen months. Once the term of accreditation has expired, the program must be reevaluated using the same process to make certain it continues to meet standards and remains current with the changing demands of the profession. Volunteer interior design practitioners and educators supported by a professional staff conduct the Council accreditation process.

NCIDQ

The primary mission of the National Council for Interior Design Qualification is to develop and administer an examination, which tests minimum competency to enter the professional practice of interior design. Through the examination process, it serves to identify to the public the interior designers who have met the minimum standards for professional practice by passing the NCIDQ examination. The Council endeavors to maintain the most advanced examining procedures and continually updates the examination to reflect expanding professional knowledge and skills. It seeks the acceptance of the NCIDQ examination as a universal standard by which to measure the competency of interior designers to practice as professionals. NCIDQ is the only examination acknowledged by the International Interior Design Association, the American Society of Interior Designers, the Interior Designers of Canada, and the Interior Design Educators Council. In addition to responsibilities for examination, NCIDQ is charged with defining, researching, and updating bodies of knowledge; conducting field surveys; analyzing candidate performance; evaluating subject areas and item validity; developing and pretesting questions and problems; improving scoring; implementing grading and jurying procedures; reviewing education and practice requirements; and identifying public health, safety, and welfare issues.

To sit for the examination, the candidate must apply to NCIDQ and meet education and experience requirements. Once the application is accepted, the candidate is eligible to sit for the next scheduled exam session. The exam is structured as a two-day test. The first day, applicants take a series of multiple-choice tests that examine knowledge of codes, standards, and technical aspects of interior design. The second-day tests are practicum problems in which knowledge is tested through application. The exam is offered twice annually at proctored test sites throughout North America. Completed exams are sent to jury sites and scored by trained review teams. The candidate may retake sections that were not successfully completed.

History

Established in the late 1960s to serve as a basis for issuing credentials qualified professional interior design practitioner, the Council has been in effect since 1972. It was formalized as a not-for-profit organization when it was incorporated in 1974. NCIDQ's founders were the American Institute of Interior Designers (AID) and the National Society of Interior Designers (NSID), the two national organizations who were then preparing to merge into what became the American Society of Interior Designers (ASID). All national design organizations whose membership was made up in total or in part of interior designers were asked to join.

NCIDQ was founded as a separate council to certify, through a qualifying examination, the interior design practitioners who were competent enough to practice. They also study and present plans, programs, and guidelines for the statutory licensing of interior design practitioners. The incorporation charter of the Council provides membership for American state or Canadian provincial regulatory agencies. It does not offer membership to individuals. Representatives from state or provincial regulatory agencies and professional societies are appointed to serve as delegates on the NCIDQ Council of

Delegates for two-year terms. The NCIDQ Board of Directors with professional staff manages the activities and affairs of the Council, which has the right and authority to manage its affairs, property, funds, and policies.

Successful completion of the NCIDQ examination is a prerequisite for professional registration in American states and Canadian provinces that have enacted licensing or certification statutes to protect the health, safety, and welfare of the public. The NCIDQ examination must also be passed by every interior designer applying for professional membership in NCIDQ's constituent member organizations: American Society of Interior Designers (ASID), Interior Designers of Canada (IDC), and International Interior Design Association (IIDA). NCIDQ is a member of the International Federation of Interior Architects/Interior Designers (IFI), an organization representing many of the interior design associations around the world.

CERTIFICATION & LICENSURE

Certification is generally defined as a voluntary form of recognition of an individual, granted by a nongovernmental organization or agency. However, minimum competency in any profession is usually a baseline standard accepted by state and provincial governments for purposes of legal recognition. In addition to the development and administration of the professional competency examination, NCIDQ also administers a certification program for interior designers. Certification is available to practitioners who meet minimum competency standards for the practice of interior design. This certification includes minimum requirements for education and experience, as well as completion of the NCIDQ examination. NCIDQ certification is included among the license eligibility criteria in all American states and Canadian provinces with enacted statutes.

Certification by NCIDQ gives the interior designer a credential that acknowledges their preparation to professionally practice interior design through education, experience, and examination. NCIDQ certification serves as qualification for professional membership within interior design organizations, and, for nonaffiliates, represents a voluntary individual accomplishment. Certified designers receive a certificate that identifies them as a qualified practitioner ensures recognition of expertise and assists development and self-improvement through the individual's understanding of a body of knowledge to competently practice interior design.

RECORD MAINTENANCE

As a part of NCIDQ's ongoing effort to provide administrative support to facilitate legal recognition for interior design practitioners, the Council's

Board of Directors approved a record management requirement effected in 1990. Individuals pay an annual fee for record maintenance that enables NCIDQ to:

1 maintain an accurate mailing list of certificate holders for ongoing notifications pertaining to NCIDQ's certification program

2 update state and provincial regulatory agencies with current certification data for residents within a given jurisdiction

3 confirm NCIDQ certification status for initial licensing purposes in states and provinces

4 act as a clearinghouse for purposes of licensing reciprocity

IDEP PROGRAM

The career path of a professional interior designer involves formal education, entry-level work experience, and passing the qualifying examination. Entry-level work experience is required of candidates for the NCIDQ examination, as well as by the major interior design organizations for professional membership. American state and Canadian provincial licensing boards require proof of quality interior design experience for licensure and/or registration. NCIDQ developed the Interior Design Experience Program (IDEP) as a monitored postgraduate internship program to assure that candidates are prepared and qualified for examination. The program is administered by the NCIDQ for graduates of interior design education programs.

The general purpose of IDEP is to reinforce the interior design graduates' education as they enter professional practice and prepare for the NCIDQ examination. The program promotes the acquisition of professional discipline, skills, and knowledge. It also provides structure, direction, resources, and support to the training experience. These contribute to the development of competent interior designers and enhance interior design entry-level work experiences. The IDEP program has been developed using the definition of an interior designer and the common body of knowledge established by the NCIDQ and FIDER.

IDEP has been developed to assist entry-level interior designers in obtaining a broad range of quality professional experience and to establish performance guidelines for the work experience of new interior designers. The program serves as the transition between formal education and professional practice, recognizing the unique differences between programs of education and diversity of practice. Most important, IDEP facilitates the development of competent interior designers who can provide professional interior design services and work as team members involved in the design of the built environment. NCIDQ also produces a number of publications to support the mission of the organization, including study guides, practice exams, jury check sheets, and studies, as well as *Analysis Of The Interior Design Profession.*

In order to ensure the continued acceptance of NCIDQ certification in existing and proposed licensing statutes, the NCIDQ examination continues to evaluate minimum competency for the profession. However, as minimum competency in any profession may change or evolve with the development of the profession and the demands of the public, the examination and other certification standards are continually reviewed and modified accordingly. NCIDQ encourages current certificate holders to periodically keep current with the profession through re-examination. At the present time, this is a voluntary action, and existing certificates are not jeopardized if a certificate holder elects to take a subsequent examination. NCIDQ will issue renewal acknowledgments to those individuals already certified who are successfully re-examined in 1990 or after. NCIDQ certification provides interior designers with peer recognition, allows reciprocity to practice in licensed jurisdictions, and promotes public acceptance through awareness of a profession with certified practitioners.

Contact Information

NCIDQ
1602 L Street, NW, Suite 200
Washington, DC 20036-5681
Telephone: 202-721-0220
Fax: 202-721-0221
Email: ncidq@ncidq.org
Web site: www.nicdq.org

Council for Interior Design Accreditation
206 Grandville Avenue, Suite 350
Grand Rapids, MI 49503
Telephone: 616-458-0400
Fax: 616-458-0460
E-mail: info@accredit-id.org
Sources for this section were provided from Council for Interior Design Accreditation and NCIDQ Web sites.

5

The Legal Environment

BY BARRY B. LePATNER, ESQ.,
AND RONALD B. FEINGOLD, ESQ.

Introduction

Over the past thirty years, design professionals have encountered a series of challenges from new and varied areas of legal complexity and exposure. In recent years, the design world has been forced to address increasing liability for claims ranging from sick-building-related illness and Americans with Disability Act violations to the more common cost overruns and change order and delay claims by owners and contractors. In addition, interior designers and other design professionals in many states have been exposed to increased civil and criminal liability for practicing in jurisdictions without proper foreign authorization and licensure, as well as penalties for unauthorized practice as a professional. And, of course, there is now the added obligatory green building environment to which all design professionals must be attuned.

It is troubling enough for designers to consider the personal and professional losses they might incur if they were to defend a claim asserted against them. But legal exposure presents a concrete financial risk as well, even when a designer is covered by liability insurance. At the same time that claims against designers have increased in frequency and complexity, the costs of defense have skyrocketed. The cost of defense, too, often exceeds the potential liability of the claim itself. Even when the designer has liability insurance to cover a claim, the diminishing coverage, exhausted by the costs of one's defense, may not leave sufficient insurance to pay the claim. In the face of a diminishing liability policy—which is what most design professionals have—a designer can be personally liable for a portion of the costs of a claim even if the settlement or judgment amount was originally within policy limits.

Designers should also be mindful about the amount of the deductible they may select when it comes to deciding upon liability insurance. With a deductible, the designer/insured is responsible to pay (i) the defense and any expert costs and (ii) the amount awarded (paid out as settlement) to compensate the plaintiff for its damages, up to the threshold amount of the deductible. The designer may prefer a larger deductible because a larger deductible translates into a reduced insurance premium (as long as no claims are filed against the designer, the designer reaps the benefits by paying lower premiums). However, a higher deductible has a negative aspect. Once a claim is filed, the designer's exposure in having to front the higher defense costs and pay out any damages or settlement up to the amount of the deductible could have a substantial impact on a firm's bottom line. Therein lies the risk. The higher deductible for a reduced premium works as long as no large claim is filed against the designer. But once a substantial claim is filed, the designer must accept responsibility and pay the higher amount for attorneys' fees and any significant payment (or settlement) awarded to the plaintiff.

Although the risk and costs of liability may seem overwhelming, designers can protect themselves if they are aware of the types of liability they potentially face and what they can do to avoid becoming involved in legal proceeding. This section focuses on the areas of the law that pose an increased liability to practicing interior designers and other design professionals. Also included in this discussion are practical steps for interior designers to take in order to help avoid liability. As a related matter, this section also sets forth a discussion addressing certain business and legal complexities facing the design world. Though this chapter is not intended to be viewed as a summary of every area of liability faced by an interior designer, it is the intention of the authors to sensitize practitioners to the need to take the appropriate steps, which can limit or eliminate, from a business and contractual standpoint, such liability. Because it is not practical to discuss the law and practices of every jurisdiction, design professionals are advised to obtain the assistance of experienced local counsel.

Licensing

During the recession of the early 1990s, many architects began to complain that interior designers were usurping the licensed field of architecture, i.e., practicing a profession for which they were not authorized by strict professional training. In order to avoid legal exposure because of licensing issues, interior designers must not only become familiar with the licensing laws and rules in the state where a project is located but also be able to distinguish the difference between the services they can legally perform and those they cannot perform.

Licensing issues can have serious consequences for designers, financially as well as personally. In some states, interior designers can be prosecuted in criminal court under penal statutes for unauthorized practice, and they may face the possibility that a client will sue them for monetary damages for the unlicensed practice of interior design, architecture, and engineering. Even if they are not sued, designers are likely to find that a court will refuse to enforce the designer's claim for the payment of fees if the court finds that the designer performed professional services without the required license.

The purpose of state regulation of design is to protect the health, safety, and welfare of the public. Twenty-six states and Puerto Rico now have laws recognizing the title "Certified Interior Designer" or prohibiting the unlicensed practice of design. At least one state commission has determined that professional association (such as ASID) and certification are reasonable expectations of a competent practitioner of design. Likewise, ASID encourages certification and association with national and state organizations and review boards.

Perhaps the most important step designers can take is to understand what services they can perform in a particular state. The distinction between permissible and impermissible services is not always as clear as it seems. Licensing laws concerning interior designers commonly stress the difference between interior design and the practice of architecture and engineering. These laws place responsibility for the building systems (i.e., mechanical, electrical, plumbing, and life safety) with the architect and engineer, who are licensed by state law to seal and stamp drawings for this portion of a project. In New York, for example, the law emphasizes the difference between interior construction "not materially affecting the building systems" and design services that affect building systems. The clear intent is that the latter shall fall within the practice of architecture and engineering. Elements such as cabinets, lighting, and shelving usually fall within the ambit of the interior designer's permissible scope of work. Where an interior design firm's services included designs for floor elevations, changes in walls and openings, and supervision of the general contractor, a New York court found that the interior designer engaged in the unlicensed practice of architecture and noted that "there is a thin—but plain—line between 'interior design' and 'architecture' services."[1] The court held that "the preparation of plans and supervision of construction work are the usual functions of an architect."

In comparison, Florida focuses on the difference between structural elements and nonstructural interior elements of a building. The Florida Board of Architecture & Interior Design defines "interior design" as:

> *Designs, consultations, studies, drawings, specifications, and the administration of design construction contracts relating to nonstructural interior elements of a building or structure. . . . Interior design specifically excludes the design of or responsibility for architectural and engineering work except for specification of fixtures and their location within interior spaces.*

The Florida Board defines "architecture" as:

> *The rendering or offering to render services in connection with the design and construction of a structure or group of structures which have as their principal purpose human habitation or use, and the utilization of space within and surrounding such structures.*

Where interior design documents are prepared by a registered interior designer in Florida, the Florida Board requires the interior designer to include a statement on the plans that "the document is not an architectural or engineering study, drawing, specification, or design and is not to be used for construction of any load-bearing framing or walls of structures, or issuance of any building permit, except as otherwise provided by law."

Designers who practice beyond the scope of a license often incur serious civil and criminal consequences. Not only do these designers lose the opportunity to make a valid defense to an owner's malpractice claim, but also in states such as California, Illinois, and New York, those who practice without a license commit a crime that subjects them to penalties such as imprisonment, fines, and the revocation of their properly obtained license. Likewise, a designer who unlawfully uses another's title or stamps a drawing could also be subject to penalties. Most states, and the rules promulgated by the American Institute of Architects, require a design professional to report any instance of licensing law violations to the appropriate regulatory bodies.

Interior designers must be careful not to mistakenly hold themselves out to the public as being able to practice beyond the scope of their license. Most states not only prohibit the unauthorized practice of the professions but also proscribe a nonlicensed individual from holding himself or herself out as a licensed person. In California, New York, and other states, an interior designer or interior decorating firm cannot include the term "architect" or any similar word in its name or on its advertising materials, including business cards, which may indicate to the public that the firm is qualified to practice architecture or engineering. Care must also be taken to avoid using terms such as "architectural" and "construction supervision," or similar expressions.

To avoid claims or liability for unlawful practice, designers should inform their clients of the services their firm will be performing and specifically exclude all architectural or engineering services. When drafting an interior design agreement, careful attention must be paid to ensure that the interior designer's services do not go beyond the allowable definition of interior design. This information should be included in the written agreement with the client so there will be no misunderstanding concerning the services to be performed.

Proposals

For interior designers, preparing and submitting proposals is a traditional approach to securing new business. The skillful preparation of a request for proposal ("RFP") can position a firm on a project's short list or, in the best of circumstances, reflect qualifications that distinguish one firm from others without similar qualifications or terms of service. The fundamentals of the proposal process are simple enough: identify prospective clients and projects; clarify the prospect's need to determine your marketing approach; transmit the written proposal; and, hopefully, learn that one's proposal has received the client's approval. Seems easy enough. Or is it? Unfortunately for designers, under certain circumstances the proposal can bind the designer contractually to terms that may be unreasonable. In order to avoid being bound by unreasonable contract terms, interior designers should understand the legal ramifications of preparing a proposal for a project.

What happens if a proposal is answered by a simple client reply stating across the bottom page: "Accepted, please commence services immediately as set forth above"? Is there an enforceable contract? Are you responsible for commencing your services immediately? Can you be sued if you do not perform the precise services outlined in your proposal? The legal answer to these questions is frequently yes. Although responding to a Request for Proposal (RFP) does not create an automatic acceptance of the offer, a designer must be aware that the prospective client can turn such response into a binding contract merely by writing "Accepted" on its face. This is so because a proposal can sometimes be interpreted by courts as an invitation or "offer" to enter into a binding contract for the described services.

Generally, whether at an auction in a gallery or on an Internet site, when a potential buyer makes a bid and the seller subsequently accepts it, a contract exists because the parties have mutually assented to be bound. It does not always matter that the parties may not have worked out every one of the contract terms or that the agreement is not in writing. And, the mere fact that the parties intend to reduce their agreement to writing in the future does not make their "agreement" nonbinding. For this reason, designers should recognize the process of responding to a potential client's RFP as serious business.

Design professionals can avoid being unwittingly bound to contract terms if they follow some steps designed to make their proposals precise and to make their intent clear. Under the law of contracts, parties are free, with certain limitations, to decide under what circumstances their assents will become binding. It is also fundamental that contract formation is governed by the intent of the parties. In evaluating the parties' intent, courts look to their expressed words and actions. Two legal rules are well established on this point: (1) if parties manifest an intent not to be bound unless they have executed a formal agreement, then they will not be bound until such time; and (2) the mere fact that the parties intend to memorialize the agreement in a formal document does not prevent the informal agreement from taking effect prior to that event.

Consequently, in order to avoid becoming bound by a reply containing unreasonable contract terms, the astute interior designer should follow these four rules for submitting proposals:

1 Review the terms and conditions contained in an RFP carefully. Include language to the effect that the proposal is not to be construed as a contract between the parties that eventually will occur only upon execution of a formal agreement.

2 Thoroughly think through fee and schedule terms with an emphasis on staffing availability. Unexpected fees and schedule delays are the main cause of owner dissatisfaction.

3 Qualify proposals to conform to or address special concerns as to how and when your firm will perform its work. Exceptions should be made based on ambiguous and incomplete information contained in the RFP. If your proposal is accepted, these qualifications and exceptions may make the difference between a profitable and unprofitable project.

4 Attach a copy of your firm's standard agreement for services. If your proposal is accepted, you will ensure a full negotiation on all contract terms after your firm has been selected.

5 Remember at all times that you may see your proposal become an exhibit in a final agreement, so be certain about the specifics of the material terms of pricing, reimbursables, staffing, and schedule.

Liability and Contractual Protections

As team members, interior designers are subject to real and imagined claims from a number of directions; many of them will stem from actions undertaken (or omitted) by another team member. This liability has two types. The first type of claim, a contractual liability claim, arises when designers fail to perform a promise that formed a part of their contract. Contractual liability is usually measured in terms of assumed or due care in the performance of a designer's contractual obligations. The second type of claim involves malpractice or professional negligence, in which clients allege that designers committed professional misconduct, provided services that fall below an acceptable local standard of care, or engaged in other improper conduct relating to their services. Like contract claims, professional negligence claims are usually measured in terms of whether the interior designer's performance fell short of applicable professional standards usually exercised by a member of the profession in the locale where the services were performed.

The law does not expect or require absolute perfection from an interior designer. Unless the parties have contractually agreed to a higher standard, the law tests the efficiency of the interior designer by the rule of ordinary and reasonable skill usually exercised by one of that profession. To prove malpractice, the claimant must almost always present evidence of the standard of care by which the designer's competence may be judged and show that the designer did something, or failed to do something, that violated accepted professional standards.

Design professionals commonly face exposure to liability related to the design, scheduling, construction cost estimating, supervising and inspecting, certification of payments due a contractor, and resolving disputes. We focus below on several of these areas and address specific steps that an interior designer can take to minimize risk of exposure in these areas.

Liability for Scheduling

If a designer fails to achieve established project deadlines, the owner can sustain substantial damages. A design professional may be liable to the owner if the project is not completed on time as a result of his or her acts or omissions. Because of the increasing number of claims for damages due to delay, designers should include in their contracts specific provisions to minimize liability for this type of claim.

Although a sophisticated owner will want the designer to assist in preparing a project schedule and be responsible for meeting all agreed-upon schedule deadlines, the designer's contract should expressly exclude liability for delays caused by other project team members. Such contractual language could read as follows:

> *The Designer, in collaboration with the Owner [and the Architect of Record], shall establish a mutually acceptable schedule for the design development and contract documents phases. The schedule shall include commencement and completion dates for such phases in accordance with the Owner's established date for*

issuance of drawings for bidding. Should there be any deviation from this schedule due to the Owner's programming changes or other causes outside the Designer's control, the completion dates for such phase shall be modified accordingly. As appropriate, the Designer shall assist the Owner [and the Architect of Record] in coordinating the schedules for installation of the work, but shall not be responsible for any malfeasance, neglect, or failure of any contractor or supplier, [the Architect of Record] or any of the Owner's agents to meet their schedules for completion or to perform their respective duties and responsibilities.

Should the project be delayed through no fault of the designer, the designer should be entitled to an adjustment in the project schedule and compensated for the extra time spent and services rendered on the project past the agreed upon completion date. The following provision will ensure that the designer is entitled to the schedule adjustment and is properly compensated for the extended time and services rendered on a project as a result of an owner or contractor caused delay:

Notwithstanding any other provision contained in this Agreement, if the services covered by this Agreement have not been completed within _____ (___) months of the date hereof, through no fault of the Designer, the Designer shall be compensated for all services rendered after _____ (___) months on an hourly basis in accordance with the Designer's Hourly Rate Schedule which is then in effect. The Designer shall be entitled to an adjustment to the project schedule for the number of days the completion of services was delayed.

Finally, designers should take the following general precautions to avoid exposure for scheduling claims: (1) be insistent that all project schedule milestone dates and turnaround times are realistic; (2) ensure that reasonableness standards for time extensions are built into your agreements and that a *force majeure*, i.e., Act of God, clause is included; and (3) immediately inform your client in writing of all delays caused by contractors, consultants, or other parties.

Liability for Cost Estimates

Often, clients claim that designers failed to prepare a design within the owner's budget. If a design professional miscalculates the anticipated costs of a project, it may face liability to the owner. In determining whether the designer is liable for cost-estimating claims, courts will seek to determine whether the designer lived up to the reasonable standard of professional skill. If the court finds that the designer did not live up to the reasonable standard, it could hold the designer responsible for damages to the client, and in addition it could deny the designer compensation for services rendered. However, the court will not usually infer liability simply because the cost discrepancy is greater than usual.

Design professionals should think carefully about employing a common protection against such claims, such as incorporating a clause in one's agreement, which limits liability for cost estimates. Such a limitation of liability shifts the responsibility for estimating costs away from the designer. The American Institute of Architects has sought to insulate architects from providing cost estimates for a project by placing responsibility for cost estimating with the owner. This position, however, will often cause an owner, especially a sophisticated one, to lose faith in the designer. Historically, design professionals gained stature in the eyes of their clients by delivering designs that matched project budgets established by the client. By retreating from this service, designers paint themselves into a corner. They provide design services with only limited construction involvement and are often unable to protect the client from being overcharged by contractors.

The other approach to cost estimates is to work even more closely with the owner and other members of the team involved in the project. By agreeing to work closely with the owner or his or her cost-estimating consultant, or with a construction manager, designers can play a more significant role in a project without increasing liability. Those concerned about risk can minimize their exposure with a specific contract provision that recognizes the designer's responsibility to make design changes to meet the project budget at no cost through the design development phase. Once the owner approves the design development documents as conforming to the project budget—based on confirmation from an outside cost consultant—there can be little or no liability flowing to the designer if subsequent bids come in higher. In addition, the designer will be paid for required design changes after the design development phase to conform the drawings to the owner's project budget.

Design professionals should incorporate provisions into their agreements that reflect their commitment to work with the owner to adopt realistic project costs, as well as protective language to minimize their exposure. Designers should explain to clients that as the result of fluctuating labor costs and the volatile price of materials and equipment, they cannot reasonably be expected to take on the risk of guaranteeing project cost estimates. Such a provision can take the following form:

> *Any evaluations by the Designer of the Owner's project budget or statements of probable construction cost represent the Designer's best judgment as a design professional familiar with the construction industry. It is recognized, however, that neither the Designer nor the Owner has control over the cost of labor, materials or equipment, over the Contractor's methods of determining bid*

prices, or over competitive bidding, market or negotiating conditions. Accordingly, the Designer cannot and does not warrant or represent that bids or negotiated prices will not vary from the project budget proposed, established, or approved by the Owner, if any, or from any statement of probable construction cost or other cost estimate or evaluation prepared by the Designer.

In order to avoid exposure for excessive cost claims, the designer should explain the cost-estimating process to the client. Before finalizing a contract for the project, designers should explain how project costs are developed and how many uncontrollable factors affect cost predictions. During design and construction, designers should inform clients about how scope or other changes may affect previous cost estimates as well as increase in fees that may eventuate from design changes at late stages of design development. Designers should become particularly sensitized in cases where an owner continually advises that its project must be constructed on a guaranteed cost basis.

Ownership of Documents

Who owns, and has the right to future use of, the written design documents created by a design professional? Do clients who pay for the production of drawings and specifications own the documents? Are design professionals merely selling their ideas to clients whereby they retain exclusive use and ownership of their documents? If another designer subsequently completes the project, can the original designer be liable for errors or omissions contained in the design documents?

Absent an agreement assigning their rights, designers generally have ownership rights to the plans and specifications they create. However, contract terms, such as those contained in standardized AIA or ASID agreements, customarily grant the owner a license or permission for the owner to copy the designer's documents and use them for particular purposes. Additionally, when a contract does not contain any terms about whether the client can reuse drawings and documents, the client generally has a right to use the documents prepared by the design professional.

Agreements with Clients

Design professionals can protect themselves from exposure should the owner reuse design documents, and from the possibility that the owner might unlawfully use or copy them, if their agreements contain language that states that the design professional is the author and owner of the design work and retains possession to and ownership in the work. Such a provision can be worded as follows:

The drawings, specifications, and other documents (including but not limited to all documents related to interior construction, custom furniture, lighting, fabrics, and carpet [add additional items here]) prepared by the Designer for this Project are instruments of service and shall remain the property of the Designer whether the Project for which they are made is executed or not. As the author of these documents, the Designer shall retain all statutory and other reserved rights, including but not limited to copyright and patent rights. The Owner shall advise its agents, employees, contractors, vendors, and manufacturers who are provided copies of these documents of the Designer's proprietary interest in such documents.

In order to reflect the owner's limited need to be able to use the designer's documents for information and reference purposes after the project is completed, the following language should be added:

The Owner shall be permitted to retain copies, including reproducible copies, of drawings and specifications for information and reference in connection with the Owner's use and occupancy of the project provided the Owner is not in default under this Agreement, except as provided herein or by agreement in writing and with appropriate compensation to the Designer. The drawings and specifications shall not be used by the Owner or others on other projects, for additions to this project, or for completion of this project by others.

Design professionals should negotiate for additional fees with any owner who seeks to utilize the design documents for any future project. If such negotiation is not possible, the design professional needs protection for claims arising out of such future use. An owner should agree to indemnify, i.e., restore any loss to, the design professional for any future loss associated with the owner's subsequent use of the drawings and specifications. The following provision will operate to reduce exposure in the event of the owner's subsequent use of the designer's documents.

In the event the Designer is not retained for subsequent adaptation(s) and the use of the design prepared by him/her for this project, the Owner shall defend, indemnify, and hold the Designer harmless from and against all claims, demands, liabilities, causes of actions, lawsuits, damages, judgments, costs, and expenses, including reasonable attorneys' fees, the Designer may sustain or incur, in connection with, arising out of, as a consequence of, or by reason of the use of the Designer's design on such subsequent adaptation(s) and new project(s).

By including such provisions in agreements with clients, designers will protect their property interests in the tangible manifestations of their work at the same time that they also recognize the owner's need to have some control over the documents concerning the project.

Copyright Laws

United States Copyright laws protect original works of authorship fixed in any tangible medium of expression. The copyright laws apply to the expression of an idea, but not the idea itself. Under the Architectural Works Copyright Protection Act of 1990, an extension of the protections afforded under the Copyright Act of 1976, an original design of a building embodied in any tangible medium of expression, including a building, design plans, or drawings, is subject to copyright protection as an "architectural work." The 1990 act granted the design professional copyrights in both the design embodied in the drawings or buildings as well as in the drawings themselves. Under the act, an original design is licensed to the client for construction for a single project. This law protects the design professional from infringement by clients who might use the design professional's original drawings for repeated projects without appropriate compensation.

Designers should be aware that the Architectural Works Copyright Act is limited to certain structures. The use of the term "building" excludes many types of three-dimensional works worthy of copyright protection, such as bridges, walkways, recreational vehicles, mobile homes, boats, and gardens. However, the term "building" includes not only structures inhabited by humans but also those used by humans, such as churches, pergolas, gazebos, and garden pavilions.

It should also be noted that a copyright is distinct from a patent. There are three basic differences between the two. First, the subject matter differs because patents are directed at physical, scientific, and technological things, whereas copyrights are directed at artistic and intellectual works. In general, copyrightable works are nonfunctional, such as a writing, painting, or a piece of sculpture. Second, patents offer considerably more protection. A patent is a seventeen-year monopoly granted to the inventor by the federal government in exchange for a complete and thorough description of his or her invention. A copyright is a right granted to the author of literary or artistic productions, whereby he or she is invested with the sole and exclusive privilege of publishing and selling his or her productions. Protection under the United States Copyright Act is secure until fifty years after death of the author. Third, unlike the patent process, obtaining copyright registration is relatively simple. An application is submitted, together with a filing fee and one original copy of the unpublished work to be copyrighted.

Copyright grants four rights exclusively to the author or owner of the architectural work: the right to transform or adapt the work into another form; the right to make copies; the right to distribute copies; and the right to display the work publicly. Anyone who violates any of these rights provided to the author or owner of the copyright is committing an illegal act, i.e., an infringement of the copyright.

All authors and owners are advised to have their designs and technical drawings registered with the copyright office. While registration with the copyright office is not essential for the creation of a copyright, the copyright holder is certainly not without incentive to register. First and foremost, a completed registration is an indispensable prerequisite to filing an action for infringement. Once the material has been registered, it is immaterial whether the infringement that leads to the lawsuit occurred before or after the effective date of registration. Additionally, the copyright holder can use a certificate that shows the work was copyrighted before or within five years after its first publication to provide *prima facie* evidence of validity, both of the copyright and the facts stated in the certificate. A court may not award statutory damages or attorneys' fees for any infringement of an unpublished work occurring before registration or for any infringement of a published work not registered within three months of publication. Other notable benefits of registration include preservation of the copyright in certain circumstances, even when the work as published bears no notice of copyright whatsoever, and protection of the actual owner's interest when the notice erroneously names another as the proprietor of the copyright.

Because of the copyright laws, even if developer-owners own the drawings, they do not have a free hand to clone a design or one of its elements unless they receive an assignment of the design copyright from design professionals or the design professionals are their employees. If the developers do not own drawings and do not have an interest in the work by way of an assignment or otherwise, they may be required to defend against an infringement action brought by the design professional. Especially if developers intend to use the design at a different location, they might consider purchasing the copyright, which is assignable like any other copyright, along with the drawings.

Health/Safety Issues

Recent health studies over the past twenty-five years have found that increasing numbers of people have contracted severe respiratory and skin diseases as well as fatigue and headaches resulting from unacceptable levels of gasses, bacteria, fungi, molds, and other harmful chemicals in the air circulating throughout enclosed buildings. These symptoms, referred to in the aggregate as "sick-building-related" symptoms, are on the rise. Across the country, physicians report that sick-building-related illnesses have increased by as much as 40 percent in the past decade alone. With the rise in awareness of indoor pollution comes the rise in litigation against owners and design professionals for building-related illness and sick-building syndrome. Both new construction and renovation projects are prone to these claims. Substantial lawsuits have been filed by sick tenants, occupants, and visitors against owners and design professionals. Even when the plaintiffs do not name the design team as defendants in such lawsuits, designers are often brought into the litigation by owners who seek to be indemnified from design professionals for the sick-building-related claims.

Illnesses caused by harmful chemicals found in buildings fall into one of two categories. The first illness is known as building-related illness, which occurs when a readily identifiable fungi or other airborne matter causes actual disease. The second is sick-building syndrome, which occurs when people report symptoms that cannot be traced to one particular cause.

Building-related illness and sick-building syndrome can be caused by a number of different factors, including poor air distribution; inadequate air intakes; sealed windows; contaminated HVAC systems; faulty air filters that fail to filter out noxious impurities; recycled air containing second-hand smoke; construction dust and paint fumes; accumulation of standing water in HVAC condensate trays; dangerous construction materials such as textile trimmings, dies, and sealants in furniture; and other materials containing heavy metals.

Additionally, the presence of asbestos in commercial and residential buildings has taken on ominous proportions for the real estate industry. The presence of asbestos in buildings has resulted in federal, state, and local legislation to limit the exposure to and handling of asbestos. On the federal level, the Environmental Protection Agency (EPA) and the Occupational Safety and Health Administration (OSHA) have promulgated exposure limits to asbestos measured over time periods. There are also special requirements for renovation, removal, and demolition, including negative pressure enclosures, supervisory personnel, worker decontamination areas, clean rooms, and equipment rooms. State and local legislatures and agencies have also enacted legislation concerning asbestos. For example, the New York State Department of Law, which oversees cooperative and condominium offerings, has enacted regulations requiring sponsors to inspect for asbestos and disclose its presence, if any, in the cooperative offering plan. In addition, the New York state legislature amended the statute of limitations for toxic tort lawsuits. Victims in New York may commence an action within three years from the date the injury was discovered as opposed to when the victim was actually exposed to the toxic material. Other states have enacted similar rules.

An interior design firm can avoid or minimize its liability by incorporating certain exculpatory provisions in their agreements. First, the designer-owner agreement should place all responsibility for air quality with the owner. Since many owners will not accept the additional costs relating to improving air quality without evidence of a real need, in projects where air quality may pose a particular problem, the designer-owner agreement should also provide that the owner retain, at its expense, an air quality consultant.

Second, the agreement should specifically exclude the designer from responsibility for all work related to toxic and hazardous material. The design firm should advise the owner before commencing services on the project that it does not have the expertise required to deal with toxic materials and a consultant should be hired for this purpose. The essence of this wording might read as follows:

> *The Project may uncover hazardous or toxic materials or pollutants including, but not limited to asbestos, asbestos-related materials and PCBs. Notwithstanding any provisions in this Agreement to the contrary, the Interior Designer and its consultants are not responsible for the performance of any services in connection with or related to such materials and the Owner hereby agrees to retain an expert or experts to arrange for the prompt identifications of and/or removal of treatment of such materials identified during the course of the Project and to indemnify and hold harmless the Interior Designer and its principals, employees, agents, and consultants from any claims, damages, losses, demands, lawsuits, causes of action, injuries, or expenses, including reasonable counsel fees, incurred by the Interior Designer arising out of, as a consequence of, or in any way related to the existence of such material on the Project.*

By including this language, on projects where existing air quality issues may pose heightened concerns, designers will be indemnified from any claims alleging liability related to the existence of toxic materials. This is especially important where known toxic airborne particles such as asbestos and lead-based paint are present on the site.

Realizing that the integrity of a building's health is important, certain practical considerations should be addressed to limit liability for building-related illness and sick-building syndrome. Designers should pay close attention to the specification of materials to be used in the building. Although designers will not usually be responsible to conduct their own testing of materials used on their projects, they should not specify materials for which the side effects may be unknown. They should also hesitate to use newly developed materials before an established testing program ensures that there are no health-related effects. Where an owner demands a substitution of materials and the designer believes it could potentially cause pollution problems, the designer should require the owner to indemnify it against any claims arising out of such substitution.

Americans with Disabilities Act: How the ADA Affects Interior Design Professionals

OVERVIEW OF THE ADA

The Americans with Disabilities Act ("ADA" or the "Act") has and will continue to have a significant effect on the design community. The Act sets forth requirements with respect to new construction and obligates property owners to modify existing structures to accommodate the disabled. Interior designers performing services on commercial projects will find that their clients will expect assistance in interpreting the provisions of the Act that relate to accessibility of places of public accommodation and commercial facilities.

The ADA is the most comprehensive civil rights legislation enacted since Title VII of the Civil Rights Act of 1964. It was designed to protect disabled individuals from discrimination in employment (Title I), public services (Title II), public accommodations (Title III), and telecommunication relay services (Title IV).

Title III of the ADA took effect on January 26, 1992. Despite its many benefits, Title III places serious financial burden on developers, owners, landlords, and tenants of real property. Many of the requirements under Title III remain unclear and confusion still exists as to how to comply with these requirements. What is clear, however, is that compliance with the ADA requirements is mandatory and persons with disabilities cannot be charged for the costs incurred in complying with ADA. It should be noted that construction standards in local jurisdictions are often more rigorous than those in Title III and, therefore, take precedence over ADA requirements. However, where Title III requirements go beyond those contained in the local law, Title III must be complied with.

Title III divides buildings and facilities into two categories: public accommodations and commercial facilities. The Title III requirements only apply to public accommodations. Public accommodations generally fall within one of the following twelve categories:

- Places of lodging
- Establishments serving food or drink

- Places of exhibition or entertainment
- Places of public gathering
- Sales or rental establishments
- Service establishments
- Stations used for specified public transportation
- Places of public display or collection
- Places of recreation
- Places of education
- Social service establishments
- Places of exercise or recreation

Commercial facilities are usually defined as nonresidential facilities used by private entities with commercial operations such as office buildings, warehouses, and factories.

The following discussion is intended to provide the reader with a general overview of the major ADA requirements and suggestions for avoiding common pitfalls associated with ADA compliance. This section is not intended to provide a comprehensive review of all ADA requirements. The Act should be examined whenever a question of compliance arises.

ARCHITECTURAL BARRIERS

Architectural barriers are physical objects that obstruct a disabled individual's access to, or use of, a facility. An example would be a narrow doorway as the only entrance to a room. To the extent that it is readily achievable, the law requires the removal of all architectural barriers in existing facilities. If it is determined that barrier removal is not readily achievable, there is still a requirement for the public accommodation to make its services, facilities, or privileges available to the disabled in a way that is readily achievable.

The term "readily achievable" means "easily accomplishable and able to be carried out without much difficulty or expense." Because there are no predetermined formulas, the issue of whether a removal is readily achievable is to be determined on a case-by-case basis. However, the following five factors are to be considered in determining whether a change is readily achievable:

1 The nature and cost of the required action.

2 The overall financial resources available at the site, the number of employees at the site, safety requirements, and the impact of the proposed action on the operation of the site.

3 The geographic separation and the administrative or fiscal relationship between the site and parent entity.

4 If applicable, the overall financial resources of the parent entity, including the number of employees and the number, type, and location of its facilities.

5 If applicable, the type of business of the parent entity.

Some examples of types of alternatives are providing a "talking directory" in building lobbies; valet parking for the disabled; providing home delivery; and relocating activities to accessible locations. A person with a disability cannot be charged for the costs of providing alternative approaches.

Title III recommends that barrier removal take place in the following order of priority:

1 Physical access from parking lots, public transportation, and sidewalks—this includes installing ramps, creating accessible parking spaces and widening doors.

2 Access to areas where goods and services are available to the public, including access to retail display areas, and adjusting display racks and cases.

3 Access to restrooms, which includes the installation of full-length mirrors and wide toilets.

4 Other measures necessary in order to remove other barriers.

Removal of a barrier will be mandated by the courts in all cases where discrimination has been proven. However, if the Justice Department has reasonable cause to believe that a practice or pattern of discrimination exists, it can file a civil suit, which can result in ordering barrier removal together with a fine. The best way to avoid such lawsuits is by making good faith efforts to comply with the ADA before problems arise.

The Justice Department recommends self-evaluation of existing facilities to identify potential barriers. Good-faith self-assessment and consultation with individuals with disabilities and the organizations that represent them can diminish the threat of litigation. Additionally, it is advisable to keep a list of existing barriers that are not removed, together with the specific reasons for not removing them. Continuous efforts over time to make buildings more accessible will demonstrate an owner's good faith and will help diminish the threat of future litigation.

While the "good-faith standard" requires positive compliance efforts, no business is exempt from compliance because of a failure to understand or receive technical assistance in implementing removal of barriers.

New Construction/Alterations

As of January 26, 1993, all new commercial facilities and places of public accommodation must be fully accessible to the disabled to the extent that it is not "structurally impracticable." The phrase "structurally impracticable" means that unique characteristics of the land prevent the incorporation of accessibility features into a facility. If a building permit for a commercial building was approved after January 26, 1992, and received its first certification of occupancy after January 26, 1993, it must be fully usable by individuals with disabilities. If the permit was approved prior to January 26, 1992, the building is not subject to Title III rules pertaining to new construction, even if first occupancy occurred after January 26, 1993. However, the building must still meet the barrier removal requirements discussed above.

When there are alterations to a commercial facility or place of public accommodation, the altered areas of the facility must be fully accessible to the disabled. Alterations are defined as remodeling, renovation, or reconstruction that affect the use of the building. Alterations do not include such usual maintenance such as painting, reroofing, asbestos removal, and most changes to the electrical and mechanical systems except for switches and controls. If the structural conditions of an existing building or facility make it impossible to fulfill the Title III accessibility requirements, those accessibility requirements shall be deemed "technically infeasible."

With respect to an alteration of a building or a facility, "technically infeasible" means that it has little likelihood of being accomplished because existing structural conditions would require removing or altering a load-bearing member that is an essential part of the structural frame or because other existing physical or site constraints prohibit modification or addition of elements, spaces, or features that are in full and strict compliance with the minimum requirements for new construction and are necessary in order to provide accessibility. Where required alterations are technically infeasible, the owner will not have to comply with the alteration requirements of the ADA. It should be noted, however, that if compliance is technically infeasible, the alteration must provide accessibility to the maximum extent feasible. Any elements or features of the building or facility that are being altered and can be made accessible must be made accessible within the scope of the alteration.

Penalties for Noncompliance with the ADA

Design professionals face considerable risk under the ADA. As a civil rights law, the ADA specifies that either a private individual or the U.S. Attorney's Office can bring a suit against a public accommodation that violates the ADA. It is not necessary to allege discrimination "after the fact." A lawsuit can be filed if the petitioner has reasonable grounds to believe that discrimination is "about to occur" in either a new construction project or an alteration.

One particular case against an architectural firm deserves mentioning. In *United States v. Ellerbe Becket, Inc.*, the United States filed an action against Ellerbe Becket, Inc., an architectural firm, for violations of the ADA.[2] The complaint alleged that Ellerbe had engaged in a pattern or practice of designing new sports arenas across the United States that failed to comply with the ADA and its regulation regarding lines of sight for disabled patrons.

Ellerbe maintained that the ADA was not clear and was open to interpretation as to precisely what was required. Although the government settled with Ellerbe in 1998 for an agreement by Ellerbe to design new stadiums so spectators in wheelchairs still have a full view when other fans stand up, the case presents an example of how easy it is for a designer to incur liability for ADA violations. In order to avoid liability where ADA provisions are unclear and open to interpretation, designers should inform their clients in writing of the ADA issues and require the owner to make the final determination concerning how far they should go in ensuring ADA compliance.

Conclusion

There is more to the art of negotiating contracts than limiting liability or deciding how to protect your intellectual property. It is widely recognized that even today's seemingly simple construction projects are far more complex than those built even ten years ago. Owners and designers alike are facing increasing choices in the means and methods of design and construction. It has, therefore, become more important then ever to integrate business and legal protections into each agreement with the client as well as to coordinate the interior design agreement with those of the other members of the project team.

This change has occurred because the costs of projects today have grown increasingly larger and owners often hire integrated teams of consultants to ensure that their projects are unique. As a result, it is important to properly ascribe to each of the team members the appropriate responsibilities and liabilities. Similarly, it is necessary to properly define all of the variables—the special features needed to match each member's scope of services with the project delivery system—and ensure that they are coordinated with the phased completion dates for each stage of the project.

At the outset of each project, the design team must meet with the client and survey what is most critical to them, what factors they most need to see to consider the project successful. Even for small and simple projects, the complete investigation calls upon the designer to work with the owner and other project team members to address goal-oriented questions before the design process can effectively begin. If designers identify clients' design and business goals, they can ensure that their agreements with owners contain the requisite legal protections as well as provisions that will coordinate their work and responsibilities with those of other members of the project team. By adopting a more businesslike approach to the drafting and negotiation of agreements, designers will limit their exposure to liability, ensure timely collection of their fees, be in a better position to meet and exceed their clients' goals, and see more of their projects successfully completed.

ENDNOTES

1. Marshall-Schule Associates, Inc. v. Goldman, 137 Misc.2d 1024, 523 N.Y.S.2d 16 (Civ. NY 1987).
2. United States v. Ellerbe Becket, Inc., 976 F.Supp 1262 (D. Minn. 1997).

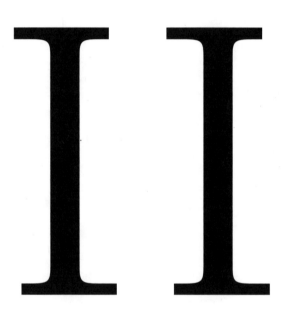

II

The Work Process

6

Scope of Service Matrix

BY EVA MADDOX

esign firms each have a unique way of approaching the design of a project. The following chapters in this section of the book focus on the designer's scope of services. These chapters are presented as narratives from a varied group of designers each describing their individual methods of approaching the process of design. While these approaches vary due to the size of a project, project type and the design firm's philosophy and resources, the basic scope of services is generally consistent from project to project and firm to firm.

Eva Maddox, principal of Perkins & Will Branded Environments, designs a broad range of project types: from residential, healthcare, and education to commercial and corporate projects. The firm has combined the best-practice knowledge they derive from their diverse practice to construct the following Scope of Service Matrix. The matrix is a "snapshot" in time, describing the current key activities generally performed during the course of a project from marketing to project closeout.

Perkins & Will Eva Maddox Branded Environments Design Process Project Phases

Key Actions	00 Proposal to Contract	05 Project Initiation
Project Coordination	· review marketing information · review scope of work · identify P+W deliverables · identify client deliverables · develop task plan · identify % profit · review w/marketing · review w/design	· conduct team kick-off/orientation meeting · establish client communication protocols · develop client "directory" · team meeting, post-client meeting · team meeting, summary report/review program · issue report/program to client for approval
Contract	· finalize scope of work · establish fee payment schedule · finalize contract · schedule contract presentation · obtain client authorization · obtain initial payment if applicable	· scope review · review P+W deliverables · review client deliverables
Fee Monitoring	· confirm fee to work scope	· review fee & project work against budget · review task plan · review profitability goals · monitor
Schedule	· establish project schedule · establish key project milestones	· review project schedule · establish critical internal meeting dates and deliverables · revise/issue client schedule · schedule client kick-off meeting and/or programming meeting(s)
Teams/Roles	· identify team · identify consultants	· assign team · assign project responsibilities · establish client contact · monitor
Objectives	· identify P+W internal objectives · establish project objectives	· define/establish project objectives · monitor
Information Gathering	· gather client background/info · identify client vendor alliances	· develop list of questions/interview forms · conduct client kick-off/progr meeting(s) · define areas of research · define client profile
Big Idea		· identify Big idea
Patterning	· determine if applicable	· identify opportunities
Presentation Formats	· identify key presentations	· establish formats for project presentations · define quality levels
Budget	· identify client's build-out budget	· obtain client's build-out budget
Design°	· define scope of work	· identify key areas of focus
Graphics	· define scope of work	· identify areas of application · define methods of output · establish vendor alliances
Documentation	· define scope of work	· establish formats for project · define quality levels · prepare summary report/program

Key Actions	Schematic Design Development	Design Development
Project Coordination	· conduct team kick-off meeting · conduct internal team meetings as required · maintain client communication · conduct in-house presentation, two days prior to client meeting · issue meeting minutes	· conduct team kick-off meeting · conduct internal team meetings as required · maintain client communication · conduct in-house presentation, two days prior to client meeting · issue meeting minutes
Contract	· monitor work against contract · monitor need for additional services · obtain client deliverables	· monitor work against contract · monitor need for additional services · obtain client deliverables
Fee Monitoring	· monitor P+W profitability · conduct team kick-off meeting	· monitor P+W profitability
Schedule	· review project schedule · establish critical internal meeting dates and deliverables · revise/issue client schedule · schedule SDD presentation meeting	· review project schedule · establish critical internal meeting dates and deliverables · revise/issue client schedule · schedule DD meeting
Teams/Roles	· monitor staffing against role assignments · monitor consultants	· monitor staffing against role assignments · monitor consultants
Objectives	· monitor SDD solutions against objectives	· monitor design solutions against objectives
Information Gathering	· conduct project research · report on findings · analyze information · chart results · identify appropriate product resources · obtain required "product" samples · identify code requirements & conformance	· obtain required "product" samples · confirm "product" availability · confirm code requirements & conformance · finalize research
Big Idea	· begin conceptual development of Big idea	· monitor design solutions against Big idea · integrate Big idea
Patterning	· develop conceptual patterning · apply to preliminary design components	· apply patterning to design components
Presentation Formats	· outline cartoon set of presentation · develop communication matrix · outline meeting agenda	· outline cartoon set of presentation media · develop communication matrix · outline presentation booklets & mtng agenda
Budget	· outline presentation booklets · outline board or other media layout · prepare preliminary statement of probable cost	· meet w/appropriate vendors · update budget estimate
Design	· establish design strategy · develop conceptual design components	· maintain design strategy · develop final design components
Graphics	· establish graphic strategy · develop conceptual graphic components	· maintain graphic strategy · develop final design components · refine methods of output · maintain vendor alliances
Documentation	· prepare all presentation materials	· prepare all presentation materials · mark up all DD info for integrated design tech, involved from Day One · develop critical details

Perkins & Will Eva Maddox Branded Environments Design Process Project Phases (Cont.)

Key Actions	Documentation	Bids
Project Coordination	· conduct team progress meeting(s) · maintain client communication · conduct in-house document review meeting(s) · conduct client review meeting · obtain client approval · issue meeting minutes	· prepare list of qualified bidders; review w/client & obtain approval · stamp appropriate documents · issue documents for bid · receive, review, & qualify bids · prepare bid summary & recommendations · review bids w/client · obtain bid authorization
Contract	· monitor work against contract · monitor need for additional services · obtain client deliverables	· issue authorized bids to successful bidders · monitor work against contract · monitor need for additional services · obtain any client deliverables
Fee Monitoring	· monitor P+W profitability	· monitor P+W profitability
Schedule	· review project schedule · establish critical internal meeting dates and deliverables · monitor completion against schedule · revise/issue client schedule · schedule client document review meeting	· review project schedule · establish critical response dates from contractors (bid time frame) · revise/issue client schedule · schedule client bid review meeting
Teams/Roles	· monitor staffing against roles, assignments, profitability · monitor consultants · adjust staffing if required	· monitor staff against roles, assignments, profitability · define responsible party to answer bid questions · monitor consultants · adjust staffing if required
Objectives	· monitor technical solutions against objectives	· monitor bids against budget objectives
Information Gathering	· obtain all design background from team · outline questions/concerns for design team review · identify missing information · obtain required technical products, samples and cut sheets · confirm long-lead items · confirm code requirements & conformance	· research qualified bidders for project scope · clarify information for bidders · obtain necessary information to respond to bidders · receive all bids · prepare addenda as required
Big Idea	· monitor technical solutions against Big idea · integrate into technical approach	· monitor bid pricing/bid alternatives against Big idea
Patterning	· integrate patterning components into documentation approach	· identify value of patterning components
Presentation Formats	· outline cartoon set of documents · outline cartoon set of specifications · outline meeting agenda & booklet	· develop bid summary format · develop budget prioritization format
Budget	· monitor technical/design solutions against budget	· monitor bids against budget · prioritize budget expenditures against bids
Design	· develop design/construction details	· monitor bids to maintain design integrity
Graphics	· develop graphic/technical details	· monitor bids to maintain graphic integrity
Documentation	· prepare all document sheets as required: engineering, permit, bid, construction · prepare all specifications · prepare all finish sample sheets · develop all critical details	· outline & develop bid forms and procedures · prepare bid packages for: construction items, exhibit components, signage/graphics, furniture · establish bid authorization log

Key Actions	11 Site Monitoring	14 Project Closeout

Project Coordination	· conduct kick-off job site meeting with all contractors/vendors
	· attend job site review meeting(s)
	· issue field reports and punch lists to appropriate parties
	· conduct client walk through's
	· conduct P+W team walk thru for "lessons learned" evaluation
		· conduct project close-out meeting
		· distribute close-out reports to:
		    marketing coordinator
		    senior vice president
		    project manager
		    finance manager
		· close-out all project files
		· distribute materials to marketing as required

Contract	· monitor work against contract · monitor need for additional services · obtain any client deliverables	· obtain copy of final contract with any change orders · obtain copy of all additional services
Fee Monitoring	· monitor P+W profitability	· obtain copy of final project progress reports
Schedule	· review project schedule · coordinate schedules w/all contractors/vendors · establish critical job site review dates · monitor contractor/vendor schedules against work progress · monitor completion against schedule · schedule client walk through/review meeting(s) · schedule project team walk through's	· schedule close-out meeting w/marketing coordinator & project team · schedule close-out meeting w/client
Teams/Roles	· monitor staffing against roles, assignments, profitability · define key field coordinator · monitor consultants · adjust staffing if required	· evaluate success of team members · evaluate success of consultants · evaluate client satisfaction
Objectives	· monitor build-out against design, budget and schedule objectives	· obtain copy of client objectives · obtain copy of P+W objectives
Information Gathering	· clarify information for contractors/vendors · respond to contractor's request for information · monitor substitutions/replacements for discontinued items · prepare bulletins as required · monitor quality of construction	· gather all data for close-out meeting from team
Big Idea	· monitor build out for quality control of Big idea	· document the Big idea
Patterning	· monitor execution of patterning components	· identify impact of patterning on project
Presentation Formats	· outline presentation of job site to customer: path, clean site, issues	· identify information format required for marketing: presentation booklets, color print outs, plans, presentation boards
Budget	· monitor cost of field conditions against bid & budget	· obtain copies of all vendor costs
Design	· monitor execution to maintain design integrity	· identify measurable results
Graphics	· monitor execution to maintain graphic integrity	· identify measurable results
Documentation	· prepare job site observation reports · prepare field condition clarification · prepare change directives as required · review change orders · review contractor's applications for payment · prepare punch lists · prepare/maintain shop drawing log · review submittals	· prepare project close-out form

7

Pre-Design Services

BY SHARON TURNER

Purpose

The value of pre-design services should not be underestimated—this is where a project can begin its life and a good start sets the standard for the quality of service and delivery for the project as a whole. Put simply, whatever the extent of the commission, this is where the goals of the project are clearly identified and understood by the project team.

Primarily, pre-design involves establishing the necessary information to design and administer the project and determining how the design firm will professionally relate to the client and the wider project team. The opportunity for developing trust and strong, collaborative working relationships in this phase will go a long way toward the successful outcome of the overall commission.

Methodology: Types of Commission

Broadly speaking, interior design firms are involved in pre-design services in three ways. The first is the project initiation phase of a standard interior design commission, where the space to be designed has already been identified and the scope of work is already predetermined by the client.

The second is strategic facilities planning, also known as a pre-lease service, where the interior design firm is a part of a wider project team tasked with identifying future space requirements in a strategic way and assisting in the identification of suitable buildings or evaluating the extent of work required in an existing building or property portfolio.

The third is consulting, where a client organization is undergoing some form of major change, e.g., a corporate relocation, merger, acquisition, or a radical rethink of the workplace, and so employs an interior design firm in a pre-design consulting role to undertake research, propose scenarios, and inform business decisions.

Typically, these three types of commission take the following approaches.

PROJECT INITIATION

In this scenario, the project typically is in an existing space already under the control of the client or the space has been bought or leased prior to the appointment of the interior design firm. Pre-design services in this scenario usually involve no more than initial meetings with the client team to establish the project reporting and administration structure and to set the work plan and schedule for the future phases. These meetings are attended typically by the principal in charge of the project or a senior project designer, the client or client representative, a client IT representative or consultant, and the MEP engineer where applicable.

Project Initiation Checklist
- Project and team organization structure
- Reporting and approval procedures
- Budget and cost control procedures
- Confirm the project size and review design scope and building constraints
- Review client corporate guidelines, space standards, and business plan documentation
- Review headcount, organization structure, and adjacency requirements
- Review a summary of existing client programming data
- Receive "as built" drawings, computer disks, and technical specifications
- Identify field survey requirements
- Identify requests for information (RFIs) and assign responsibilities and timescales
- Develop the work plan and schedule
- Review fee invoicing and payment procedures

A word of caution, however: where the interior designer has come late to the table, there have been many instances of clients having underestimated their space program. I recall a case in which a client and his broker had been searching for and negotiating on 75,000 square feet of commercial office space for four months. Three buildings had been short-listed prior to the appointment of the interior design firm, who subsequently proved the real space program was 10,000 square feet. This is a sobering example—one that had serious consequences for the client organization.

This project initiation phase is then followed by the detailed programming phase, and the project proceeds in a traditional phased way. Fees for project initiation are included in the overall interior design fee for the project, which is commonly quoted as a dollar-per-square-foot rate.

The Strategic Facilities Planning Approach

Successive economic recessions have resulted in clients taking a very cautious approach to acquiring real estate, and they are looking for increased value from the buildings they occupy. Both end user clients and the brokerage community are now retaining the services of interior design firms earlier in the real estate acquisition process. The pre-lease team often consists of the client representative, the real estate broker, legal representation, an architect/designer, and an MEP engineer.

The objective is for the architect/designer to contribute to the decision on which building or space the client buys or leases. This is done by identifying the client's strategic space requirements program, undertaking a technical evaluation of short-listed real estate and testing how well the program works within each building.

In large corporate sector projects, the interior designer, with the assistance of an MEP engineer, establishes the clients' "big picture" space requirements and develops an ideal building footprint (this is also known as a strategic program). Once signed off by the clients' senior management, this plan is used to begin the real estate search. In the case of a build-to-suit project, the information will be used to solicit responses for developer's proposals.

The outcome is an assessment of how well individual buildings perform in terms of space efficiency and operational effectiveness for a particular client.

Typical Building Appraisal Checklist
- Building footprint and loss factor efficiency
- Architectural arrangement and core provision
- Building services review with engineer
- Planning authority/local code compliance issues
- Construction challenges
- Stacking diagrams and space planning test fits
- Rating how well the building meets the client's program

The designer adds value to the client in this type of pre-design service by developing a clear space strategy, criteria for a space search, the analysis of short-listed sites or buildings, and professional advice in supporting negotiations and decision making. The value to the interior design firm is that this type of commission, when properly executed, often leads to a full service interior design commission following the leasing or building acquisition.

Because the time spans for this type of commission can often be a year from the start of the strategic programming process to making a final decision on a building, this pre-design service is offered as a stand alone commission based upon either a fixed or not-to-exceed fee.

The Consulting Role

This third type of pre-design service involves understanding how design and environment can contribute to the alignment of business goals, corporate culture, and real estate. This rarely takes the form of a traditional design project. These projects are more likely to be feasibility studies for large accommodation strategies or feasibility studies exploring new ways of working with a view toward implementing major space occupancy changes in a client organization.

Accommodations strategies consist of reviewing and analyzing buildings to establish existing conditions, space efficiency, and effectiveness. The analysis would attempt to answer the questions of what is working, what isn't, and why not. The review of existing conditions, especially environmental conditions, requires measuring existing performance against preset guidelines or best practice criteria. Obtaining this data requires the services of engineers— almost always MEP & FP, and sometimes structural. The data are presented in report format with recommendations for upgrades, costing information, and implementation logistics.

The findings are best reported in the form of a spreadsheet so that comparisons between building and/or locations are easily understood. The report should also contain "big picture" occupancy-stacking scenarios and test fits of typical building floors to establish efficiency and loss factors.

Pre-design feasibility studies are projects that exist outside of a "live" interior design project and involve the design firm providing knowledge-based advice to set new goals and guidelines for workplace design and occupancy targets. These projects are nearly always driven by the need to occupy less space, use existing space more efficiently, and provide a better-quality environment for staff and customers.

These projects are invariably for large-scale corporate clients. Virtually, all large relocation projects involve a pre-design feasibility study prior to the real estate decisions being made or the appointment of the interior designer to design a given space. These studies are usually carried out with the client's facilities management team and the interior design consulting team, and more frequently, with the input of business or management consultants who report on improving business processes and operational criteria. Many large corporate clients are amending their design services criteria to exclude design firms that cannot offer this type of consulting service. The fees for these projects are usually on a fixed fee or not-to-exceed basis.

Who Is Involved With the Pre-Design Process?

All three types of pre-design services are influenced by the tangible project parameters of schedule and budget with key issues such as "We will pay double rent if we are not relocated by," or, "There can be no down-time for our operation." These can be understood and planned for by the design team.

Less tangible, yet critical to success, is the definition and understanding of what the true goals and objectives of the project are and what the measures of success for the project are in the eyes of the Board, the stakeholders, or the employees. The design professional needs to understand how the client views the situation, including the history, the boardroom politics, the perception of themselves in their market place, and the degree of potential change to be planned for from the outset.

Any pre-design phase reports and recommendations must come to clear and impartial conclusions to be credible with one's direct client and their senior management and responsive to the needs of the business. The methodology for gathering information, the analysis, and presentation of recommendations is extremely important for the establishment of consensus on what the project is truly trying to achieve—quite a tall order for an outsider to come into a client organization and accomplish. But the design professional can identify, without bias, the issues surrounding the client's existing situation and/or proposed project. Because we are not from "in-house," our opinions are often more readily accepted as being impartial and therefore more credible.

Establishing a Project Strategy Development Team

In the second and third examples of pre-design services, the interior designer forms a part of a wider strategy development team. Ideally, this should consist of the client's corporate real estate team, facilities management, IT, human resources, and the interior designer, with input from engineers, real estate professionals, and other consultants on an as-needed basis.

The strategy development process involves:

- Holding strategic planning sessions with the business heads

- Determining the business objectives and change/flexibility targets

- Asking where the opportunities are for change and how design can contribute to them.

- Keeping space programming macro—. Detail is not required at this stage—think "big picture"

- Undertaking research where applicable—e.g., time utilization studies, satisfaction surveys

- Questioning the real need for physical proximity between people, departments, and business units

- Establishing the IT and services infrastructure requirements at the earliest opportunity

- Establishing the level of amenities to be provided and operational strategies

- Establishing existing conditions if appropriate

- Establishing the real drivers behind the project and what defines project success

Even if the client has chosen to outsource the management of the project to a client representative or project manager, it is critical that a strategy development team is set up in this manner. Building credibility with one's client and their senior management is key to a successful project. The finalized accommodation strategy or feasibility study report is signed off on by the client, and the information forms the yardstick to highlight the challenges foreseen to implement a "live" project and sets out the criteria to measure project success.

The Role of the Real Estate Professional

The real estate professional represents the client and finds and screens prospective locations and buildings that meet the client's criteria. He or she will liaise with the strategic facilities planning team and provide the interior designer with base building floor plans, technical specifications, and services information. He or she brings to the team the market knowledge and negotiating skills to obtain for the client the best lease terms, landlord contributions and incentives, building management, and services provision. We, as the design professionals, are as expert witnesses to what is on offer in terms of existing conditions, upgrade requirements, and compliance of the building with the client's needs. This collaboration between interior designer and real estate professional very often leads to an advantageous negotiating position for the client if a building is spatially inefficient, loss factors are exceptionally high, or specifications fall below those "reasonably" expected.

Real estate brokers expect designers to provide a quick turnaround on the performance and viability of short-listed buildings. To make this process credible, the bases by which one judges a potential building must be consistently applied by using an "ideal" benchmark. The designer and engineer determine these benchmarks in the project initiation phase at the outset of the commission.

Working with Other Consultants

In addition to the designer, the primary consultants on pre-design projects are the MEP/FP engineers, and sometimes a structural engineer who may need to confirm structural loading and provide supplemental design.

It is this group of three consultants who provide the primary professional licensed service to the client. They take the legal responsibility for their portions of a project and are held accountable by the state that granted them a license to practice. Quite often, code consultants help expedite the filing of the documents with statutory authorities having jurisdiction over the project while providing expert advice on a design's compliance with city, state, and federal codes.

Whether the client contracts directly with these consultants or they are contracted through the interior design firm on behalf of the client, these consultants should follow the directions of the interior design firm regarding meeting deadlines and coordinating their work.

If the pre-design commission includes a search for new buildings or locations, the engineer provides a scope of service that can be summarized as a due diligence study to investigate whether enough capacity exists in the base building systems to meet the client's needs. If the services provision falls short, the engineers need to quantify that shortfall. At a later stage this can support the client's lease negotiations with the building owner.

In projects where the client is considering an equity stake in a new building, the number of consultants in the strategic facilities planning needs to be expanded to include specialty consultants who will advise on specific building elements such as structure, sustainability, vertical transportation, and acoustics, in order to insure that the building complies to the specifications and drawings prepared by the owner's consultants. For projects of this nature it is common for a client to retain a construction manager to review and advise on the owner's contractor and their methods, logistics, and costs. If the client's design team requires building modifications, they need to be properly priced as additions and deductions by the owner for charge-back to the client.

Where any type of property search is involved, the client should have a professional real estate advisor involved as well as legal counsel. With today's reliance on IT, the client's communication and IT advisors (in-house, outside, or both) should be involved in the project from the beginning. How those are managed vary from being completely in-house to completely outsourced, depending on the client's organization and the size of the project.

As you can see, these teams can become quite large. How they are organized, the reporting structure, and the approval processes differ greatly with different clients. The Internet and project management software enables us all to communicate more efficiently and deliver information that is readily accessible to all parties.

Regardless which of the three typical pre-design services one may be performing, the common thread through them all is to gather the right information at an early stage to truly understand the objectives of a project. This, in turn, will result in a more informed design process and better design solutions.

8

Programming for Change

BY PAMELA ANDERSON-BRULÉ

Process

At the commencement of any project, when one begins the process of discovery into their clients' needs, wants, and desires, one thing is surely present no matter the project or client type, and that is change. Whether it is a residential client in search of a home, a corporation in search of a headquarters, a government agency in search of a public facility, or a new project or remodel, there will be change.

Change is a very powerful occurrence and has notable effects on the humans whose lives are wrapped around its events. Change brings with it every spectrum of emotion, from excitement and expectation to fear and apprehension. It is in the presence of the unknown that these emotions can often be magnified and affect the quality of communication and understanding that needs to be present to successfully design a project.

In order to begin to discover the effects of change on the client and on their future needs, one must consider the effects of change on the client's entire system. If you are designing for a family, the effects of change will be different for the husband than they were for the wife or the children. What might work well for the finance department might cause an issue with the human resource department, for example. Therefore, we must look at our clients as a whole system and we must also understand their parts, their structures, and their strategic objectives if we are to assist the client in making successful decisions about its future.

Programming, in a broad sense, is the process, methodology, and tool used in the discovery and/or creation of the unknown to the known. Depending on the complexity of the problem, the magnitude of change, and the emotional and factual understanding of the client for their own future desired state, it can be simple and straightforward, or it can be extremely elaborate, with a multitude of interrelated or interconnected parts.

"Traditional" programming records a description of space needs and documents the elements within a project that are necessary to successfully meet the client's requirements. The process used to establish this document is typically an interview, or sometimes a questionnaire, between the client and the designer, recording their responses. The client is then asked to review the information and confirm the content of the program, which then becomes the guide and checklist for the designer.

This traditional method assumes that the client is capable of understanding its own circumstances, analyzing the effects, re-planning and re-organizing for its future, and then clearly communicating this to the designer in terms of building needs. It also assumes that the client's representative has a thorough understanding of its entire system and the complexity of its own cultural, technical, financial, and organizational needs, etc. Certainly, in most cases, the clients do not even completely understand their own current state and are often responding to their existing physical space or cultural archetypes in a way that may no longer be valid.

How, then, do you begin to build common understanding of the "change" that will occur, and how do you assist your clients through a process of discovering the unknowns?

Process Design and Development

You must begin with a planned process that is designed around the end results that you and your client seek. Similar to the way you would design a project, you must start with a conceptual idea of the process, explore areas for analysis, and determine what level of effort and cost the client is willing to invest in its own development. Once these concepts are outlined and agreed upon, a game plan with agendas must be created to guide you through the process. It must be facilitated in a way that allows for open exploration, honest feedback, and well-thought-out direction. The process must address the emotional, cultural, operational, and/or functional needs of the client. It must include the analysis of existing conditions as well as the projection of the client's future needs, which will support their strategic objectives.

It is important to understand that the discussions need to be highly interactive, participatory, and open to questioning by all. In the 1999 publication, *Excellence by Design: Transforming Workplace and Work Practice*, by Turid Horgen, Michael Joroff, William Porter, and Donald Schon, in association with Space and Organization Research Group (SPORG) of the Massachusetts Institute of Technology's School of Architecture, there is a discussion of "process architecture." The book describes the necessary steps to providing process leadership to accomplish the goals of transforming a workplace. "Process architecture requires openness to creative tension between the user and practitioners. This approach is much more demanding than traditional programming. . . . Process architecture demands a tolerance or zeal for open-endedness and persistent uncertainty. For the process architect, the design is never entirely complete . . . however, one characteristic of the design process in that one rips apart what has been, looks at it with different eyes, and puts it together in a way it has not been put together before."

There is a variety of facilitation methods that can be used in an interactive manner for information gathering. They include one-on-one interviews, focus groups (structured discussion with pre-selected participants both internal and external to the organization), open forums, workshops (internally focused working sessions), and benchmarking (guided tours of similar or relative projects, with focused discussions). It can also be appropriate to use questionnaires, surveys, etc., to gather information that can provide valuable data to the project, where an inclusive process does not affect the outcome of the information.

The concept of facilitating a process rather than just doing one is fundamental to reaching a superior level of service to our clients. It is as important that the building is ready for an organization as it is that an organization is ready for the building. Facilitating a client through this interactive process can often be the catalyst for change to begin and can encourage it to continue even after they occupy their space.

In the example of the San José Martin Luther King Jr. Library, a large joint use facility was envisioned where city and state university libraries were integrated into a single facility. Their vision was to create seamless service, a united culture, and a project unique in the nation between two distinctly different organizations. A facilitated process allowed for the discovery and acknowledgement of complexity and initiated the necessary steps to cultural and operational development years before the completion of the facility. In this way, the architecture of the organization was developed in unison with the architecture of the facility, and alignment was reached between the organizational objectives and their vision.

Systems Analysis

To begin to truly understand your clients' needs, you must understand their current state or system. In order to accomplish this, you must go through a discovery process, which will allow you to gain enough insight about them to be able to record their current state. This is typically done through an interactive process, involving individuals within the organization to ensure that you have accurate data and information.

One example of this might be the programming of a public health clinic. If you were to interview the administrative staff and ask them to map out their current work process, you could get a completely different outcome than if you ask the same task of the nurses, and yet another if you asked the doctors. The reason for this is that each of the participants sees the system from a different perspective and, in fact, may not understand exactly what actually happens. Through this example, we can see why it is so important to use "cross-functional" teams of individuals when you are working with organizational complexity.

It is also important to talk to each of the departments or groups individually so that you can understand their individual perspectives and needs in isolation of the whole, or you could easily miss an important issue. Even in the case of residential design, if you discuss the client's needs with only a couple, you may never discover an unspoken but truly important need of one of the individuals.

Also, through the interactive process of defining the existing conditions, one needs to record what works and what does not work within the system. Often times, in a designer's excitement to create a new space, things that worked quite well and are truly important to the client are lost and not missed until the project is complete. By asking questions about what works and why, the designer can gain a deeper level of knowledge into a variety of conditions for the clients organization. This will make the designer more astute when the program is finally complete and as the design is being developed.

Work/Live Flow Analysis

Work-Flow Analysis or Live-Flow Analysis (for residential projects) is one tool that helps record the day-to-day reality of an organization or group. Every aspect of the organization or group must be discussed as you walk through a typical day, week, month, and year. It is important to capture physical, cultural, emotional, financial, technological, and organizational needs that are attributed to the way one leads one's life and work.

If any one of these aspects is forgotten, the user and the designer will not be fully aware of how change might affect them and will be unable to plan a design that will support them fully. As our lives become more complicated, as change becomes a constant, and as time becomes more in demand, the way we work, live, share knowledge, and survive will become more dependent on the quality of the spaces in which we live. The ability of the design space to nurture our personal and professional needs will be paramount to our survival as a society.

External Factors and Drivers

Once this information is captured, the discussions should expand to external factors that will drive the system. Something as mundane as how the garbage is stored and collected, how supplies are delivered, or how the children enter the house on a rainy day can often lead to process discoveries that have real and serious design implications.

Logistical Issues

Another level of analysis that should be performed is the review of logistic issues that will affect the project and the client in the process of completing design and construction. Does the project need to be phased? Will your client occupy the space during a remodel? How will move coordination be handled? What contingencies need to be included in the schedule? All these may seem to be more construction-related questions, but in fact, they may lead to the discovery of elements that will need to be considered in the program design, and certainly in the project planning from the very beginning of the project.

Conclusion for Systems Analysis

The concept of doing a full investigation into all of the matters that might affect your client in the process of change leads to the discovery of unknowns and allows for you to collaboratively work with your client to design the next steps. It should be noted that one should never be married to the end result while proceeding through this process. The real solution to the need for change may in fact not be in a built project, but in organizational change.

It is not until we have gone through these interactions with our clients that we will be able to rebuild a new system for them that will support them in the future in every aspect of organizational success. Inevitably, the journey that you will go on with your client through this discovery process will be in and of itself more valuable to them and you than the actual end result. As important as it is to plan out the process, it is equally important to continually monitor your progress and be completely open to redesigning it when the need arises.

Cultural Development

In the current state of the world of acquisitions, mergers, blended families, joint use projects, etc., there is a real need for the development and understanding of a client's culture if a designer is going to have an appropriate level of insight to design the project. Even when working for existing companies, organizations, agencies, and individuals, there is often a "cultural void" to their own understanding of themselves. If there is not an alignment on this level, the project is at constant risk of inherent conflicts that can develop from the individual whims of participants.

It is important to make sure that there is the right level of participation in a project of key decisionmakers. A core team of key representatives and stakeholders who will validate the proposed plan and provide direction and leadership throughout the process should be selected at the very beginning of the project. If an organizational vision exists, it must be reviewed and validated, and if it does not, it must be built. The core values of the client must be articulated and aligned to their stated vision. This provides the framework for decisionmaking, and should be constantly present as the programming decisions are reached. The success of the programming effort can then be measured by the degree to which the program supports the organization's core values, vision, and objectives.

Ideally, development of the client's new system will include the "right people" at a deep organizational level, at the right times. However, not everyone in an organization will have been involved, and communication is necessary to ensure that nonparticipants will accept and support the proposed changes to their environment. A plan can be developed that will address the needs of the whole organization as it moves toward implementation, and might include ongoing communication, an input and feedback loop, and individual and team training where needed to prepare for future operations.

The Space Program

The space program document can reflect both the programming process and its outcome. Elements of a comprehensive space program for a complex organization might include all of the following components, where as a residential space program might only contain a few of them in a reduced format.

1 Introduction
Description of how information is organized within the document, a glossary or definition of terms, general assumptions, etc.

2 Organizational Vision, Core Values, and Strategic Objectives
Vision statement, core values, and objectives that provide the framework for the decisions that led to the space program and should guide the designer throughout the project. For a residential project, this might be a written "dream" by the client of their future home.

3 Process and Methodology
A summary of the process and its participants. Future users of the document will gain an understanding of how and why decisions were made.

4 Operational Plan
Documentation of future operational and functional scenario(s), developed through the systems analysis, which form the basis for the space requirements. An operational plan could also include an implementation strategy (the necessary steps to achieve the future scenario), and address resource allocation (budgeted time and expense for staff, consultants, and any other necessary resources to implement the operational plan).

5 Critical Issues List
A description of any issues or elements that are critical to the success of the project, or that must be addressed or resolved in design.

6 Space Program
a) Space Allocation Standards
Where appropriate, standards for space allocation can be developed based upon functional requirements, hierarchy, etc. Especially in large facilities, standardization of the size and technical requirements of conference rooms, workspaces, etc., creates modular spaces that support future reconfiguration or alternative use.

b) Qualitative Spatial Requirements
A narrative that describes the vision for the quality of the space, which can include "how the space should look or feel."

c) Building Standard Assumptions
i) Technical Standards
Includes structural, mechanical, electrical, technology, lighting, plumbing, security, communications, audiovisual, and acoustical requirements.

ii) Departmental Grossing Factors
A factor applied to net square footage of each department that accommodates interdepartmental circulation, etc., and creates the total departmental gross square footage.

iii) Building Grossing Factors
A factor applied to the sum of the departmental gross square footage and accommodates building systems, building circulation (department to department and vertical, where applicable), wall thickness, etc.

d) Quantitative Spatial Requirements
i) Quantity, Square Footage Allocation, and Function for Each Type of Space
For each type of space, the total quantity, net square footage, functional and use comments, and staff projections.

ii) Space Data Sheets for each Type of Space
   1) Technical and Building Systems Requirements *(Reflects conditions atypical to building standards)*
   2) Projected Furniture, Fixtures, and Equipment

e) Space Layout Diagrams
Typical conceptual space diagrams—conference rooms, training rooms, workspaces, standard office layout, etc.

f) Functional Adjacencies
Describes the primary, secondary, and tertiary adjacency requirements of individual spaces in relation to other spaces.

g) Functional Stacking Diagrams
Describes the adjacency requirements of individual departments or subdepartments in relation to other departments both horizontally and vertically (multiple floors).

h) Site Development Criteria
Site requirements developed through the systems analysis such as accessibility, parking and transportation, and amenities such as proximity to other services, etc.

7 Appendix
a) Meeting Memoranda
b) Participant Listing

Tools

The level of information collection that has been outlined can be overwhelming. Yet if any of the details are forgotten, the outcome can be a missed detail, an inaccurate assumption, a design with flaws, and an unsatisfactory end result. If we accept the notion that the quality of the project is equal to the quality of the process and that information management is the key to meeting the functional as well as the quality goals of the project, then we must find a way to collect, record, change, track, measure, and learn from information.

The current means available to effectively accomplish this is through a relational database. Development of a relational database, which is designed to support the process and includes the specific types of information required, acts as both a repository and a checklist for information. When a database is used, it can be designed and programmed to capture specific information as well as to allow change tracking and program reconciliation to development of the design. The most important aspect of inputting information in a database is to ensure that its integrity is maintained over the life of the project.

Program reconciliation is accomplished by comparing design documentation at periodic intervals (i.e., 50 percent design development, 100 percent construction documents, etc.) to the initial space program. Tracking the initiation and approval of changes to the space program, as reflected in the actual design, is necessary to ensure that the original goals are eventually met at completion of the project or are revised to accommodate the change.

Conclusion

Programming is really the art of knowledge management, which is constantly changing and expanding with our ability to manage information. We need to creatively collect, record, and manage this information if we are to accomplish the act and art of design. Innovative design must be fundamentally functional and in alignment with the vision, goals, and objectives of our clients and their organizations. In essence, it must not only align to their strategic needs, but also to their cultural and even emotional needs. We can never reach this objective if we are not willing to expand our thinking, invest in our tools, and train ourselves in the art of facilitating and designing process. We must be willing to involve ourselves at an emotional level if we are going to achieve meeting the emotional needs of our clients through design.

9

Schematic Design: Communicating the Design Spirit

BY ORLANDO DIAZ

S chematics are the most inspirational and creative phase of the design process. Schematic design is when you communicate three-dimensional and decorative ideas about the space to the client. To reach a point where you actually have ideas to communicate, you will need to have completed the programming and the planning phases, not only from the quantitative information, but the philosophical as well.

While the entire design process is a collaborative one, schematic design should be the responsibility of a single mind. This phase of the process is the most creative expression of the project: schematics illustrate the spirit of what the space will become; therefore, it should express the designer's insights and intuition. In the case of a collaborative or group effort, there must be a designer who synthesizes the various points of view. When all the individuals are creators of their own ideas, the master coordinator must synthesize the different ideas. It is not easy to be the single creator of an architectural expression, and it is even more difficult to be the orchestrator of differing opinions.

Programming also includes finding out what the social behavior of the company is and what image the company wants to project to the public. In residential projects, how do the clients live now and how the new environment will change them in the future?

The information gathered during the programming phase should also capture accurately the identity of the client. The planning phase of the project should begin to express the potential architectural character. However, sometimes the reality of design practice gets in the way and the individuals who gather and plan the space are not necessarily the persons who develop the schematic design. The designer should be assessing or participating in the assessment of the purpose of the project through the programming and planning phases.

Schematics are expressing to your client what the solutions will look like in a general sense. You need to be able to express your ideas both verbally and visually. Verbalization gives or transfers immediately your expression for the project.

Visually, there are several techniques for presenting schematic designs, like renderings or models or virtual computer realities. My hesitation about them is that they make a very detailed perception, especially in the case of computer-generated drawings (they don't call it virtual reality for no reason) where the definitions of the lines create the impression of a finished idea. I prefer to use hand drawings that show not only the reality but also the illusion of the ideas conveyed. The client is going to interpret exactly what he or she sees. With the schematics, you want the client to see a general picture and get a feeling about how the space is going to look. Schematics illustrate—they don't document. It's important for clients to realize that the specifics of the interior (architectural details, finishes, materials, furniture, fabric, paint color, flooring) have yet to be precisely determined.

The most important factor for the designer is to understand and be emotionally involved in what he or she is about to create. No good solution comes out of dislike (of the project or the client). Empathy with the project is of extraordinary importance.

Great ideas don't execute themselves. A design is what you build, not what you think you wanted to build. The compromises and the limitations are integral parts of the design. The big idea is a reflection of two equally important components: the first is how well the designer integrates the desires and requests of the client into the solution, and the second is how experienced, talented, and creative the designer is in such interpretations.

Creativity for its own sake doesn't necessarily constitute a viable solution and often results in ideas that are out of sync with the program. One has to reevaluate the solutions as well as the program. The idea might be so strong and unique that it conflicts with the program, or the idea might be so weak as not to represent the desired goals of the project.

Our programming is always tainted by our own and the client's experiences, and without careful attention, can produce preexisting solutions. The designer should evaluate when the end result for a project may be close to a preexisting solution. The designer's task is not to reinvent the wheel; rather, it is the designer's obligation to make sure that every effort has been made to ensure that client's individual characteristics and preferences are expressed in the program, in the schematics, and, ultimately, in the finished space.

One should always begin programming by asking: What makes you different from anyone else? What do you tell your potential clients? What image do you want the public to have of you? Those questions help us begin to analyze our clients, their perspectives, their philosophies, and their images.

The most important and eventually most satisfying aspect of the project for any client is creating a building or a space that truly represents them. In order to achieve the desired effect, the designer has to resolve a variety of conflicts, even when a client might have a clear vision of who they are and have strong opinions of what they like. For example, the CEO of the company understands the company's image and the demands of the budget, but someone who is only concerned with the dollars may give the designer instructions based only on financial concerns, which may result in design decisions that don't produce what the company needs. Another type of conflict happens when the business partner of the design company gets information from the client about programming and budget and then translates that information to the designer in a way that omits the client's philosophical concerns or his or her own opinions. The designer has to be involved in the pre-schematic phases of the project; the designer will hear and discover things about the client that other people won't.

There is the tendency to begin a project with predisposed ideas—for example, open or closed plan offices, etc. One must make an effort to integrate those considerations into discussions so that we don't take solutions for granted.

A commercial client (a corporation, a financial firm, a law firm) is much more apt to define its identity. Commercial clients do this all the time because they have to define to their customers what they do and what they make. Hospitality clients have a better perspective because they know when they engage a designer who their customers are, who they want to attract, what image they want to portray, and what their economic parameters are.

Residential design clients, for the most part, are couples with different upbringings who have lived in different environments most of their lives. Aesthetics are one of the last things that any couple ever discusses. They might talk about how nice it would be to have a house in the country, or that they'd like a larger place in the city, but they rarely talk about what kind of house or place they might have. Most residential clients tell you what they want, but not who they are.

Most design programs are concerned with quantity of space and how that space is distributed. A program generally maps out the working relationships among people, but it rarely touches on how people performing any given function interact on a personal basis or the degree of privacy or social interaction they need to have.

We should recognize that economics and time are integral factors that affect the possible solutions. One should not design for solutions that create delays and discomfort for the client unless the client accepts that they are for their own benefit. Nor should one design beyond the economic parameters pre-established by the client.

When doing schematics, the designer must be responsible for both budget and time. An experienced designer knows when he or she is pushing the boundaries of one or the other. Sometimes you know that the best solution requires extending the time, expanding the budget, or both. It is then the designer's responsibility to present to the client the repercussions of their ideas and to reassure that he or she is suggesting these changes not to fatten their own ego or wallet, but because they are actually the best solutions for the client.

It is a designer's responsibility to adjust the creativity of the designs to the economic means of the client. A great idea without the money to execute it is not a great idea. It is imperative that at least general information is obtained before beginning the schematics to know how to budget for the proper expectations. There is no truth to the statement, "I don't know." Clients always know, or they at least know what their limitations are. A client who says to you, "Give me ideas and the price, and I will tell you if I want it," offers more drawbacks than you might suppose, since it can easily result in solutions that lack a cohesive point of view.

The amount of time it takes for a project to become reality is the factor least within the designer's control. While, in general, we know how long the normal design and construction process takes, approvals and construction considerations are outside the designer's control and often create the most undesirable results. The designer's responsibility is to create solutions that can be accomplished within the reasonable and customary time that it takes to execute an idea of similar complexity within standard practice.

Creating things that work is not a real criterion. Functionality is an integral quality of whatever is created. A good idea is only a good idea if it serves the purpose for which it is created. The most confusing attitude in design for the client is that aesthetics and functionality are forces that work against each other.

Aesthetics are the most esoteric quality of a good solution, but they are by far the most easily perceived and appreciated qualities of any project. They are also, in the end, the most emotionally fulfilling. There is no human pleasure deeper than emotional pleasure. Aesthetics are not contradictory to time and money.

Uniqueness is a responsibility of the designer, who takes a vow of creativity just by choosing this profession. The designer does not just issue formulaic solutions; he or she applies his or her mind and experience to the particulars of each specific client and problem. No two people, no two businesses, or no two families are alike. Therefore, no two solutions should be alike. Being unique is not necessarily reinventing the wheel with each and every project. The human mind is the greatest computer in the universe, with the ability to create infinite combinations of all the available resources. The designer must use his or her mind to the fullest to strive for the best answer. At the same time, uniqueness is the quality the client most frequently inhibits inadvertently. People have a picture in their minds of what they want, and intrinsically it is what they have already seen. In contrast, the designer's ability is to see what has not been seen before. While knowledge of what the client wants provides a great starting point (it can set a general direction), it can also impede creativity. It takes time to explore, converse, and prove to the clients that multiple possibilities exist in addition to those they've seen. It is extremely important that the proper time be allowed for the designer to get to know and prepare the client for all possibilities.

A good idea doesn't build itself. The designer needs to know or understand all of the existing physical conditions, as well as the new conditions to be created. This information is critical to the designer in the course of generating ideas, in addition to during the design process itself. Consultants, therefore, are very important because they can analyze the physical limitations as well as the physical possibilities of all components of the solution—both materials and technologies. The proper knowledge of materials old and new and the unlimited ways to use them should be part of the designer's vocabulary while preparing a solution.

Designers need to understand that the original concept might change during the course of the project because of unforeseen circumstances. No one can expect the schematic design to cover all the possible conflicts; rather, it should set a good path for design development of the project.

10

Design Development: Designing the Project

BY STUART COHEN

esign development is the process of taking the work produced during the schematic design phase of a project, the conceptual design sketches, and other forms of information or research and continuing its development. This is usually done through design decisions that go into greater detail with respect to the quantifiable aspects of a project such as size, materials, and methods of construction. Depending on the type of project and the design professional's role, the work to be done may include a first attempt at generating dimensioned floor plans and wall elevations, the selection of materials and manufactured products, and the design of construction details showing how different materials and finishes come together. Because we are architects as well as interior designers, during this phase of our work, we are concerned with the development of both the exterior and the interiors of the buildings we do.

As architects, we are often puzzled by the conceptual separation between the interior and the exterior of a building and the separation of professional services that characterizes the work of most architects. We believe that the same formal and compositional ideas that generate the exterior of a building should inform its interior. Our practice is primarily custom residential architecture. While most of our clients will work with an interior designer or a decorator on the selection of furnishings, we define the scope of the services we provide as extending to the design, selection, and specification of everything that is permanently attached to a building. Because we are designing both the building and its architectural interiors, we usually deal with the building's basic planning rather than issues related to interior design during schematic design. During this phase we are establishing basic plan organization and exterior massing in freehand sketches. Window locations are always considered from the inside as well as the outside, but the interiors are still thought of as spaces rather than being fully conceived. These spaces may have unique characteristics because of their configuration in plan or section, but the materials, finishes, colors, details, and other features we associate with the work of interior design are rarely considered at this point. Occasionally we will make thumbnail interior perspectives to examine a special feature of a space that we want our clients to understand in three dimensions. This usually happens when the space or element being sketched is integral to the floor plan strategy we want to convince the client to accept. The real work of conceiving the interior features of the houses we design begins during the design development phase.

The computerization of the drawing process requires precise dimensional information to be entered into the computer to draw each line. Thus, early in the design development phase, the plans and exterior elevations of the building have been drawn and quite a lot of technical information has been established. Decisions about exterior wall construction, exterior materials, floor-to-ceiling heights, and window types and sizes have been established through the simple need to enter real dimensions into the computer. Design questions such as whether the windows go floor to ceiling or sit on top of base trim or an apron can be addressed. It becomes evident that something as simple as establishing the height for the tops of windows and interior doors may depend on selecting, designing, and detailing interior trim conditions. This is true whether these are profiled millwork or drywall and plaster corner beads. After these decisions have been set, the work of conceiving the interiors can really begin.

Like in the schematic design phase, we conceive the interiors in freehand drawings. These are usually perspective drawings that show the features of a space such as vaulted or angled ceilings, clerestory windows, interior windows and doorways connecting interior spaces, fireplaces, and built-in cabinetry. These freehand sketches will be made for all the principle spaces in a house. These sketches are never constructed perspectives. They are developed in the same manner as sketch plans: through successive layers of tracing paper on which alternatives and revisions are drawn over the original drawing.

A sketch may be redrawn and revised to look at alternative ideas. The process continues until the drawing looks good. This may result in revisions being made to the floor plans. The perspective sketches are idiosyncratic in that they may have multiple vanishing points in an attempt to unfold or view the space as it might appear to us when we turn our heads to take in things that fall outside our normal field of view. In many cases the finished space is remarkably like the initial sketch. This can happen because the finishes and

Library Perspective Sketch (Cohen & Hacker Architects)

details suggested in the sketch are conditions that have been worked out before and are completely understood architecturally and in terms of their detailed construction. We will then meet with our clients. Reactions are usually very positive, and often a client will say, "Oh, now I understand what you were trying to describe."

With the main features of the interiors approved on the basis of perspective sketches, development can proceed. On the computer, each interior elevation is laid out from the plan. The perspective sketches plus information already established are used as the basis for this step. Here because each line drawn represents a corner, the edge of a surface, or a joint between materials, typical finishing details can be solved in a new layer within the floor plans, which were already drawn on the computer. These are conditions that are unlikely to change, and this allows the interior elevations, which are drawn and refined as a part of the work of design development to be converted directly into working drawings after any client directed changes have been incorporated. For us the final step is to model the main spaces in three dimensions. These models are great presentation tools for our clients and design tools for us. They allow us to see visual adjacencies and potential relationships between interior elements that cannot be imagined looking at plan or elevation drawings and might be missed in 3-D computer models and animated walk-throughs. For the time being, we are biased toward the construction of real physical objects, although as more powerful 3-D programs become available, this could change.

The models we make are constructed rapidly by printing floor plans and interior elevations from the computer at one-half-inch-equals-one-foot scale. These are glued down to Foamcore board, cut out, and quickly assembled. They can be rapidly modified on the basis of client comments or visual problems with the design identified by studying the model. Like all the other materials prepared during the design process, they serve the purpose of showing us what our ideas will look like when constructed. They are interactive tools that we can alter, correct, and improve until the information they present to us convinces us that our designs will look good when actually built. At one-half-inch scale, the models are dollhouse-like in their ability to engage a client's attention. We encourage our clients to handle them, to hold them up to eye level, to look into them from different angles, and to use them the way we do: as aids to visualization.

The model then becomes the primary frame of reference in subsequent client meetings when materials are presented and chosen. These are referenced back to the appropriate surface or location in the model. While a client may not really understand issues of continuity between adjacent surfaces, they are easy to see and explain in a model. Often we will make sample boards, however, presenting materials is usually less formal. We will lay out wood, tile, and stone samples on our conference room table, along with catalogue sheets for lighting fixtures, plumbing fixtures and fittings, and hardware. While we try to get our clients to make all of these decisions during design development, many may be put off into the working drawing phase. Although the difference

Tile Layout for New Arts & Crafts Fireplace (Cohen & Hacker Architects)

between natural wood and painted cabinetry is enormous in its visual impact, rarely does a construction detail change when one is selected over the other. However, changing tile or stone thickness or size can necessitate the redrawing and redesign of detail conditions, so we are always uncomfortable when these decisions are put off until later in the project. We have redrawn and redimensioned entire residential kitchens when a client decided they wanted to use Delft picture tiles or some other patterned tile that cannot just be cut at any point along its dimension. I can still remember spending days as a young intern architect working out the tile layout and bonding for floor and wall tiles in the public toilets in Philip Johnson's IDS Center in Minneapolis. This was done so that all the tile joints on the floors and walls would align. We now do this by computer, including scanning the patterns on picture tiles.

As fixtures and fittings are selected, they are added into the elevation drawings. Drawing these elements to scale keeps us from making embarrassing mistakes, such as a medicine cabinet in a bathroom that won't open because the spout on the lavatory set the client selected was taller than the height allowed for the back-splash. Drawing all the elements to scale can save us from aesthetic mistakes as well as functional ones. A very talented interior designer with whom we work tore out and moved a pair of antique wall sconces three times. With antique fixtures or special items of furniture, working from a photo and some measurements, we will draw an object to judge its location and position against a wall or to visualize its scale. Is the chandelier going to be to big or is it so small in a space that it will look silly? Drawing a light

Finished Library Shown in Perspective Sketch. (Cohen & Hacker Architects)

fixture in an interior elevation can help with the decision about what height to hang it.

Drawing fixtures and fittings to scale has become easier to do as many manufactures now supply graphic catalogues of their products on CD-ROM. These allow a drawing of the product to be imported directly into the design development drawing. As mentioned above, we've found this very useful with wall and ceiling hung light fixtures, although few lighting manufactures supply drawing of their fixtures on disc. Drawing other elements such as electrical switches, outlets, and HVAC wall registers is usually done during working drawings. This extra work can save unhappy moments in construction coordination.

In the history of design development there is a cachet afforded to drawing or modeling full size details. Mies van der Rohe's office built full-size models of the details of exterior curtain walls. Kevin Roche had an entire conference room from the Ford Foundation building constructed and furnished. LeCorbusier, the great twentieth-century French architect, had a twelve-foot-tall chalkboard on the rear wall of his studio on which he sketched details and full-scale building wall sections. During design development, we often call in favors from cabinet shops and other suppliers we with whom we work on a regular basis to make us sample cabinet doors or samples of custom-milled running and standing trim. Because the millwork and trim assemblies in our houses play a key factor in determining vertical heights as well as plan dimensions at openings in walls and at inside and outside corners, it is important to us to determine these profiles and dimensions early in the design development phase. To do this, we plot computer drawings of trimmed window and door openings full-scale, including base and crown moldings. These long scrolls of computer plots are taped up to the walls of our office or to the walls of a house we are remodeling. Interior features such as cabinetry and fireplace mantels are printed and considered full-size. This allows us to consider the contour and profile of details, but more importantly it allows our clients to determine how much of an upper kitchen cabinet they can reach without standing on a stool, or where the mantel of a fireplace should fall in relation to their eye level.

Throughout this process, our objectives are to study all aspects of the design in greater detail, to flesh out areas of the project that have not yet been considered, and to guide our clients through the process of understanding what their building will look like and how the it will function for them. With most of the design decisions made, we are ready to start the construction drawing phase. However, before we begin, we need to know if the project is still on budget. During schematic design, estimates of probable construction cost are based on cost information from comparable projects and on unit costs (cost-per-square-foot allowances). In the schematic design phase, we are primarily concerned that the scope of the work and the size of the project are not out of line with our client's budget. Because of the detailed information now available on interior finishes, fixtures, fittings, millwork, and cabinetry, it is important to determine that preliminary assumptions and allowances haven't been exceeded. Because the choices made during this phase of the work can have such large financial ramifications, we usually ask our clients to pay for a detailed cost estimate. While we are capable of providing this service, we usually prefer to employ a cost estimator or a general contractor. If the project is over budget we then must go through the often painful and difficult process of backtracking and reconsidering the decisions we have worked so hard to convince our clients are the right choices for their project.

Below is a list of the steps in the design development process.

1 Work out floor plans, equipment, furniture, and fixture layouts to scale from schematic or freehand sketches. Review any resulting changes in size or layout with client.

2 If you have not previously done so, conceive and communicate to the client your visual ideas for the interiors. What is its character, ambiance, etc.?

3 Draw to scale elevations of all interior surfaces and elements, including built-in cabinets and custom furniture.

4 Do research necessary to select all materials, fixtures, fittings, and furnishings.

5 Draw construction and finishing details for all typical and atypical conditions in the project.

6 Prepare or commission a sufficiently detailed cost estimate to determine whether the cost of the project design, as you've developed it, exceeds the original cost estimate or the budget established by the client.

11

Contract Documents and Working Drawings

BY TOM BOEMAN

Contract documents are comprehensive documents prepared by the architect/design professionals as part of the contract between the client and a contractor for the bidding and constructing of a project. These include documents prepared by the architect and designer as well as documents prepared by the mechanical, electrical, plumbing, and fire protection engineers and other technical consultants. Generally, contract documents include both drawings and written content. The drawings are commonly referred to as "working drawings" and the written documents are commonly referred to as the "specifications."

The purpose of the working drawings is to provide a graphic depiction of the physical components of a project including their relationship to each other and their context. The purpose of the specifications is to provide a summary of additional requirements for executing the work. The specifications include a summary of acceptable products and manufacturers, standards of performance for materials and systems, and their methods of installation or application, as well as requirements for product submittals and mockups as appropriate.

The working drawings and specifications are complementary documents that, together with the owner/contractor agreement, define the contractor's obligations to the owner. The remainder of this chapter will be limited to a discussion of working drawings.

The Intentions of Working Drawings and the Architect/Designer's Responsibility

Working drawings are prepared with two distinct intentions, each with a distinct set of associated responsibilities and obligations. The first intention is to communicate the design intent to the contractor for the bidding and construction of the project. Unlike other design drawings prepared for the client's review, working drawings are prepared for an audience that is already familiar with construction and experienced in the interpretation or the "reading" of working drawings. The working drawings are both technical and conventional in the sense that they employ a specialized language of graphic representations, symbols and language shared by both the design professional and others in the construction industry. The architect/designer has a responsibility to his client to faithfully reflect the design intent and client's expectations in these documents. In fulfilling this obligation, the design professional is expected to perform to a standard of reasonable care for licensed design professionals providing similar services.

The second purpose of the working drawings is to document the conformance of the proposed design to local building regulations or building codes. Many projects will require a building permit from an agency or department of the municipality, county, or other local governing body with the responsibility of protecting the safety and wellbeing of the general public and have authority to grant building permits. Securing a permit usually requires the submission of a few sets of the working drawings bearing the architect's seal for review by the agency. Approval of the plans and granting of a permit are necessary before the contractor can begin the work. These agencies often have specific requirements as to how certain aspects of the project are documented. As a licensed design professional, the architect has an obligation to the general public for its "health, safety, and wellbeing." Conformance of the design to local building codes as well as federal regulations such as the Americans with Disabilities Act (ADA) is a minimum standard for this responsibility.

The Content of Working Drawings

Because working drawings are intended to convey the information necessary to accurately bid and construct a project, there is essential content necessary in every working drawing set. This content includes:

- Identification of all materials to be employed in the construction.

- Details and elevations indicating the correct relationships of these materials.

- Dimensions indicating the proper physical relationships of building elements.

- Identification of manufactured items such as light fixtures, equipment, and appliances.

Content that is typically *not* included in the working drawings includes design drawings such as overall sections and perspectives prepared for the client's understanding and benefit.

The Structure of Working Drawings

Working drawings consist of individual drawing sheets collected into a single "set." The sheets are all prepared using the same title block. The title block includes three major groups of information. The first is information about the firm preparing the drawings. This includes the firm name, address, telephone number, and perhaps the URL of the firm's Web site. The second group of information is the project information, including the name and address of the project, the project number as established by the designer or architect, and the name of the client. Third and final is information for the specific sheet such as the sheet number, sheet name, and the date the drawing was created, as well as space to track information for each drawing issuances and revision. Title blocks are typically arranged on the right side of the sheet so they are easily accessed in rolled-up drawings. The set normally includes the designer/architect's drawings, followed by the mechanical, electrical plumbing, fire protection, and other technical consultant's drawings. Often, the designer/architect provides a title block and sheet format for use by the technical consultants. The technical consultants add their firm information to a space on the title block provided for that purpose.

The working drawing set may include the following components:

Cover Sheet

A cover sheet generally orients the contractor to the project and the drawing set. Accordingly, it includes a brief description for the project, a location plan, and an index of drawings in the set. The cover sheet also may include locations for the designer/architect's stamp and other seals required for permit.

Legend and General Notes Sheets

The legends and general notes provide guidelines in interpreting the rest of the drawing set. They include legends of symbols and abbreviations used in the set and how they are to be interpreted for this specific project. They also often include general notes indicating what the contractor is to provide in the absence of specific direction otherwise. These notes often begin with "Unless otherwise noted . . ." Legend sheets may also include information specifically pertaining to the permit requirements such as the building occupancy classification, construction class, and exiting capacities, as examples.

Plan Drawings

For interior projects, plan drawings may include a demolition plan, construction plan, power and communications plan, reflected ceiling plan, wall finish plan, floor finish plan, and furniture plan for each floor of a project. All plans should be prepared to the same scale, typically ⅛"=1'-0", or in some cases, ¼"=1'-0". Usually, the engineering consultants will provide several plans as well. These may include mechanical (HVAC) plans, electrical floor plans, lighting plans, and fire protection plans. In addition, the designer/architect is responsible for coordinating the engineer's drawings with their own to confirm consistency in quantities and placement.

Elevation Drawings

The elevation drawings include all elevations necessary and sufficient to describe work not communicable on the plans and/or in the schedules. For clarity, it is recommended that all elevations are prepared at the same scale—typically ¼"=1'-0"—but sometimes larger, as needed, to provide more information. In many cases the plans and schedules are sufficient to completely describe the material and finishes for an individual room or space and elevations are not required. An example is a room consisting only of painted walls, wall base, and doors. Since these items are indicated on the plans and finish schedule, an elevation would contribute no additional information and is not necessary.

Enlarged Plans

Enlarged plans are prepared for areas that cannot be clearly delineated and dimensioned on the plan drawings. Enlarged plans are cross-referenced from the plan drawings.

Detail Drawings

Detail Drawings include wall sections, cabinet sections, and other construction assemblies. These drawings are typically prepared at a 1½"=1'-0" or 3"=1'-0" scale.

Schedules

Schedules are matrices containing additional information about project components that are referenced in the plans or elevations via a key or coded symbol, for convenience. For example, while the construction plans may include a symbol with a door number at each door opening, the door schedule supplements this information with information pertaining to the size, construction, fire rating, and hardware components for each door.

The Qualities of Working Drawings

Working drawings are one of the most substantial work products of the design professional. Their quality has a direct impact on the quality of the final built project as well as the contractor and client's experience of the entire construction process. Irrespective of the type of project or the nature of the design, there are distinct qualities that all good working drawings share. These qualities are clarity, sufficiency, and consistency.

CLARITY

Clarity refers to both the graphic legibility of the drawings as well as how lucidly they communicate the relationship between the construction elements. Quality working drawings are easily read and immediately convey their intentions. The drawings must contain a great deal of technical information while being orderly and clear. For the designer/architect, the goal for the drawings is to inspire confidence and trust that the design intent is clearly defined.

There are several practices that contribute to clarity in working drawings.

- Understand what it is you're drawing. There is no effective way to draw or detail without a working understanding of the construction systems or scope of work you're depicting. If you copy materials from other sources, you must make sure you understand exactly what's being illustrated and assume full authorship.

- Employ common industry-standard graphic symbols and language to the highest extent possible.

- Keep related information together.

- Visually align notes, details, detail titles, leader lines, and other graphic elements within a detail and on a sheet where possible. Maintain a consistent location of items, such as plans, from sheet to sheet.

- Avoid cutting and pasting from other drawings without carefully considering if the contents are appropriate and specifically relevant to the current project.

- Understand what every line on a drawing represents.

- Use varying line weights for emphasis and legibility.

- Graphically distinguish, in a clear manner, work that is the contractor's responsibility and existing conditions not part of the contractor's scope of work. For example, in construction plans for interior projects, the new interior walls should be of a heavier line weight and should "pop out" from the existing core, shell, and interior walls.

SUFFICIENCY

Sufficiency in working drawings means that the scope of work is completely defined without redundancy. That is, the work is documented without being over-documented. Over-documenting undermines both efficiency as well as clarity in the drawings.

Practices that contribute to sufficiency in working drawings include:

- Understand that the contractors will only provide/include items indicated on the drawings and/or described in the specifications. If your intention does not appear on the drawing or specification, it will not be included in the scope of work.

- Look for opportunities for misinterpretation in the drawings and provide additional information as needed.

- Understand any and all relevant existing conditions of the project and be sure those conditions are clearly distinguished in the drawings. However, don't document conditions that do not contribute to an understanding of the contractor's scope of work.

- Understand standard methods of construction. Consider what results you will get if you don't draw an elevation or detail. Pay close attention to those conditions where you are expecting something other than standard construction.

- Detail when and where different systems and the work of different trades come together and must be coordinated.

- Understand what is written in the specifications and avoid replicating it in the working drawings.

- It is not necessary to detail standard manufacturer's systems when those systems are specified and are expected to be installed in accordance with manufacturer recommendations and instructions.

CONSISTENCY

Consistency refers to avoiding contradictory information within the set of working drawings, as well as consistency of the drawings with the physical conditions they represent. A lack of consistency creates confusion and, if extreme, can diminish the contractor and owner's confidence in both the drawings and the designer/architect.

Practices that contribute to consistency in working drawings include:

- Avoid replicating the same information in different sections of the working drawings. As drawings evolve, alterations or corrections made in one area must be replicated in all parts of the working drawings to avoid conflicts.

- Carefully review elevation and detail references to make sure they remain intact for the life of the construction phase of the project. As the preparer of a set of working drawings, you may have a familiarity with the documents that allows you to navigate through the set without actually following the detail reference. It's important to be careful to avoid creating "broken" references since the contractor, who is trying to navigate the set of documents, may be confused or may skip some critical information.

- Always confirm existing geometries and conditions. Although it is common and acceptable to include notes such as, "Contractor shall verify all dimensions and conditions in the field," these notes do not excuse negligence on the designer/architect's part. The designer/architect is expected to exercise due diligence with respect to the conditions that inform the preparation of his or her drawings.

- Avoid drawing details that include speculation or assumptions about existing conditions that have not been tested or observed without noting on the drawings that the conditions require verification in the field.

The Production of Working Drawings

For full-service interior design projects, working drawings may represent between 20 and 40 percent of the firms total billings on a project. As such, efficiency and cost-effectiveness in producing working drawings is critical to the competitiveness and financial wellbeing of a design firm. In addition, a lack of thoroughness or diligence in preparing working drawings can be a key source of construction change orders, cost overruns, and client dissatisfaction. This dissatisfaction can lead to errors and omissions claims against the design firm, which can then impact the firm's costs for insurance and damage the firm's reputation. Therefore, doing the construction drawings right is an integral part of a healthy firm's practice.

Today, most working drawings are digitally produced with computers. Irrespective of the means of producing the set of working drawings, by hand or digitally, the tenants of quality, clarity, and consistency equally apply.

Currently, the most common types of digital applications used to develop working drawings are CADD (Computer Aided Design and Drafting) and BIM (Building Information Modeling) applications. There are several different applications available for CADD (available on most computer platforms), but somewhat fewer for BIM. The applications differ in how the files are organized; how the drawings are created, customized, and automated; and the degree to which they support other design deliverables, such as models and renderings and area reports. In discussing CADD applications, it is useful to distinguish between what are referred to as "basic CADD applications" and "object-oriented CADD applications."

Basic CADD Applications

Basic CADD is close to a literal adaptation of the manual or hand drawing process to the computer. Today, basic CADD is still the most dominant model of production for working drawings, although it is quickly yielding to object-oriented CADD and BIM. In basic CADD applications, two-dimensional drawings and three-dimensional models are created using graphic primitives such as lines, hatch patterns, text entities, and simple volumes. Each graphic primitive is drawn on "layers" and assigned "pen weights" for printing. Drawings are ultimately designed for printing on paper and to a scale. Some of the distinct advantages that basic CADD promises over manual drafting include:

- Easy reuse of graphic components and design assemblies between projects.
- Ease of making changes to drawings.
- The possibility of automating the production of sets of drawings.

Object-Oriented CADD

Object-oriented CADD applications include tools for creating "intelligent" objects in the drawings, which behave in some respects like the object they represent. For example, instead of drawing parallel lines to represent walls, the application presents walls as entities with properties such as height and thickness that can be edited or changed numerically. Once the change is made, the graphic representation will adjust automatically. Wall intersections automatically "clean up," and it is possible to insert doors into walls. The walls automatically break to accommodate the door, and should you delete the doors, the walls will "heal" themselves. Object-oriented CADD applications are often a supplement set of tools or an "overlay" to a basic CADD application. As a supplement, the object-oriented tools are additional drawing entity types to the repertoire of lines and other graphic primitives. Some of the distinct advantages that object-oriented CADD promises over basic CADD are:

- Enhanced productivity in drawing architectural objects.
- Ability to automatically generate schedule for standard objects.

- Ease of making global changes to multiple instances of an object in a drawing.

- The ability to generate coordinated plans and elevations from the single 3-D model.

- The automatic enforcement of drawing standards.

BIM

Although on the surface BIM and object-oriented CAD look alike, they are fundamentally different in the way project content is created, stored, managed, and presented. Whereas CADD is an adaptation of drawing and sometimes 3-D modeling processes to a computer environment, BIM is an adaptation of computer database and information management applications to the building industry.

In BIM applications, the user does not use drawing primitives, such as lines, to build graphic representations of construction items. Instead, the software models the properties and behavior of the construction components, and the user directly interacts with these modeled components in assembling a comprehensive model. Therefore, drawings, sections, renderings, and schedules are all "views," or representations of one single model, and the model can be accessed and manipulated through any one of these views.

For example, a user may change the height of a door in a door schedule. Because the door schedule is a view of the same model shown in the elevations, the user, on returning to the elevations, will find the height of the door in agreement with the schedule.

BIM isn't intended strictly as a production tool, but rather as a comprehensive environment to manage all aspects of a project through the entire design process. The BIM model goes beyond the 3-D representation familiar in even basic CADD applications. It is a highly intelligent parametric model that can include nongraphic information such as product manufacturers and product numbers, as well as special characteristics like weight or recycled content.

The ability to extract this type of information is helpful specifically for projects attempting LEED certification, where, for example, it may be necessary to calculate the total recycled content of a project as a percentage. Extracting this type of information is very difficult with manual drawing or even CADD applications. The distinct advantages of BIM include:

- The ability to add, manage, and extract overall performance data for the design model such as total cost and percentages of recycled content.

- The ability to set up sophisticated relationships between model components.

- The ability to extract quantities of materials.

- The ability to extract calculated quantities such as total "R" values of a building envelop or total recycled content of a project.

- Complete synthesis of drawing information between graphic drawings and schedules.

It is important to clearly distinguish between the final distributed working drawings and the CADD or BIM files used to create them. Only the printed or otherwise controllable uneditable versions such as PDF files should be distributed as the project's working drawings. The CADD or BIM files should never be distributed as working drawings. However, the designer/architect, either as a courtesy or as a contractual requirement, may provide CADD files to contractors for their use in preparing shop drawings or to their clients as part of a contractual obligation. In either case, it is important that the designer/architect provide disclaimers attached to the media and, ideally, in the files themselves, to protect them from improper use and modification and to assert that the material is either "in progress" or "not for construction." This protects the designer/architect from responsibility since he or she is no longer in a position to review the progress of the information.

Selecting the Right Tools

Selecting the right production tool for creating working drawings is a challenging and important task. Initial setup and ongoing maintenance of the software can be costly. Additionally, firms must invest in personnel time to train employees on the use of the platform and to develop standard details, legends, and other graphic components. Currently, the costs for CADD and BIM may range from free to several thousand dollars for each computer installation or "seat." Therefore, careful consideration must be given to the software purchase. Some of these considerations include:

- Ease of use.

- Initial costs.

- Suitability of the application for the design firm's type of work and design.

- Ongoing costs to maintain licenses.

- Ability of the software to integrate seamlessly into the design process including its ability to support 3-D modeling and visualization tools.

- Compatibility with consultant's applications or the broader industry.

- Availability of staff already trained in and familiar with the application.

- Ease of customizing the software if necessary.

- Compatibility with the operation system and other applications in use by the design firm.

Consistent Quality of Working Drawings Across an Organization

Uniformity in the way that working drawings are produced within an organization is a key to the consistent delivery of quality working drawings. Practices that support uniformity in the production of working drawings include:

- Standardization of common graphic elements.

- Creating templates for sheets and project setups.

- Libraries of commonly used details and project components.

- Customizing the application interface to provide ready access to preferred ways of doing things. Make it difficult for the user to do things wrong.

Working Drawing Production and Firm Organization

In addition to the tools used, firms vary widely in how they manage the staff responsible for the production of working drawings. In many offices, particularly smaller ones, the project designer and the technical staff are one and the same. However, in some organizations, the design team and working drawing team are distinctly different teams. In this case, the design drawings are turned over to the technical staff for the development of the working drawings. In either arrangement, practices and policies must be in place to assure that the design intent and client's expectations as established in the earlier design phases are preserved though the working drawing phase and that a substantial durable and serviceable set of documentation is provided.

12

Contract Administration: Getting Started

by Gregory T. Switzer and Robert Sutter

L ike contract documentation, the contract administration phase of a project requires a different set of competencies from the earlier phases of a project. The competencies required during this phase are less about the aesthetic of the project but more administrative focused and look at issues of costs, schedules, and code compliance.

The administration phase is critical to the success or failure of the project. Contract administration, the last phase of a project, is often one phase the client remembers. If this phase is successful in the client's mind, the client will likely consider the entire project successful. However, if this phase is unsuccessful, no matter how well the team performed in earlier phases, it is this failure that the client will likely remember.

The Permit Process

Navigating the myriad of regulations and actually receiving approval to construct your design can be a daunting challenge. The skilled designer will be fully armed with an understanding of the process and be proactive in addressing possible issues that can disrupt the construction process or the design itself.

Each project location will have its own particular procedure for gaining approval for permits. It is essential to determine the Authority Having Jurisdiction (AHJ) for your particular project. In certain cases, there may be multiple AHJs, on the basis of the project location or nature of the work. The customary AHJ will consist of the local building official from the Building Department and fire marshal from the Fire Department. Most jurisdictions have Internet sites that identify the AHJs and requirements. A skilled designer will investigate the AHJ early in the design process and determine which aspects of the design will be subject to the AHJ's approval for permit. While the primary need for AHJ approval and permitting is to ensure the health, safety, and welfare of the public, this process also represents a source of revenue for the jurisdiction. As such, it is important to recognize the responsibility for accurately identifying project costs, and to do so for those specific elements of the design that each AHJ may require. For instance, most jurisdictions only require that capital improvement items (i.e., partitions, doors, and ceilings) be identified. However, there are certain jurisdictions that state, "building permits are required for everything except painting and pressure cleaning." This means that the AHJ wants to review, permit, and take a fee on decorative items such as carpet installation. Knowing all the AHJ requirements beforehand will save time and aggravation later in the process.

Advance planning for the AHJ permits and approval process is essential to ensure timely implementation of the design and construction. Knowledge of the submission requirements, and possibly a preliminary review with the AHJ, may actually help to speed the process along and ensure permit issuance on the first review. It is not unusual for the AHJ to have conflicting requirements that can prove troublesome later on if not investigated before application for permit. Building officials typically use codes written by the International Code Council (ICC) for their review, while fire marshals sometimes use codes written by National Fire Protection Association (NFPA). There are numerous situations where ICC and NFPA differ. In the case of accessibility, the International Code Council references its own guidelines, which can be more stringent than the ADA Accessibility Guidelines for Buildings and Facilities (ADAAG) that some AHJs choose to follow. While you may think these differences are inconsequential, think again. If you have just designed and sold your client on a beautiful full-glass entry door to their suite, the AHJ follows the International Code Council's A117.1 guideline (and not the ADAAG), and that door is considered to be on the accessible route, it may not be approved because it will need to have a kick plate at the bottom.

Equally important as the content of your design will be certain non-design-related matters. Know in advance the "use" or "occupancy classification" of your design and what is allowed in the building. Planning and zoning ordinances govern the activity that can take place inside a building, and it is essential that your design not be for a prohibited purpose. Likewise, it is essential that your design not create an occupancy condition in conflict with the certificate of occupancy for the building, either by exceeding the number of occupants or by being designed for a nonapproved use. Typical "use and occupancy" situations in office planning involve meeting spaces for more than fifty persons, cooking areas using open flame, and certain storage rooms.

Conflicts of planning and zoning can involve significant time and effort, public hearings, and delays to the construction of your project. While infrequent, it is not unusual that a nonconforming interior design can trigger a requirement for additional parking spaces and even new landscaping at the building exterior.

Another nondesign matter involves the scope of work represented by your design. The ICC Codes classify work into three categories or "levels" of alteration. Know in advance how your design will be classified, as certain scopes of work trigger additional upgrades outside of your space and can involve common areas or other tenant spaces. For instance, an office design that has a work area exceeding 50 percent of the aggregate area of the building may require life safety upgrades in egress corridors from the work area floor to the floor of exit discharge. Conversely, a residential design of such size will require the entire residence to be brought up to current code in what is known as a "reconstruction."

Permit applications involve much detail, not only in terms of who can make the application but also the information that must be provided and the administrative steps through which each application must pass. Most AHJs require that a contractor licensed with the jurisdiction be the applicant. This may pose a time constraint on your project if there is to be an extended bidding process. Some AHJs allow an architect or engineer to make the application, then hand it off to a contractor when selected. It is essential to know who can submit plans for permits, and this varies by the state and AHJ. Research these requirements carefully to avoid substantial delays. For instance, some states require that an architect or engineer submit plans where the cost of work exceeds a set value (for instance, New York state's value is $20,000) or where the design involves changes to egress or an engineered building system. Some states, such as Florida, give a licensed interior designer full authority to submit plans so long as the work does not involve structural, fire rating, or life-safety changes. Some AHJs allow a permit processor (formerly known as "expeditor") to be the interface during the permit process. A permit processor may alleviate the designer or Owner from the burdens of the permit submission, including preparing forms, standing on lines, and making plan review appointments. The permit processor may also be invaluable in assisting on the cost of making the application. For instance, most AHJs assess a permit fee in the range of 1 to 3 percent of the cost of the proposed work. However, there may be other substantial fees imposed for seemingly inconsequential items such as adding a sink or making an office out of a storage area. These fees are generally imposed to increase revenue for the jurisdiction. For instance, Florida imposes "impact fees" and Oregon requires "systems development charges." Since these fees may create havoc with a project budget, the designer will want to know in advance if his or her design will trigger these fees.

Be certain to consider the following elements when submitting your design for a building permit:

- List applicable codes and local requirements on the cover sheet of your construction plans.

- Identify the governing accessibility regulations for the project, ANSI 117.1 or ADAAG.

- Indicate the proposed "use" of the facility.

- Provide a key plan showing the area of work and applicable area calculations (gross, net).

- List the scope of work and show the legal description of project premises (lot, block).

- Obtain building owner approval in the case of projects in leased space.

- Research the review process of the AHJ (i.e., planning board, building department, fire department).

- Have the owner or contractor ready the funds for the cost of making the application.

- Identify any streamlining options that may be available (i.e., self certification, special inspections).

- Make sure the construction plans have all necessary code data to ensure a prompt review (i.e., occupancy group, construction type, construction cost, egress and fire resistance data, critical dimensions).

- Know in advance who can make the application and obtain required information on forms (owner, applicant, contractor, insurance requirements, notarization).

- Determine whether the AHJ has a permit checklist and complete during the design phase (see sample).

Even when a building permit is physically issued, the process itself has not ended. Designers must remain vigilant to make certain that the project is completed according to all conditions imposed by the AHJ. During construction, there will be required inspections of the work. Know in advance whether or not the AHJ will allow the use of special inspectors. These are private companies that are often available to conduct inspections in less time than the AHJ. Know in advance what parts of the work are required to be inspected. If contractors build past the point of a required inspection, the AHJ may demand the work be uncovered, which can lead to unnecessary delays. Last, you must know in advance all of the AHJ's requirements before occupancy can take place. While not the norm, it has been noted that overdue payments to the jurisdiction, such as for a water bill, can delay occupancy.

The Bidding Process

The interactions of various codes and the complexity of a project involving multiple systems and many inspections complicate the permit process. The same complexity is experienced throughout the bidding process. In what follows, we detail some key considerations that can help designers control who is likely to bid and how they will respond, and identify potential problems with the project in advance.

Preparation of Bid Set

Part of the design professional's interaction with the client involves completing construction documents, even if they are only for bidding purposes (i.e., 75 to 100 percent completion). Designers should always review in great detail and as a separate task the construction drawings that are used for purposes of pricing. This pricing review must take into account the expectations of the other parties involved, namely the general contractors and their subcontractors, and building or property owners and managers. To generate the best results from the bidding process, designers must understand that they will need more than a comprehensive set of construction documents—they will need to provide more detailed information about various components. At first glance, the drawings will always illustrate the level of detail and information that the contractor needs to construct the project, but often the designer should include basic information that may not effect the architectural essence of the project but will provide for a more complete interpretation by the contractor of the designer's submission. The key is to leave as little as possible for interpretation. With this in mind, there are a few simple methods that have proven themselves ideal for projects of any size or type.

Projects involving a construction management process will require special consideration for bidding. In these projects, trades may be split apart from the overall job and from one another. Without information from the design professionals, individual contractors will not have information about how the work they are bidding upon may be impacted by others' work. This type of bidding process requires unusually tight coordination, since bids may be solicited at different time intervals.

Contractors find it useful when, in addition to the actual contract documents, they receive an itemized list of key items to be considered in their take off and costing exercises. Typically, this detailed list should be organized in accordance with the room or area numbers for interior finishes and requirements and general notations, which should reference the plan. An example of such would be:

ROOM 100: RECEPTION AREA

- Non-building-standard carpet (upgraded from building standard/ cost: $20 uninstalled) with marble surround
- Three-way switch for general lighting
- Two core drills for power/data
- Electronic strike and release to reception desk. Programmable keypad for door release at public corridor side
- Class E tie-in
- Fire strobe
- Four outlets
- Emergency lighting with battery backup
- Paint all walls and door frames
- Drywall ceiling
- Twelve down lights
- Millwork reception desk
- Herculite doors with accessible hardware and concealed closers
- Building standard hollow metal door to adjacent interior corridor

Your list can be as detailed or as simple as you like, but it should be synchronized with the level of detailed information in your construction documents. Other things to consider are fire extinguisher enclosures, egress signage, blinds or special treatments for windows, and ADA compliant hardware and appliances. Remember that the more details you provide, the less room there is for oversight by the contractor. Similarly, know what contractors look for on drawings for cost, and even more importantly, where they look for certain information within a set of construction documents.

The next rule of thumb is quite simple: place notations or special requirements on the documents where they are most obvious. That is, a note about a special requirement should appear on the sheet to which it pertains. This is a good habit, especially for bid documents, and it can help to eliminate the problems that arise when design professionals write catch-all general notes at the beginning of the set. These general notes can be overlooked, confusing, redundant, or irrelevant to the actual project. In contrast, page-specific notes allow contractors to bid realistically.

Professional trade organizations such as the AIA, ASID, and AGCA have published detailed methodologies on the bidding process in their respective handbooks of professional practice and by-laws.

Contractor Pre-Qualification

Before bids are taken, the design team should compile a list of possible contractors for consideration. It may identify firms through advertisement, past experience, lists maintained by the building owner, or other means. In addition, the team should prepare a list of criteria that are important to them in selecting a contractor. Consider such things as financial stability, years in business, reputation, on-time and on-budget completions, assigned staff, quality of work, references and satisfaction, and any requirements for union labor. Once the team has evaluated each long-listed firm, it can then narrow the number of possible contractors to a reasonable number. Consider market conditions and size of the job in determining the number of contractors. We suggest a minimum of three and a maximum of six for the typical interior fit-out project.

RFP Preparation

Request for proposal (RFP) preparation is perhaps one of the most important items of the entire bidding process, and designers must follow a standard process, with very little deviation if possible. The RFP will succeed only if the design team conscientiously prepares a form of request that is comprehensive and project specific. The form of request should include the following key elements:

1 Project Description
Briefly describe the project in terms of location and size. Include a general scope of work to be performed by the contractor. Keep it simple. It is not important to be very detailed here. Just describe the essence of the work to be performed.

2 List of Drawings
The RFP should always incorporate a comprehensive list of drawings and their issue dates. It is important for the contractor to know that the set of drawings received is complete.

3 Bid Form
The RFP should include a bid response form. This form allows you to specify how you wish to receive the bid information back from the contractor. Typically, each trade is broken down into its constituent

parts with unit and or line item costs for the project. The bid form is provided for the purpose of evaluating bids equally and to determine the appropriateness and completeness of each submission.

4 Terms and Definitions

Incorporate a list of definitions for terms used in the RFP, regardless of how rudimentary they may seem. Such a list leaves little room for interpretation.

5 Scope of Services

Provide a detailed scope of services indicating the responsibilities of the contractor.

6 Project Schedule

Indicate the project start date and any other critical project dates.

7 General Provisions

General provisions includes project guidelines for bid submission, requirement of site visits prior to bid submission, and contractor due diligence.

8 Substitutions

Provide a clear policy on how substitutions will be addressed.

9 Insurance Requirements

10 Other Project Requirements

Other requirements that should be considered as part of the RFP include an attachment of building, landlord or property requirements, and rules and regulations.

11 Other Attachments

A particular project may require that the RFP include additional attachments. The standard form of contract between owner and contractor, such as the AIA Document A101 or A107, should also be considered.

12 Submission

In the interest of competitiveness and discretion, sealed bids, delivered to the client at a time and place of mutual agreement, are essential. Submissions on municipal projects may require special procedures and they may also involve purchasing units or agents.

Again, the RFP preparation process will establish how contractors interpret project concerns, parameters, rules, guidelines, and form of contract. It is very important to follow a cohesive format and to always provide parameters for submission.

The form of response, as previously mentioned, is essential in the evaluation of bid responses. Typically, one of the most difficult tasks of the design professional during the bid phase is to evaluate what is and what is not included in the contractor's submission. If your submission guidelines are clear and include the above structure, this process becomes quite simple. The following exhibit is the culmination of a well-prepared request for proposal.

Request for Proposal
General Construction

Services of General Contractor
Date: January 1, 2015

I.   PURPOSE:

    A.   On behalf of our client, **Design Firm XYZ** seeking to obtain bid proposals from General Contractors, to be retained as a member of the project team, responsible for the completion of the project as described herein.

II.   PROJECT DESCRIPTION:

    A.   Interior alteration for retail space located at PROJECT ADDRESS. Consisting of the Construction of demising partitions, plumbing and HVAC infrastructure as indicated on the attached drawings.

    B.   The contract documents are as follows.

        1.   Architectural Drawings

No.	Description
A-001.00	Cover Sheet
A-002.00	General Notes
A-003.00	General Notes, Structural Details & Calculations
A-004.00	Full Apartment Floor Plan
A-005.00	Door and Hardware Schedule
A-101.00	Removal Plan
A-201.00	Construction Plan and Partition Types
A-301.00	Reflected Ceiling Plan
A-401.00	Power and Telephone Plan
A-501.00	Finish Plan
A-502.00	Enlarged Ceiling Plans
A-801.00	Elevations
A-802.00	Elevations
A-803.00	Elevations
A-901.00	Ceiling Details / Millwork Details
A-902.00	Millwork Details
A-903.00	Details

        Engineering Drawings

No.	Description
P-001.00	Plumbing Notations, Sanitary & Water Riser Diagrams
M-001.00	Mechanical Drawings and Notes

2.   Documents

    A.   This RFP
    B.   AIA A101 Owner-Contractor Agreement - Stipulated Sum (Provided By Contractor)
    C.   AIA A201 General Conditions of the Contract for Construction (Provided By Contractor)
    D.   Alterations Guidelines
    E.   Building Contractor Calendar for 2009

PROJECT NAME
Request for Proposal - General Contractor
Page 2 of 6
1/1/2015

III.   **TRADES INVOLVED (BID FORM):** FIRM NAME:_____

The following form is provided for our convenience in bid analysis. **Omission of a line item or consolidation of items under multiple lines does NOT relieve the performance of work called for in the contract documents.**

General conditions including insurance, filing, permits, etc.	$_____
- Permit Pick-up all work-types	$_____
Demolition	$_____
Concrete	$_____
Masonry	$_____
Metalwork and structural steel	$_____ N.I.C.
Millwork	$_____
Waterproofing	$_____
Fireproofing and fire-stopping	$_____
Roofing	$_____
Hollow metal work	$_____
Hardware	$_____
Glass	$_____
Acoustical ceiling	$_____
Drywall and carpentry	$_____
Flash patching	$_____
Wall base	$_____
Tile and resilient flooring	$_____
Carpet	$_____
Painting and wall-covering	$_____
Specialties	$_____
Signage	$_____
Equipment	$_____
HVAC	$_____
Plumbing	$_____
Sprinkler	$_____
Fire alarm	$_____
Electrical	$_____
Communications cabling systems	$_____
Security systems	$_____
Audio/visual systems	$_____
Subtotal	$_____
Overhead and profit	$_____
Total Bid	$_____

Note: "NIC" denotes work, Not included as part of this scope.

DO NOT RE-TYPE THIS FORM. FEES MUST BE SUBMITTED ON THIS PAGE. ALL OTHER FORMS WILL BE DISCARDED AND RESPONSE <u>WILL BE WITHDRAWN FROM RFP PROCESS (NO EXCEPTIONS)</u>.

Please provide a separate sheet explaining all exclusions. No substitutions will be allowed. Contractor and Subcontractors performing work on this project are responsible to adhering to the requirements outlined in the drawings, general notes, and manufacturer specifications. All parties must carefully study all notes and items that pertain to their trades. Failure to read the drawings, notes, and specifications does not permit the contractor to deviate from the outlined project requirements.

IV.   SCOPE OF SERVICES

If you are the successful Bidder, the scope of services shall require execution of AIA A101-Owner\Contractor Agreement, Stipulated Sum. Work shall be in accordance with AIA Form A-201 General Conditions of the Contract for Construction attached hereto. Your scope of service shall also include the following items. The listing of these items as an omission or exclusion on your proposal shall NOT relieve the performance of the required services as a part of the stipulated sum base contract.

1. Full-time site supervision and construction management of day-to-day operations and schedules including but not limited to weekly project meetings, as well as establishing and coordinating meetings with subcontractors to expedite the construction process as required.

2. Project expediting and administration to assure proper scheduling of trades, materials, and supplies. Identification of any long lead items and pre-purchasing of same as required to meet project schedules. Preparation of guarantees and operation documents and commissioning of all systems and components with the Property Owner prior to final completion.

3. Obtaining all necessary permits required of jurisdictions having approval over the project, pulling of all permits & securing inspections.

V.   TIME

A. Time is of the essence, but shall not give rise to any claim for non-workmanlike performance or quality other than a "first-class" installation. Critical dates are as follows:

- Start construction no later than or about INSERT DATE with all major trades, long lead items, etc., and finish on accelerated schedule as soon as possible.

B. Completion of all punch list work, if any, must be performed no later than thirty (30) days after substantial completion. Failure to achieve final completion by this period may result in a forfeiture of retainage.

C. Provide Gantt schedule for entire project breakdown by all trades including required time for permit approvals, shop drawing turnaround, and all "NIC" trades.

VI.   CONTRACT INFORMATION

A. See Part IV Scope of Services.

B. General Requirements:

B.1 By making and submitting a Bid Proposal, the Bidder represents:

a. That they have carefully examined and understands the Bidding Documents, and his Bid is made in accordance therewith.

b. That the Bidder has visited the site of the proposed Work, is fully familiar with local conditions and other conditions and regulations where the Work will be performed, and has correlated his observations with the requirements of the proposed Contract Documents and has included such requirements in his Bid.

c. That the Bidder has utilized complete sets of Bidding Documents in preparing Bids; neither the Property Owner   nor DESIGN FIRM XYZ. and Consultants shall assume any responsibility for errors or misinterpretations resulting from the use of incomplete sets of Bidding Documents.

d. That the Bidder has included all sums to cover the cost of the Work and any portion thereof, including all fees, coordination fees, overtime, shipping, freight, delivery, and other added sums as required and specified within the Bidding and Contract Documents. After the execution of the Contract Agreement, no consideration will be given to any claim of misunderstanding of Bidding and Contract Documents.

The submission of a Bid will be construed as evidence that such examinations and stipulations in the Bidding Documents have been made and that all amounts/costs for performing the proposed Work or portions thereof are included. Any later claims for labor, equipment, materials, fees, or for any difficulties encountered on any item stipulated in the Bidding Documents shall not be recognized.

B.2 Bidders shall promptly notify DESIGN FIRM XYZ, and the Property Owner of any ambiguities, inconsistencies, errors, or discrepancies in, or omissions from the Bidding and Contract Documents. Any clarifications or interpretations required shall be requested in writing at least five (5) calendar days prior to the date for receipt of Bid. In addition:

a. The Property Owner and DESIGN FIRM XYZ along with the Consultants shall be the sole judges of the interpretations of the Bidding and Contract Documents.

b. Any interpretation, correction or change of the Bidding Documents will be made by Addendum. Interpretations, corrections, or changes in the Bidding Documents made in any other manner will not be binding, and Bidders shall not rely upon such interpretations, corrections, and changes. Each Bidder shall ascertain prior to submitting his Bid that he has received all Addenda issued, and he will acknowledge their receipt in his Bid.

c. In all cases where a discrepancy between items, description and model number, assemblies, details, engineering vs. architectural coordination, and between drawings and specifications exist, the Contractor shall include in his bid price the more expensive nature. This shall hold true of all work throughout the entire course of the work.

d. Substitutions:

1. The materials, products and equipment described in the Bidding Documents establish a standard of required function, dimension, appearance and quality to be met by any proposed substitution.

2. No substitution will be considered prior to receipt of Bids unless written request for approval has been received by DESIGN FIRM XYZ at least three (3) days prior to the date for receipt of Bids.

3. Approval or disapproval of requested substitution is by DESIGN FIRM XYZ, any decision will be final. If DESIGN FIRM XYZ approves any proposed substitution prior to receipt of Bids, such approval will be set forth in an Addendum.

4. No substitutions will be considered after the Contract award unless specifically provided in the Contract Documents.

B.3 All other work shall be considered as occurring in normal working hours. Bidder shall identify any additional expected overtime costs as a separate line added cost in his Bid, stating the scope and nature of each such costs.

B.4 The Bidders will include in his Bid all costs (including overtime) for removal, new installation and reinstallation work for any plumbing, ceiling (take-down and reinstallation), electrical or telecommunication work, mechanical work, or other work under his Scope of Work included in the Bidding Documents that is required on the vacant, or occupied and operational floors above, below, or adjacent to the Demised Areas.

B.5 Bidders will include in his Bid a listing of all Insurance Certifications, Bonds, Release of Liens, or other requirements per the Property Owner. Procurement of same will be required by the time of Contract and Agreement. Costs of such items shall be included in the Base Bid sums of this Bid submittal.

B.6 The Bidders will include as part of his Bid any costs stipulated in the Bidding Documents that pertain to filing, controlled inspections, etc., as set forth in the drawings.

C. The General Contractor shall conform to all Building Rules and Regulations.

D. The General Contractor shall comply with all obligations outlined in the attached Alterations Guidelines, attached to this RFP. Proposals must include all costs reflecting insurance requirements, delivery hours, etc. as specified in lease or Rules and Regulations.

E. No hazardous materials, as in the case if asbestos is present, will be utilized/installed in this work.

F. All invoices shall be subject to a retainer of ten percent (10%) to be released upon final completion of the work as provided for in the Contract Documents.

VII. INSURANCE

Upon signing of the Construction Contract, the General Contractor shall furnish to the Property Owner and DESIGN FIRM XYZ certificates evidencing the existence of the following:

A. Workmen's compensation insurance covering all persons employed for such work and with respect to whom death or bodily injury claims could be asserted against Landlord, The Property Owner and DESIGN FIRM XYZ, or the demised premises.

B. General liability insurance naming Landlord, its designees, and DESIGN FIRM XYZ. as insured, with limits of not less than $1,000,000.00 in the event of bodily injury to any number of persons in any one occurrence, and with limits of not less than $100,000.00 for property damage. The General Contractor, at its sole cost and expense, shall cause all such insurance to be maintained at all times when the work to be performed for or by the Property Owner is in progress. All such insurance shall be for company authorized to do business in New York, and all policies, or certificates therefore, issued by the insurer and bearing negotiations as evidencing the payment of premiums, shall be delivered to the Derivative Solutions.

C. Contractor's Insurance: The contractor shall secure, pay for, and maintain until all work is completed, such insurance as will protect him and the Property Owner and DESIGN FIRM XYZ. from claims under Workmen's Compensation Acts, Workmen's Occupational Diseases Act, and from any other claims from damages to property or for bodily injury, including death, which may arise from operations under this contract whether such operations be by this contractor or anyone directly employed by either of them.

Such insurance shall cover all contractual obligations, which the contractor has assumed including the "Indemnification of The Property Owner" agreement.

D. Indemnification of the Property Owner and DESIGN FIRM XYZ. The contractor shall defend any and all suits brought against The Property Owner and DESIGN FIRM XYZ, by any employee or other person (whether employed by the contractor or not) for damage or property and/or injury to persons (including death) alleged or claimed to have been caused by or through the performance by the contractor of the work, and shall indemnify and hold harmless The Property Owner and DESIGN FIRM XYZ, Inc., from and against all claim or claims arising out of the work performed by the contractor; also, the contractor shall pay, liquidate and discharge any and all claims or demands for bodily injury (including death) and/or loss of or damage to any and all property caused by, growing out of, or incidental to the performance of the work performed by the contractor, including damage to the building and other property of the Property Owner and including all damages for the obstruction of private driveways, streets, and alleys and all cost and expenses of suits and reasonable attorney's fees. In the event of any such injury (including death) loss or damage (or claim or claims therefore) the contractor shall give immediate notice thereof to The Property Owner and DESIGN FIRM XYZ. Insurance required above, A., B., C., shall be maintained continuously during work. Certificates shall provide for notices of cancellation of not less than 90 days. Indemnification, above D., shall survive the completion of work.

VIII.   **SUBMISSION OF PROPOSALS**

The following submission requirements shall strictly be adhered to. Because of time constraints, if proposals are not submitted exactly as indicated, proposal will be rejected. **No exceptions will be made.**

A. Proposals shall be submitted on company letterhead and signed by an authorized representative.

B. Proposals shall be submitted in the exact format per Article III of this RFP.

C. List of Project Team Members and their qualifications to be included.

D. The Property Owner reserves the right to reject, with or without cause, any or all proposals submitted, to waive any formalities therein, or to accept any proposal where it may appear to be in the Client's best interest to do so. The cost of Contractor's bid proposal submission is to be borne by Contractor regardless if the proposal is accepted, cancelled, or rejected.

E. Delivery - Sealed proposal shall be delivered no later than **Monday, February 16th, 2009 2:00 PM**.

Attention: Individual Name
                                            Principal
                                            DESIGN FIRM XYZ
                                            ADDRESS
                                            New York, NY 10018

Late or incomplete proposals will be rejected. All proposals shall be binding for a ninety-day period after submission.

F. For all inquiries, information, clarifications, and visits to the site, etc., contact Individual Name at (212) 555-1212.

END OF RFP

WALK-THROUGHS AND CLARIFICATIONS

No project will succeed if the contractor cannot easily interpret what the design professional intends. Designers can greatly assist contractors to better understand the project and the work required to complete the project if they hold pre-bid conferences or walk-throughs (preferably at the proposed new project location). It is here where the design professional and the potential bidders meet and discuss issues or clarify questions pertaining to the project.

The design professional should be very conscious of the questions asked and provide not only oral replies but written ones as well. Questions and responses given during the walk-through should be forwarded in writing to all in attendance. This practice alleviates any misinterpretations about what was said during the site visits and again allows for written documentation of what is required for a comprehensive submission. The same should be done for all questions or clarifications asked pertaining to the project throughout the bid process.

BID OPENING/COMPLIANCE

The design professional should establish a formalized procedure for the receipt and opening of bid materials. Regardless of project type, bids should be opened in the presence of the owner or a designated owner's representative. Before the submissions are evaluated, the bids should be recorded and submitted to the project file as received for future reference.

Further, all submissions should be governed by simple guidelines for compliance, in an effort to ensure the timely receipt of bids, format of bid content, and how bids are received. Designers should consider the standard requirements:

- Proposal cost information should be completed in the exact format provided in the RFP.
- Proposals should be submitted on company letterhead and signed by an authorized representative of the GC.
- Telephone, telegraphic, electronic submissions, and unsealed proposals should not be accepted.
- Ask for key project staff (GCs) to be assigned to the project.
- Establish a deadline for submissions. Be detailed.

EVALUATION OF BIDS

Bid evaluation requires the time and expertise of someone familiar with the project and the construction process. It is important for this individual to have authority to address the corresponding contractors with questions for the purposes of determining whether their bid submissions are complete. As a rule of thumb, the evaluation process requires that the responsible person prepare a spreadsheet to compare the line-item costs of each bidder.

The following is an example of the level of information such a spreadsheet may entail.

COMPANY XYZ

1600 Broadway, 10th Floor

New York, NY

BID ANALYSIS

Level Spreadsheet

Date: 4/20/00

Design Firm Project # 48804

	CONTRACTOR #1	CONTRACTOR #2	REMARKS
1. Demolition	$ 750	N.I.C.	
2. Concrete & Masonry	N.I.C.	$ 900	
3. Fireproofing	N.I.C.	N.I.C.	
4. H.M. Doors & Frames	$ 2,100	$ 2,000	
5. Hardware	$ 6,500	$ 6,489	
6. Drywall & Carpentry	$ 47,000	$ 48,700	Includes blocking
7. Lath & Acoustics, Metal Clg.	$ 55,000	$ 53,000	
8. Metal Work & Steel	$ 20,000	$ 9,100	
9. Millwork			See Below
10. Paint/Wallcovering	$ 14,000	$ 11,918	
11. Carpet V.C.T. Base			See Below
12. Window Treatment	$ 2,000	Included in #17	
13. Stone Work, Ceramic	$ 20,000	$ 25,245	
14. Glazing/Glass	$ 58,000	$ 59,102	
15. Appliances	$ 600	Included in #17	
16. Convector Enclosure	$ 14,000	Included in #17	
17. Projection Screen, Specialties	$ 1,650	$ 35,270	
18. Fabric Panels	$ 2,750	Included	
19. Signage			See Below
20. HVAC	$ 60,000	$ 55,000	
21. Plumbing	$ 8,000	$ 8,875	
21A. Flash Patch	Included	Included	
22. Electrical	$ 300,000	$ 295,000	
23. Fire Alarm	Included	Included	
24. Roll Down Grill	$ 2,400	Included in #17	
25. Permits	Included *	Included	*No price submitted - Estimated Cost
26. Filing	Included *	Included	*No price submitted - Estimated Cost
27. Insurance	Included in #28	Included in #28	
28. General Conditions	$ 51,476	$ 70,000	
29. Overhead & Profit	$ 20,287	$ 19,646	
TOTAL BASE BID	$ 686,513	$ 700,245	

Millwork	$	165,000	$	156,497
Carpet V.C.T. Base	$	30,000	$	32,500
Signage	$	4,417	$	4,858	*No price submitted - Estimated Cost
N.I.C Totals	$	199,417	$	193,855
Total including NIC Trades	**$**	**885,930**	**$**	**894,100**
Alternates				
1. Delete Glass Transom and Channel at Desk - Add Gyp-BD & Paint	$	(5,500)	$	(500)
2. Delete MDF Board & Base Beyond Door #27	$	(4,000)	$	(4,600)
3. Metal Convector Cover in Conference Room	$	(10,000)	$	(8,500)
4. Install Sub Zero	$	3,300	$	5,610
5. Skim Coat Elevator Walls - Mount Buttons	$	3,200	$	990
6. Delete Glass Above Soffit in Reception	$	(500)	$	320
7. Install Gyp Board Furring At All Walls, Ceilings & Beams	$	85,000	$	77,000

Schedule

EXCLUSIONS

* Elevator service, building charges (Electrical Shutdowns)
* Overtime (Except for building Standards)
* Fire Watch
* Asbestos Removal
* Sales Tax (Submit copy of capital improvement)
* Controlled Wiring & BMS System Wiring

This process of bid review is also called "leveling" and is a critical step in understanding the contractor's view as to the value of the job. It allows the design team to see how the bidders have thought through what is really required to construct the project. Pay very close attention to any list of exclusions, alternates, and substitutions submitted in their response. The leveling process should address any exceptions to the RFP, including:

- Omitted items
- Clarified items
- Missing items
- Conflicting terms and conditions

In each case, the bid leveling review should result in removing the exceptional item or placing an add/deduct cost next to the item. In this manner, all bids are equally compared.

COMPANY XYZ
1600 Broadway, 10th Floor
New York, NY

Design Firm Project # 48804

BID ANALYSIS
Leveling Spreadsheet
4/20/00

NIC BIDDERS		
BIDDER	BID	REMARKS
MILLWORK		
Millworker #1	$ 160,000.00	* Cushions not included
Millworker #2	$ 149,900.00	
Millworker #3	$ 146,420.00	
Millworker #4	$ 220,300.00	* Cushions not included
CARPET		
Carpet Installer #1	$ 36,072.75	* Includes Sales Tax
Carpet Installer #2	$ 28,145.00	* Includes Sales Tax
Carpet Installer #3	$ 29,221.82	* Includes Sales Tax
Carpet Installer #4	$ 30,692.12	* Includes Sales Tax
SIGNAGE		
Signage Vendor #1	$ 2,485.00	
Signage Vendor #2	$ 2,300.00	
CARPET		
Addendum #4 (Stone to Carpet)		
Carpet Installer #1	$ 42,116	
MILLWORK (Painted Doors)		
Addendum #4		
Millworker #2	$ 148,400	
Millworker #3	$ 142,420	

Award of Contract

The design professional should always send a letter to the unsuccessful bidders to thank them for their interest in the project. Similarly, it is customary to provide the successful bidder some form of written notification to officially inform them that their bid has been accepted before the signed agreements are returned. This letter should also include any information regarding the project kickoff meeting, start dates, and any forms or additional information required before construction commences.

SUMMARY: BID PREPARATION AND RFP

In short, the following should serve as a brief guide for design professionals during the bidding and negotiations portion of a project.

- Review contract documents for biding purposes
- Pre-qualify a long-list of possible contractors
- Prepare the invitation to bid document
- Prepare instructions to bidders, forms of agreement, and solicitation of bids or negotiated proposals from reputable contractors and suppliers known to and deemed appropriate to the project
- Conduct pre-bid meetings with all trades
- Handle questions and clarifications through a formal process with all bidders
- Conduct formal bid opening with client
- Prepare a detailed spreadsheet leveling of all trade bids and assessment of submission
- Confer with client on submissions/evaluation of bids
- Award the contract

Selection of the Contractor

Important as the process of selecting a contractor is to the project, it is a tedious task. Still, the design professional should always be proactive in this process and become intimately involved with the client in establishing pertinent criteria in accessing contractor qualifications. The following are recommended criteria in evaluating the qualifications of a contractor: quality standards, construction and technical expertise, communication and service, experience and viability, references, and willingness to be responsible in terms of price, insurance, and dispute resolution.

CONSTRUCTION AND TECHNICAL EXPERTISE

The owner and design professional should make a conscious effort to look for a contractor who is familiar with or who specializes in the proposed project type. It is important to understand that a contractor who is familiar with the project type understands important issues, such as the material specifications and scheduling required to finish the job within the proposed project schedule.

A reputable contractor will also have an in-depth knowledge of the permitting and safety processes of the local jurisdiction. The more familiar a contractor is with the project type, the better equipped he or she is to deal with issues that may arise during the construction process. Further, a contractor who is familiar with the project type is most likely to prepare reliable estimates for the overall project scope.

Because of his or her vast knowledge of local construction practices and procedures, the qualified contractor should also assist the design professional and the owner with knowledge of products and materials that are readily available for the project and be capable of suggesting supporting information to the design professional and client when selecting products, materials, and techniques. This is extremely important where there can be a cost or time savings.

COMMUNICATION AND SERVICE

It is very important for a contractor to listen to the design professional and owner in order to understand what they need and want. During your initial conversation with contractors, look for a level of enthusiasm and interest in the overall project. Be particularly aware of their ability to interpret design ideas and their ability to suggest ways to make them work within the project budget. A good contractor should possess the ability to alleviate concerns about the project process. The owner and the design professional should always ask the potential contractor for examples of how similar projects were implemented and solved.

Communication is essential. Make certain that the contractor maintains a viable place of business and is readily accessible in an effort to foster maximum communication. There will always be questions and concerns during the project process, and they will often require a response most expeditiously. Communication of this sort is key to a successful relationship.

A contractor who prides him- or herself in customer service is a key attribute in overall customer satisfaction. The general contractor and their employees should always be courteous, competent, professional, and attentive to detail. Always check references and ask questions about the contractor's performance and the level of customer service provided.

When the construction documents are finalized, the bid process is over, and the design professionals have decided on a contractor, there are still several important factors, which should be addressed before construction begins. For instance, the construction process may change the conditions of inhabitation for the duration of the project. Though in most cases these changes or inconveniences will be minor, the owner should be on the lookout for any such potential problems, which may arise prior to the start of construction.

Let's face it: quality takes time and should be remembered throughout the process. This may constitute a wait for special-order materials, long-lead items, or a particular specialty trade contractor (such as a specialized wall finisher) that is known to be reliable. We know that delaying construction may have cost implications to the client and should be avoided.

The best way to educate your client to prepare for construction process is to allow for communication among the entire project team, which includes the contractor. It is important to remember the contractor is fully aware of the detailed activities that take place during the construction process.

Experience and Viability

Before design professionals consider a contractor for a particular project, it is important that they confirm whether or not the contractor has an established presence. A general rule of thumb suggests that if a contractor has been in business five or more years and has been involved in projects of similar scope to the project under consideration, then the construction firm most likely maintains a solid practice and is capable of establishing a solid level of workmanship and providing warranties for work performed.

In addition to being a presence, a contractor must be able to meet obligations if something goes wrong on the project. The design professional may be able to gather some information by talking with other experienced trade contractors such as subs who may have worked on previous jobs with the contractor in question. The design professional will want to know about factors that will provide a level of comfort about a contractor's business experience. Look for such things as licensing and insurance coverage.

References

Design professionals should never hesitate to request a list of references from contractors. Believe it or not, references will almost always be the most reliable source in determining a contractor's level of experience and their ability to perform the work required. Take time to follow up on references, and try to visit one or more of the contractor's recently completed projects. Seeing a completed project may be very telling about the contractor's workmanship and ability to complete a project.

All references are not the same; there are various types of references to be considered in evaluating contractors. In requesting references, also pay close attention to long-term relationships with clients. References can refer to:

1 Jobs in progress

2 Projects completed over the past year

3 Projects completed four or more years ago

Also verify through local authorities whether a contractor has been named in any lawsuits or illegal activities.

List of questions to ask when checking contractor references:

- Would you use the same contractor again on future projects?

- Did the project meet your scheduling requirements?

- Were you presented with change orders? If so, how were they justified?

- Were you pleased with the level of workmanship and quality?

- Did the project go over budget?

- How were the subcontractors on the job? Were they knowledgeable and reliable?

- Was the project site kept clean and safe throughout the construction process?

- Was the contractor principally involved on the project site, and if so, how regularly? If not, who was involved on behalf of the contractor?

SELECTION BASED ON PRICE

Clients and design professionals always approach a project with cost in mind. However, it is extremely important that the design professional and owner not engage a contractor by price alone. Although the lowest price may be particularly accommodating, other issues should be factored into the decision-making process. The designer and owner should also consider the ability of the contractor to perform the required work within the client's schedule, as well as his or her track record, workmanship, and references. In addition, the design professional should consider a detailed examination and breakdown of each bid to determine whether or not the bid includes all project requirements. Mistakes have been known to happen. It is extremely important to check and double-check each submission to ascertain its accuracy. Remember, the lowest bid may initially appear to be the lowest price, but in practice, it may involve serious cost increases. Only detailed bid analysis can determine whether an apparently low bid will translate into low costs in reality.

INSURANCE REQUIREMENTS

In the interest of protecting the client and the design professional it is highly recommended that a contractor maintain proper insurance throughout the entire project process. The design professional should be aware of basic coverage of that should be required for most projects. Additionally, the design professional should also be aware of the requirements established by the property owner and place as a requirement that the contractor request such requirements directly form the property owner to ensure that all requirements are met. Types of coverage typically required include:

- **Workman's Compensation Insurance** protects the owner and design professional in case a worker is injured on the property.

- **General Liability Insurance** covers the owner and design professional in the event the contractor damages the owner's or building owner's property.

- **Automobile Insurance** protects the owner in the event a contractor's vehicle damages another vehicle on the property under construction.

The design professional must receive a contractor's certificate of insurance. Request that a certificate of insurance be provided by the contractor's insurer and delivered to you directly from the insurance provider. This practice protects both the design professional and the owner/property owner. Receipt of a certificate of insurance generally suggests that the insurance is valid and is in the form of an original. Further, all insurance should name the owner of the project (or the building owner) and his or her directors and employees as additional insured to maximize the coverage umbrella.

LICENSING

Design professionals should always verify whether or not a license is required to perform the services being offered to their clients. Check governing authorities to confirm such requirements and confirm whether or not the contractor's license is valid and up to date. Where law does not require licenses, it is vitally important to investigate all references and business practices of the contractor in great detail.

DISPUTE RESOLUTION

Before a design professional engages a contractor, it is very important that all parties understand the rights of your clients concerning dispute resolution. This policy should be clearly established in writing as part of the contract between the owner and contractor. If you, as the design professional, are responsible for engaging the contractor on the client's behalf, you too should have a clear understanding of how disputes are to be resolved and how they may affect you. It is extremely important to have a legal professional review all such contracts to ensure that a reasonable means of dispute resolution is covered. Typically, clauses contained within the agreement between the design professional and the client, the agreement between the client and contractor, and the agreement between the design professional and the contractor provide for mediation or arbitration if a disputes occurs. Mediation and arbitration are generally less expensive than lawsuits as means to resolve disputes.

CONTRACTOR SELECTION SUMMARY

The process of selecting a contractor is not an easy task and requires a great deal of diligence on behalf of the owner, the design professional, and the contractor. Keep in mind the following key components in establishing a process that is fair and reasonable in the selection process:

- Quality standards of the contractor should be evaluated

- Refer to industry standards from AIA, ASID, and AGCA

- Construction and technical expertise

- Communication and service should always be explored in certifying contractor qualifications

- Experience and viability are key factors in selection process

- References should always be checked

- Selection based on price should not be the determining factor, but track record and reliability should be considered as part of the selection process

- Insurance requirements

- If required by authorities having jurisdiction over the project, always verify the validation of licenses required of the contractor

- Dispute resolution makes sure this issue is clearly defined in the form of contract between the owner or design professional and the contractor

Managing the Buildout

Once the contractor is chosen, design professionals may have the contractual responsibility to manage the actual work done on the project. Make sure the service provided during the contract administration portion of a project is clearly defined in the proposal of services provided to the client. Further, it is important for the design professional to discuss these services with the client at the onset of the project. This is extremely important in an effort to alleviate issues of responsibility between the owner and the design professional. Design professionals typically provide the following sorts of oversight and communication responsibilities during contract administration.

- A representative of the design firm should periodically visit the project premises to assess the progress and quality of the work performed by the contractor. During these visits, the design professional should visually inspect the premises and determine whether the work is proceeding in accordance with the construction documents.

- Representatives of the design firm should at all times have access to the work and has a fiduciary responsibility to recommend to the client the rejection of any work that does not conform to the contract documents.

- A project representative of the design firm should attend regularly scheduled job meetings with the contractor to review overall project progress and assist with any required clarifications.

- The design professional should also prepare field reports, bulletins, and field orders, if required.

- The design firm should always review and take appropriate (in a timely manner) action upon contractors' submittals such as shop drawings, product data, and samples for conformance with the design concept of the work as outlined in the construction documents.

- On the basis of field observations, the design firm should always review the contractor's application for payment to confirm the percentage of completion.

- Change orders for design and scope impact for uncovered conditions or approved revisions should be reviewed by the design professional and should always be discussed and agreed upon with the client prior to providing approvals to proceed with the change request. However, it is important to stipulate that the design firm should have authority to order minor changes to the work scope that do not involve an adjustment in the contractor's contract cost or schedule.

- At the completion of the work, the design firm should always prepare a punch list of deficiencies for remedy by the contractor and should, upon completion of the punch list, attend a compliance walk-through.

The following services are usually recommended as an additional level of support during construction to oversee the activities of general contractor/subcontractor. Often, these services provide the client an extra level accountability for a timely project delivery.

- Act as the client's project representative with respect to management of the project during construction

- Receive, analyze, and process payments for all approved invoices
- Review and negotiate all change orders for necessity, time, and cost impact
- Provide daily field presence as may be necessary during construction
- Maintain a spreadsheet of project costs
- Interface with the contractor, subs, and suppliers to a degree practical to assess project performance
- Monitor shop drawings, material orders, and deliveries by the contractor
- Monitor contractor's schedule for sub-trades
- Source alternative suppliers for discontinued, late, or damaged material shipments
- Coordinate client vendors (i.e., Datacom/Telecom providers, movers, furniture installers) with contractor and arbitrate any back-charges or scheduling issues
- Provide item-by-item monitoring of contractor's punch list completion
- Resolve all final payments and claims

Professional trade organizations such as AIA, ASID, and AGCA have published detailed methodologies on managing buildouts in their respective handbooks of professional practice and by-laws. These methods may govern the process on the basis of the form of contract used to retain the design professional and contractor.

Conclusion

There are myriad tasks the design professional takes on to realize their efforts of the design phases of a project. Careful attention to detail will always be the key factor in the implementation and the successful completion of any project.

The preceding sections were written to illustrate the various components of the post-design process of which design professionals should follow. The exact process may vary from firm to firm, but it is important to understand that a level of order and consistency should be maintained from project to project, regardless of the project size or scope. This allows the design professional a system of checks and balances and, thus, a level of comfort, throughout the bidding and negotiations phase into the actual project buildout.

The sections of this chapter were written to illustrate various components of a thorough approach to the administrative portions of the project process. Of course, several processes may be modified to compensate for existing internal workings, but the end result is typically exemplified by strict adherence to a formalized process. The following should serve as a brief list of those things to which special attention should always be paid.

1   Always review contract documents thoroughly before sending them out to bid. If possible, have a checklist in place to review the basics as far as format and critical filing information.

2   Know your jurisdiction as it pertains to codes, which may impact your project.

3   Know the capabilities of those who are to perform the work for you. (Namely, contractors—always check references.)

4   The owner and design professional should make a conscious effort to look for a contractor who is familiar with or who specializes in the proposed project type.

5   Leave little room for interpretation. Bid documents should be clear and concise.

6   Know from whom you are soliciting bids. Prequalify your contractors at all times.

7   The format of proposal requests should be comprehensive and project specific.

8   Time and expertise of someone familiar with the project being designed and the construction process should be allocated to evaluate contractor proposals.

9   Written correspondence should be the only method of notification that a bid has been accepted.

10 Educate your client throughout the project process and allow communication among the entire project team.

11 The design professional should be very conscious of the questions asked and provide not only oral replies, but also written responses.

12 The design professional is always aware of basic coverage required for projects.

13 Design professionals should always verify whether or not a license is required to perform the services being offered to their clients.

14 Before a design professional engages a contractor, it is very important that all parties understand the rights of the clients concerning dispute resolution.

15 Make sure the service provided during the contract administration portion of a project is clearly defined in the proposal of services provided to the client.

16 Document the entire process.

III

Management Issues

13

Managing the Marketing Process

BY LISBETH QUEBE

Marketing: A Guide to Securing Work

In the beginning, interior designers, architects, and engineers would never have used the words "marketing" or "sales." The words had an unsavory connotation, calling up images of used-car salesmen in checkered coats or encyclopedia peddlers in scuffed shoes, rather than urbane design professionals. In fact, until the 1970s, the canon of ethics of the American Institute of Architects (AIA) expressly forbade blatant promotion, and the organizations that preceded the International Interior Design Association (IIDA)—the Institute of Business Designers (IBD) and the American Society of Interior Designers (ASID)—were of similar mindsets. So how was work secured? Through connections and visibility—sometimes known as the "old-boy network." Talent and a striking portfolio were imperatives, but a design professional's practice expanded on the basis of whom he or she knew. A professional's merits were extolled by friends and colleagues, and for a fortunate few, through news stories and magazine articles written by others. As a professional, your eyes were kept suitably downcast.

Today it's a different story. Of course, the old-boy network still plays an important part. Designers must still be both visible and connected. In a profession where commissions are granted on the basis of trust, recommendations and references are forever the gold standard. Yet, over the past four decades, design professionals have accepted professional services marketing as an important part of their business. There is a thriving association, the Society of Marketing Professional Services (SMPS), comprising individuals whose prime responsibility is marketing and sales. It was founded in 1973 and now has nearly seven-thousand members, including principals and marketers from interior design firms, architectural firms, and other allied professions. Today, there are myriad methods for promoting designers and their firms to potential clients. Designers can choose from elective methods, such as advertising, exhibiting, sponsorship, publishing, speaking, and Web site promotion. And they must respond to strict requirements from potential clients for formal qualification packages, proposals, presentations, and project tours. Fortunately, advances in technology have allowed design professionals to make quantum leaps in both the quality and speed of delivery of marketing submissions and materials.

Even though design professionals are aware of these techniques, there is often hesitancy or even real reluctance to move aggressively into a proactive marketing program. Such a program requires work and resources. Marketing, business development, and public relations do cost money, in the form of time and actual dollars. Lots of heated debates occur about marketing expenses and what the "industry average" is or ought to be. In truth, there is no pat answer. But if marketing is thought of as an investment, the picture will become clearer. Just as individuals pick the amount of money they want to invest, and just as they pick the stocks or bonds they wish to use to reach their financial goals, design professionals must determine how to invest in building their practices. They must decide what they want to do and how much they want to spend. If they're smart, they will keep track of what they invest, and what they get in return, in the form of new fees. Periodically, they should compare the two. In a new effort, one dollar may be spent to make five. But in two to four years (depending on the sector being entered), tangible results should be seen. Marketing efforts should yield a return on investment that allows a practice to flourish.

What is Marketing?

So what is this thing called marketing? "Marketing" is used as an all-encompassing word, but it can be really broken up into three components. *Marketing* generally refers to all of the activities that prepare us to approach a prospective client sector. *Business development* refers to the activities in which we directly interact with these prospects, which leads to sales—those activities that actually close the deal. *Communications*, of which public relations is a major part, refer to those activities that garner visibility in the clients' worlds.

Business development and sales are activities that we will examine later in this chapter. In brief, business development begins with identification of a potential client and the qualification of the lead (is it viable, and is it right for the firm?) and continues through a period of "courtship" until the time comes for a sales pitch. Networking—keeping in touch with friends in the industry—is another important activity that falls under business development.

But before we get to that, we will examine the aspects of marketing related to developing and maintaining a company identity and making plans.

These components of marketing include determination of company position, preparation of a strategic plan (which generally looks forward some three to five years), a marketing plan (which is prepared annually), and a marketing budget (which supports the marketing plan). Market research, which may be associated with exploring a new type of client, a new location, a new service, or the firm's current image, is also included. Finally, to market effectively, designers need to develop and maintain certain systems. These may include lead-tracking systems, project/personnel databases, visual resources (photographs or digital imagery), and brochures.

This chapter will also address marketing communications. The part of communications called branding affects both how the work is done and how the work (and the firm) is perceived. The part of communications that is more outwardly focused is called public relations. The goal of public relations is to garner visibility in a positive way and, to the largest extent possible, control the content. Such control is not particularly easy when an editor or critic writes about us or one of our projects. But we can create our own advertisements, news releases, articles, exhibits, and speeches and, with some effort, get our story out in the way we want it to be heard.

Self-Definition

IDENTIFY THE FIRM'S PRACTICE MODELS

The first step in marketing is to have a clear sense of the company's identity. The design firm should evaluate just what type of company it is—what kind of work it values, the degree of specialization, the practice model, and what differentiates it from other design firms. Only when the firm has identified its position within the industry can it develop a brand identity for the firm.

Design firms are like snowflakes; no two are exactly alike. Yet it is possible to place firms in broad categories. In 1987, Weld Coxe, founder of The Coxe Group (consultant to the design industry), and David Maister, a Harvard professor, did just that. They postulated that most firms were driven by one of three values: ideas, service, or product. All were perfectly proper, and none was superior to the other. They also recommended operational and marketing approaches suited to these different values. The design profession has evolved significantly since then, but there is still much validity in their thesis.

In Coxe and Maister's model, a firm driven by ideas tends to do projects that are unique. This type of firm is hired to create a specific solution to a specific problem. There will be no other like it—one Hayden Planetarium, one Guggenheim Bilbao. Idea-driven firms get much of their work through the notoriety they gain through publication. A service-driven firm generally works on complicated projects for clients that need a lot of attention. These firms often work for large corporations, hospitals, universities, or government entities. Service firms sell most effectively through the person(s) who will do the work, often supported by business development representatives. A product-driven firm knows how to do a particular type of project extremely well. It has the systems and processes in place to pump out a perfect Wal-Mart store or Chase branch bank every couple of days. To sell this process, it relies on a sales staff that can bring in signed contracts. Every firm may not be described perfectly by any of these models, and most firms are hybrids of a sort. But it is still worthwhile to examine the firm's staff, projects, and style of service in fashioning a marketing approach, and thus Coxe and Maister's model remains a useful tool.

Identify the Firm's Degree of Specialization/Globalization

Besides a firm's values, there are other important areas of practice to examine. One of the most important is specialization. Although designers like to think of themselves as Renaissance men or women, that's hard to achieve in today's world. Things have gotten a bit more complicated; there's a lot to know about just one subject, let alone five or six. Clients are less apt to hire a generalist with just two or three of a project type on his résumé than they are a specialist, who can show a long history with a type of facility or client. There is a rationale for this. When designers are retained, clients put their trust in them. Clients want designers to understand their industry—its protocol, its processes, its language, its technology, and its competitive environment. They want to be assured that the designers know what they are doing. After all, their jobs—or businesses—are on the line.

It is wise and quite necessary to have a specialty, but it is a little scary—and perhaps foolish—to have all your eggs in one basket. Keeping a firm healthy and protected is always a balancing act, driven by the design professional's vision of its size and breadth of practice. What if a specialty area experiences a recession, or even disappears? So does the practice, if it has only one specialty. The safest position is to have a limited number of specialties and to have no more than 50 percent of the practice in any one area. That way, if the hospitality sector experiences a downturn, a firm still has corporate or health-care clients to feed the business.

Even though the world is becoming more complex, it seems to be getting smaller. Today, a U.S.-based firm is as likely to be doing work in Barcelona or Beijing as in Baltimore. The normal course of practice is to develop a specialty that is first local, then regional, then national, and finally, international. As the portfolio deepens and recognition as an expert is gained, the breadth of practice will expand. A firm may then export its knowledge in ever-broadening circles. Technological advances are making it easier for more and more firms to work on a global basis.

DIFFERENTIATE THE FIRM FROM THE COMPETITION

Being a good—or even a great—designer isn't enough. A firm's potential client base needs to know it exists. More important, it needs to know why this particular firm is better than its competition. As clients evaluate design firms, they generally go from a long list of candidates to a short list. And whether designers like it or not, it is generally a fact that any of the finalists has the ability to do the job. So why should clients pick any one firm from among the competition? The successful firm will be the one that can articulate why it is better—what sets it apart. That is the differentiation message.

A design firm must develop a message that differentiates it from the competition for a marketing communications campaign or for a specific client pursuit. Without such a message, the campaign or presentation will lack direction and punch. A message may center on a distinctive process, a certain area of expertise, or an especially talented individual. To be most effective, it must be something no one else can claim. Because process is easiest to duplicate, messages built on process are harder to sell. Many firms talk about "the charette process" or their "unique" programming methodology (in truth, rarely unique). A message about expertise is effective, given the facts to back it up, but others can make similar claims. After all, there *are* ten firms in a top-ten ranking. A message about the firm or its people ensures uniqueness. No two people have worked on the exact same projects in the exact same role, or have the same degree of recognition.

A message may have several levels, but it must have one clear theme. That theme must resonate throughout the presentation, beginning it and summing it up. The theme must also carry consistently throughout an advertising campaign, creating a series of ads building on one strong idea. It must repeat throughout a comprehensive marketing communications campaign so that exhibits, advertisements, talks, and even nametags deliver a consistent image and idea.

BEFORE MARKETING: DEVELOPING A BRAND AND A STRATEGIC PLAN

The theme a firm chooses to carry through all of its marketing messages is a key component of the concept known as *branding*. About a decade ago, the idea of branding began to intrigue the design industry. Long associated with product marketing, branding migrated into the service realm, led by the major consulting firms and real estate organizations. So just what is the concept of branding, and can it work for a design firm?

Simply stated, a product or a service is transformed into a brand when there is an emotional connection with the customer. A brand creates a strong product/service personality, one that transcends the product or service itself. Rolex isn't about keeping time; it's about status. McDonald's isn't about hamburgers; it's about lifestyle. Nike isn't about gym shoes; it's about fashion. Brands can be applied to companies, products, and even people (like Michael Graves or Martha Stewart). A brand is a promise. A brand implies both authenticity and differentiation. A brand is about trust; it makes a continuous promise of future satisfaction.

Positioning is an important first step to the branding aspect of marketing because developing a brand requires a clearly articulated vision of the company or service and an absolute commitment to long-term execution. A brand does not happen overnight simply because someone develops a clever advertising slogan or an eye-catching logo. The product or service itself creates the brand, and design professionals are more likely to understand the implications of their brand by talking to their customers than by debating the subject internally. To develop a brand, designers must understand what their clients expect, and deliver on it continually and consistently. They must keep the promise implied by the brand.

Maintaining a brand takes continuous attention and constant improvement. Companies that manage their brands successfully change their corporate culture to support the brand, infusing enthusiasm for the brand into every employee. They make their product different, not just their advertising. Public relations and advertising are used to support their product or their actions.

The most important aspect of branding is third-party endorsement. How people feel about a brand is more important than what they actually know about it. Branding exemplifies loyalty at the gut level. It is a concept well worth implementing with clarity and perseverance.

Making Plans

STRATEGIC PLANNING

A wise design professional will recognize that having a well-defined company identity is not enough. Designers must make careful, thoughtful short-term and long-term plans for their companies. In business school lingo, they must make "strategic plans" and "business plans." Just the words "strategic planning" can strike fear into the most stalwart of hearts. This phrase implies exhaustive market research, a maze of calculations, and hours spent in dimly lit conference rooms arguing with colleagues over wordy mission statements that end up so generic as to be meaningless. In truth, strategic planning can be a simple process that brings designers back to the fundamentals of their practices.

A strategic plan is a broad vision. It looks out over the next three, five, or ten years. Given the rate of change in the design industry, three to five years is the more sensible option. A strategic plan is a positioning exercise in establishing the long-range goals of the firm. It addresses the desired culture of the organization, its position in the industry, its project delivery processes, issues related to people, and, perhaps, financial performance objectives. It is largely the product of the leaders of the firm, with input from selected senior staff. It can be one page or ten. Ideally, the strategic plan is part of a planning continuum, preceding and lending direction to the annual business and marketing plans.

Marketing Planning and Budgeting

A marketing plan is a written document that outlines specific performance goals related to marketing for a specific period of time, and establishes a plan to meet those goals. You can write a marketing plan for the firm as a whole, for a specialty sector within the firm, for a service, or for a specific location. A marketing plan is a valuable communications tool, as it puts in writing the expectations and the rules for the marketing effort. It serves as a common roadmap, by assigning responsibilities in an understandable way. It makes people accountable and enables designers to measure their marketing performance.

Marketing plans are doomed to fail unless the people who are responsible for their implementation are involved in creating them, and that means principals as well as marketing and business development staff. When designers participate in the planning, they feel a sense of ownership. It is important to include the firm's principal officers (who have access to financial data) in market planning so the marketing plan will make business sense. The plan must generate enough revenue from new sales to make good business sense, and the marketing budget must be affordable. A marketing plan should be written annually and tied to the firm's fiscal year.

The Basic Components of a Good Marketing Plan

- *Audit*: "Where do you stand? What are you good at?"
- *Outlook*: "What's out there? Where can you be effective?"
- *Goals/Objectives*: "What do you want to achieve?"
- *Strategies*: "How are you going to do that?"

- *Tools/Resources*: "What do you need to do that?"
- *Budget*: "What will it cost? Can you afford it?"
- *Implementation*: "Who's actually doing what, and when?"

The Audit

In the audit, you assess your current situation. You can't figure out where you're going if you don't know where you stand. First, take a look at the sectors you serve. To protect yourself from a downturn in any one market, give some consideration to maintaining at least two (and preferably three) strong "core" sectors. Each core sector should generate at least 20 percent of your sales, but it should be no larger than 50 percent. If one market gets too big, you don't work to make it smaller, but you do invest more in some of the others to get back in balance. Examine your services. Evaluate the effectiveness of the ones you are currently providing, and determine whether there are others you should add. Look to see where your projects are geographically located. Look at the profitability of your sectors. Try to identify project types on which you consistently perform well. Examine your technical strengths and weaknesses. Strengths can include such things as innovative planning, specialty knowledge, award-winning design, and a strong record of repeat commissions. Examples of weaknesses include an inability to meet budgets or schedules, lousy references, overextended staff, and no depth of experience. Look at your competition to ascertain what they are doing and how it could affect you.

In this phase, you can also analyze your marketing effectiveness. First, examine your sales in terms of fee. Look at what you sold this year and in previous years. Compare this to your goals. Look at your "hit rate."

Note how many times your proposals got you to the interview, and how many times your interviews got you the job. This tells you where you have to improve. Look at what you spent on marketing. Compare it to what you sold to see whether you received good value.

The Outlook

In developing the outlook, try to determine what markets offer the best opportunities. This can be a project type, a geographic area, or a service. When you think you know where the opportunities lie, try to determine the best opportunities for you. Just because an area is strong doesn't mean you should be in it. You may not be capable of—or interested in—serving it.

To define the outlook properly, it may be necessary to do a little market research. Market research involves determining what kind of work you want to do (a task made easier by the self-definition exercises mentioned earlier) and finding where to get it. What do you focus on? It may be a new client type (such as Fortune 500 companies); a new project type (such as law offices); a new service type (such as environmental graphic design); or a new geographic area (such as the Southeast). What do you consider? You consider forces and trends that drive the market. You evaluate the size of the market and its maturity. You investigate funding—there can be great need and no money. You look at the competition. You examine the cost to enter the market.

There are several ways to conduct market research. There are "indirect" methods, which can be as simple as a literature search or a questionnaire. There are "direct" methods, which can be via telephone or person-to-person. You don't have to talk to 300 people, either. If you get consistent answers from a half-dozen knowledgeable people, you've probably got the answers you need.

Setting Goals

The third component, goal setting, forms the basis of the marketing plan. Goals must be specific, realistic, measurable, and limited. "Do good design" is not specific—who decides what's "good," anyway? Goals must be realistic, meaning they must be attainable and within reason. There is no faster way to get discouraged than by setting goals so grandiose that they can't possibly be achieved. Your goals must be measurable; not, "Make a profit," but "Make a 15 percent profit." Goals must be limited. Prioritize—don't try to do everything at once. It's a short twelve months. Last, goals must be collective. Acceptance by the people responsible for implementation is absolutely critical.

Goals may touch on many things. You may target the amount of net fee to be generated. You may describe the types of clients you would prefer to secure. You may delineate types of projects you would like to add to your portfolio. You may define geographic areas for penetration. You may allude to your desired reputation or level of recognition. You may enumerate a desired size in staffing or position in a ranking.

The strategic section of a marketing plan details the means by which you reach your goals and objectives. In developing your strategies, you should take advantage of your strengths, offset your weaknesses, and respond to marketing opportunities. Strategies define action. They may address any number of things: your activities with past or current clients; contact campaigns; networking activities; participation in client organizations; involvement in community activities; and public relations activities, including advertising, announcements, articles, award submissions, direct-mail campaigns, special events, exhibits, news releases, speeches, and seminars.

Determining Tools/Resources

In the tools/resources portion of the marketing plan, you determine the resources and tools necessary to carry out your strategies. Your resources are your people. Look at your strategies and try to determine whether the proper people are in place (at the principal, technical, and marketing levels) to both get the job and do the job. Your tools are your collateral materials. Look at the things you need to implement the strategies—such as project photography, brochures, direct-mail pieces, a Web site overhaul, or even a database.

The Marketing Budget

The marketing budget prices your strategies. It tells you whether you can afford the time and money allocation required to meet your firm's marketing goals. It ultimately tells you whether or not your goals are realistic. The first time you prepare a budget, it seems a daunting task. Over time, as you get to know the marketing habits of your particular cast of characters, and the costs to accomplish certain tasks, it gets easier. First, you choose your approach. There are three basic methodologies for creating a marketing budget: the projection method, the percentage method, and the goal-based method.

The projection method, also referred to as the comparison method, relies on using prior year costs for development of the upcoming year's budget. You must determine what has been spent year-to-date on marketing labor and expenses and project the final year-end costs. The challenge is to decide whether that line item will stay the same, increase, or decrease in the upcoming year. Add the line items, and you have your budget.

The percentage method, also called the top-down method, simply allocates a set percentage of the firm's total operating revenues to marketing. That percentage will generally range between 5 and 15 percent, although some firms report costs as low as 3 percent and as high as 18 percent. The accepted average, at present, is probably between 7 and 9 percent, but then, what firm is average?

The most accurate method, goal-based budgeting, is a "bottom-up" method that assigns costs to each item in your marketing plan. Although more time-consuming to set up initially, it is by far the most accurate and manageable budgeting methodology. With a detailed marketing plan, you will be able to estimate the funding required for completing any identified task. Once you have priced what you want to accomplish, you can test this number against available dollars. If you can't afford the marketing program identified in your plan, you can cut specific items intelligently. Thus, planning continues throughout the budgeting process.

Implementing the Marketing Plan

The final step of the marketing plan is implementation. Smart firms complete an "action plan," which can be a simple matrix or calendar that covers three things. It defines specific tasks ("What is to be done?"). It assigns responsibility ("Who is to do it?"). It sets a timeframe ("When will it be done?").

MEASURING RESULTS

Too many firms go to all the trouble of creating a marketing plan, file it neatly away, and go about business as usual. Smart firms monitor the plan or, as so eloquently put by Society of Marketing Professional Services (SMPS) past-president Thomas Stokes Page, "determine the degree of plan disintegration." A good marketing planning process requires a systematic method of evaluation. Did you do what you said you would do? Did you get the results you wanted?

There are a number of methods for monitoring and evaluating the entire marketing effort. Keep a sales report that tells you the amount of fees you sell each month. Track your marketing costs and compare them to your budget. Use your sales report to identify the new commissions brought in, and compare those fees to what you spent on marketing in the same time period. These exercises allow you to evaluate your return on investment. Create a "hit rate" report that tracks your success from proposal to interview and from interview to commission. Use your firm's financial statements to determine what percent of your net revenues are being expended on marketing.

So is all this planning and measurement really necessary? There are certainly many firms with no organized marketing plans or tracking systems. You *can* survive in a wholly reactive stance (for a while, anyway), but consider this: a marketing plan provides direction. It instills accountability. It builds teamwork. There is simply no more effective means of getting everyone moving in the same direction, and it allows measurement of progress year-to-year.

MARKETING COMMUNICATIONS

Once you have developed a clear sense of your firm's identity and crafted a strategic plan and written a marketing plan, it is crucial to work on how your company's image is conveyed to the world beyond your office doors. You must work to manage the representation of your firm through use of the media and effective public relations—activities that are often grouped under the umbrella of marketing communications.

Your Audience

As a design professional, you have a number of audiences—your professional peers, associated members of the design industry, your community—but no audience is more important than your current and prospective client base. Later, we will discuss client interaction from a business development standpoint. However, there is a "softer" way of influencing existing and potential clients, and that is through various media.

Your next most important audience is your network, and here, too, media can be influential. Clients look to your network—which should include brokers, architects, engineers, contractors, program managers, and specialty consultants—for information about you. What your network sees, reads, hears, and conveys about you is critical in the marketplace.

The community at large is also your audience. You have an opportunity to be known by people who are not part of the design and construction industry, or who may not even be potential clients. But if "six degrees of separation" has any validity, many people can affect your business through introductions, recommendations, or recognition.

Internally Produced Material

Historically, design firms use printed brochures as a means of communicating their experience and expertise. Volumes can be printed on this subject, but suffice to say that the best brochures express the firm's work by showing how it addresses specific client needs. The pre-printed portfolio of images that was used predominantly in the past is being supplanted by just-in-time electronic project pages, combining the requisite photographs with text that can be customized for any given situation. These types of pages can be reconfigured and recombined, creating a brochure system that is flexible and responsive to customer issues. A base brochure system like this can be supplemented with smaller custom pieces that apply to a specific market sector, project type, or service offering.

With the advent of the Internet, electronic media has made rapid gains in acceptance and importance. A Web site offers the opportunity for unlimited worldwide access to your people, portfolio, and "pitch." A Web site is a dynamic tool, but one that requires a skilled writer, a superb designer, and a technology guru to help get the message across. And unlike a brochure, it's never finished. It must be changed, updated, and periodically reinvented in order to draw people back for multiple visits.

Exhibits are another great way to be seen. Some sectors, albeit not all, offer great opportunities to promote your projects and your people. Both "unmanned" exhibits and exhibit booths are accepted tools for marketing professional services. Opportunities to exhibit include MIPIM, a yearly world summit on real estate; annual conventions of the American Society for Healthcare Engineering; various meetings of the Urban Land Institute; and the annual convention of the International Council of Shopping Centers.

Advertising has become more accepted by the design industry. To be most effective, an ad campaign must be coordinated and repetitive. For the majority of firms, this is just not financially feasible. A full-page, four-color ad may cost between $4,000 and $15,000 (and that doesn't include the national business magazines, where a page may run upwards of $30,000 for a regional edition and over $100,000 for a global edition), so a few a year is a major investment, especially for a return that's difficult to measure. Still, some firms are making the foray into building a brand through advertising.

Externally Produced Material: Getting the Press to Cover You

You work hard to secure new projects. You should work almost as hard at getting them featured in the press. As design professionals, we struggle mightily to get the eye of our own industry publications. And while it is a definite coup to be featured in *Interior Design, Interiors,* or *Architectural Digest,* it is just as useful to be featured in your client's trade press. An article in *Modern Healthcare* or *Facilities Design and Management* can be very influential, and is likely to be seen by those who can hire you. It is also beneficial to land in the local newspaper, not to mention the *New York Times.* You must court editors and writers as you court clients. Get copies of their editorial calendars, and see whether they are contemplating any articles that might logically include one of your projects or a sage quote. Let them know about work in progress. Think about storylines that would garner interest. Send press releases about new projects at selection and at completion. Send press releases about promotions and awards, too.

Print media—magazines, newspapers, or trade journals—are a potent means for conveying information about you and your firm. The fact that someone would write about you or your projects is a powerful endorsement, worth many times what you can say about yourself. Enclosing reprints from recognized trade publications (both design and client-focused) lends credibility and cachet to qualification packages and proposals. A monograph or book on the firm, published by a third party, is an unparalleled marketing tool.

Be an Expert

If a client is to entrust you with a project, he or she must feel you are an expert. It won't do just to tell him or her; you have to provide evidence of it. A stellar list of projects is the best way, but it's icing on the cake if your *curriculum vitae* includes a nice list of publications and speaking engagements. Authoring an article, either on your own or with a colleague or client, gives you instant credibility. If you are taking the time to research and write an article, find the opportunity to speak about it, too. Professional organizations (preferably your clients') are constantly seeking speakers for their conventions and meetings. Get on their agenda. Why not present as an authority to thirty potential clients rather than grovel for admittance to the office of a single one?

Teaching is another way to add to your credibility. If Harvard University puts you on the roster, that says something. It's equally true of any credible university or technical college. Teaching has a bonus. It not only helps in marketing; it helps in recruiting the stars of tomorrow.

Sustaining Client Relationships

You can hire the best marketer in the universe, create the most brilliant of ad campaigns, deliver the most compelling of interviews, and not get work. Why? Bad references. There are no marketing tricks that can overcome poor performance. Your past and current clients—and their references—are your most effective allies in bringing in new work. Your clients must be willing to speak to others about your performance. They must be willing to tour your prospective clients through their space. Your articles and speeches will be doubly effective if delivered in collaboration with your client. All this takes their time and energy, so they'll have to be enthused about helping you. You have to have made them your trusted friend.

Marketing is not cheap. It can consume anywhere from 5 to 15 percent of your revenue. The best way to reduce marketing costs is by keeping the clients you have and securing more work from them, without an onerous marketing process. If you don't have to market and sell every project, your marketing costs will naturally be less. That doesn't mean you don't "market" your existing clients. You must nurture existing relationships with the same level of energy and focus as you do new ones. Take the opportunity to socialize with your clients. Get to know them on a less formal basis. You are likely to find the relationship rewarding on a personal as well as a financial level.

The more you can learn about your client's world, the more you can help them succeed in their business, the more valuable you will be. Expand your vision to include theirs. You'll not only design a better facility; you'll help them reach their goals, and in doing so, reach yours.

Seeking and Securing Work

No design professional would disagree with the advice of the wise soul who pointed out that the most important part of any project was getting the job: without the job, there isn't much to fuss about. When designers set out to get the job, the work of business development can seem to involve a lot of fuss: identifying a market with growth potential; identifying a prospect within that market; getting on that prospect's long list; submitting qualifications; presenting your team in a formal interview; touring projects; proposing a scope of services and fee; negotiating the terms of the contract; and exploring why you did or did not get the commission. That's an exhausting amount of work before the design firm even starts the project, and it may seem to a busy designer to be a huge investment of resources for an uncertain return. But designers who think of business development solely in terms of the single project miss real opportunities. Getting one job done *well* is a key to starting a good and ideally lasting association.

The design professional's goal should be not simply getting the project, but establishing a long-term relationship. This relationship is created not through marketing the project, but by marketing the client. Maybe only one project will result—some clients build only one house, one school, or one office—but the reference is forever. If the project is an award winner, but the client is disgruntled with the process, you have only half-succeeded.

Marketing and business development activities are exercises in building trust. It is only when designers earn the trust of the client that they receive the project. Designers can earn the client's trust by demonstrating that they have current, relevant experience, talent, strong processes, and the ability to listen and to interpret the client's goals. And to prove that they have these assets, designers must understand and use the business development process. We'll now describe the process of developing clients, selling your services, and preparing proposals. At the core of all of these activities is a focus on a rewarding and enduring relationship with the client.

Business Development

The primary focus of the remainder of this chapter is on business development, which is an "external" activity in that the design professional interacts with potential clients. Yet designers should start the business development process with some internal activity—market research. Before a member of the firm picks up the telephone, gets in the car, or boards the airplane to get in front of a potential customer, it behooves the firm to do its homework.

Market Research

Market research involves determining what kind of work a design firm wants to do and finding where to get it. Design professionals might undertake market research for any number of reasons. They may want to explore a new client sector, such as healthcare or public work. They may want to explore a new project type or service offering in an existing area, such as sustainable design within the corporate sector. They may want to explore a new office location. They may want to see whether adding a new service would be attractive to clients and prospects. No matter what the motivation to do market research, designers should take four steps to do the research well: First, determine what the firm wants to know; second, determine the ideal source of the information; third, determine the method by which the firm will gather the information, and last, decide who will do it.

To determine what they want to know about a market, design professionals should write out their questions. These questions can deal with any number of issues: trends in the market, current projects, anticipated projects, desired services, performance criteria, competition, and even favorite periodicals (the firm's future PR focus). Next, the firm should develop a list of people who can provide this information. This list can contain three to 300 people, depending on the purpose of the research. Three savvy observations from well-placed observers can be just as valuable as the thoughts from the 5 to 20 percent who may respond to a larger survey.

Once the issues are identified and potential respondents identified, the firm must decide upon a methodology. It can do a literature search (a smart preparatory move, even if the firm plans to employ other methods). Literature, however, tends to look backward, and is therefore in danger of being dated. In comparison, the Internet is a marvelous research tool. It gives design professionals access to corporations, hospitals, public entities, and associations—instantly. Using this current information, they can then prepare a questionnaire and mail it out with a prepaid return envelope. The questionnaire should be simple. If essays are required, people are likely to throw the questions away; if only yes/no answers are required, people are likely to respond. The design firm may also use the telephone, either by enlisting an employee or by hiring a market research firm. The in-house route uses valuable resources, but puts the most knowledgeable person on the phone with the prospect. It affords the chance to start building a relationship, but it may stifle the prospect's candor. The consultant route provides anonymity, but designers need to be assured that a professional and knowledgeable person will conduct the interview.

When have the interviews produced enough information? When they have given the firm the input of enough decisionmakers to indicate a fact or a trend. Only when design professionals have identified a trend can they talk knowledgeably about the situation in the market and use their precious resources in the smartest fashion.

Finding the Prospect

To get work, designers must know that an opportunity exists, and the more they know about the opportunity (including the client and the potential project), the better their chances of being short-listed and of winning. Any useful information about a potential client or project can serve as a lead. Lead-finding begins with talking to the right people. Two valid ways to obtain good leads are networking and cold-calling.

Networking

To most savvy marketers, the most important element in their lead-finding efforts is an effective network. A network can provide information about markets, potential projects, competition, and just about anything else design professionals want to know. A well-constructed and actively used network can significantly improve a firm's efforts to get additional projects.

Networking usually comes to mind as a means of obtaining leads, but it can be used for much more. Networking allows design professionals to:

- *Trade reliable information on new projects.*

- *Generate project teams or partnerships.*

- *Implement market research.*

- *Get information about competitors.*

- *Confirm or discount rumors.*

- *Uncover hidden relationships, or real decision-makers.*

- *Alert others to changes within your firm.*

- *Obtain post-interview feedback.*

- *Save a lot of time (and a lot of money) because the firm won't be chasing jobs that aren't real or for which the firm is not qualified.*

Every design professional already has a network. The "law of 250" says that everyone interacts with at least 250 people on a relatively constant basis. Part of this network is friends, family, and fellow employees. Part is a network of brokers, consultants, contractors, and professional peers. In this professional context, associations and societies can be very useful, and the most useful are those made up of potential clients, such as the International Facility Management Association (IFMA), CoreNet Global, the National Association of Industrial and Office Properties (NAIOP), the Urban Land Institute (ULI), and the American Society for Healthcare Engineering (ASHE). Other helpful associations are professional societies such as American Society of Interior Design (ASID), the International Interior Design Association (IIDA), and the American Institute of Architects (AIA). Designers can also network productively with civic and government groups such as boards of major institutions and chambers of commerce, as well as suppliers of products.

In order to make the most of networks, designers should follow a set of simple rules. To network well, design professionals must be good listeners, aware of not only the words being spoken, but also the atmosphere in which the words are uttered. They must seek to build trust; networking is focused as much on helping others as helping yourself. Designers who constantly take information but who do not return anything helpful will find that their networks will cease to exist. And networking *is* work, work that requires persistence. But compared to cold-calling, networking is also the quickest source of warm or hot leads. And it pays off. One well-known architect kept meticulous lists of contacts in every city. To him, his greatest asset is not the pictures of his work, but the names in his network.

Cold-Calling

People in the design industry develop many of their leads over the telephone. When the contact involves someone the designer does not know, the contact is referred to as a "cold" call. Design professionals make cold calls to do research on a given market and to uncover leads. The goal of a cold call is not to make a sale, but to make a friend. No one buys professional services on the basis of a brief telephone call. The specific goals of cold-calling are to establish a relationship and a dialogue, to get enough information to make it possible to decide whether or not to pursue the project, and to set up an appointment.

The first step in cold-calling is to target. Decide on the type of client to be reached and the geography to be covered. Next, before the call is made, use association guides and the Internet to conduct a minimum amount of advanced research on the prospects. Identify the best person to speak with, and don't hesitate to go right to the top. Develop a list of questions to be asked. Finally, make the call.

The goal of cold-calling is to make the person want to help. Callers should identify themselves by name, company, and a short tagline that identifies what they do. They then have approximately twenty seconds to establish rapport. They should express the need for help in a friendly, courteous manner, and set the stage for asking questions. Rather than simply reading off their list of questions, they should branch off and have a natural conversation, and return to the list to make sure everything has been covered. The conclusion of a cold call may be a simple agreement just to keep in touch, or it may seem reasonable to ask for an appointment, where face-to-face selling can begin.

Cold-calling is not finished when the call is complete. It may be a good idea to send something: a note of thanks, a brochure, or a reprint. The goal of the cold call is to make the prospect open a file on the caller's firm. The designer who calls must also make a record of the call. If a contact record form is filled out (manually or electronically), it will help the designer remember the call when it's time to make a follow-up call, allow the firm to track the caller's activity, and make others in the firm are aware of the calling activity so that the firm's efforts are coordinated. Design professionals should set aside a regular time for cold-calling. Firms should set objectives—five calls a day, five calls a week, or five calls a month—and urge staff to keep at it; their comfort level will grow with experience.

QUALIFYING THE PROSPECT

Through networking or cold-calling efforts, a design professional has uncovered a lead. It's a highly desirable commission: the design of a new museum wing. But this designer has spent a career designing patient rooms in hospitals. Should this designer pursue the lead anyway? An important part of the business development process in design firms is making go/no-go decisions. Not every client is right for every designer or every firm. The design professional who has spotted the lead on the museum project could spend a lot of money to get to the interview, working connections, and writing convincing qualifications, but 99.9 percent of the time, the designer will be bested by a competitor with a half-dozen museum projects to his credit. If by some miracle, the designer is selected (perhaps the designer's Uncle William is the curator), the hospital design firm will probably lose a bundle of money learning on the job and irritate the museum client in the process.

Design professionals should understand that it is smart to walk away from a project opportunity when:

- *The designer or the firm does not have the right kind of experience.*
- *The firm cannot put the right staff on the project.*
- *The client is notoriously difficult.*
- *The designer knows that no profit can be made.*
- *The designer is sure that the job will go to a favored firm.*
- *The prospective client won't permit contact before the interview, and the designer knows nothing about them.*
- *The designer enters the hunt much too late.*

Yet there are instances when it is a good marketing decision to go after a project that the firm is likely to lose. When a design professional has targeted a desirable client, and wants to make a good impression, the firm may decide to go after a project even though its chances are slim. That is, design professionals may make a conscious decision to gain visibility and credibility through a well-crafted proposal and interview process. This exercise is very different from chasing something the design professional has no business chasing at all.

Courtship/Relationship Building

When design professionals market clients as opposed to projects, it may take some time before an appropriate project presents itself. Rather than bemoaning this situation, designers should consider it an advantage. The "market clients" approach gives design professionals plenty of time to learn the culture of the organization and establish a relationship. It's much easier to do this now than in the frantic week before the interview.

When it finally comes time for the prospect to make up a list of firms, a design firm that markets clients will be one of the names that comes to mind first if it:

- *Works diligently at the relationship.*

- *Telephones on a periodic basis.*

- *Better yet, visits.*

- *Sends interesting articles that pertain to the client or project type, or even to personal interests.*

Qualification Packages

As a result of a long courtship, a referral from a broker, or a stellar reputation, a design professional is asked to submit qualifications for a particular project. The client issues a Request of Information (RFI), Request for Qualifications (RFQ), or Request for Proposal (RFP). The industry uses these terms interchangeably, although the latter (RFP) is more likely to request a scope of services and fee, addressed later in this section.

In an RFQ, the potential client poses specific questions that the design professional answers in a qualification statement, a written exhibit of experience. Always customized, the qualification statement is a sales tool that can put a firm ahead of the competition. The main objectives of a qualification statement are to communicate how well design professionals understand the client's concerns and to show how they will address those concerns. The client determines the elements of qualification statements and proposals. Design professionals should follow the order in which the questions are asked, and answer the questions directly and as briefly as possible. They should adhere to the client's format because clients often compare submissions side by side. If clients can't find designers' responses easily, those designers will be eliminated.

Even though every RFQ is different, designers are likely to be asked for certain components. One extremely important component of the qualification statement is the cover letter that precedes the qualification package. The letter may be the only thing a client reads, and it certainly can serve as a refresher after he or she has waded through a dozen or so weighty submissions. The designer should make the letter an engaging, concise summary of key selling points.

In the first part of the submission, the design professional will introduce your firm. This introduction should be brief—one page at the most. It should be relevant to the project, and emphasize the project type for which the RFQ was issued. Next, the submission should present the project team—the individuals who will work on the project. The designer may want to precede this section with an organization chart or a written preface that clearly states names and project roles, and follow with the individual resumes of the team. Résumés should be kept to one or two pages. The designer should use project roles, not corporate titles, and tailor the individual's project experience so that it is related to the proposed project.

The design professional will definitely be asked to present relevant experience. The submission should include only the most relevant examples and it should explain why each example demonstrates the design professional's capability to do the client's job. The client may ask how the designer will approach the project. This question affords designers the opportunity to tell how they will address (and solve) the client's concerns. They may wish to briefly restate the problem, so it is clear that they understand the issues involved. They may want to state a planning or design philosophy, relating it directly to their individual situation. The client may even require that designers develop a preliminary work plan that identifies specific tasks, responsibilities, and timeframes. They may also ask designers to provide references. Designers will find it well worth the time to call every reference they list, tell them to expect the call, educate them about the potential project, and cue them about important points of emphasis. These calls to references also give design professionals an opportunity to touch base with their references.

What should the design professional do with all that marketing material in the submittal? Use a "Supplemental Information" section for pre-printed project pages, reprints, project lists, and award lists. The client may choose to look at it or not, but he will not have to wade through volumes to get to the information he really seeks.

A good submission produces results, and the client:

- *Knows that the designer understands his concerns.*

- *Knows that the designer has the team, the experience, and the approach that can address those concerns.*

- *Looks forward to meeting the designer in person.*

Selling Your Services

Presentations depend less on technical expertise or experience and more on personalities and planning. They can be in many different formats, from simple meetings to multimedia events. Regardless of format, there are two major objectives. The first objective is to deliver a clear message. Design professionals do that by developing a theme based on their and their firm's strengths, making the theme seem beneficial to the audience, and focusing on what the client wants and needs to know. The second objective is to establish team chemistry. A team's selection is based on trust. The design professional should strive to make the client think that they would be comfortable working with the design professional and that the firm is eager to solve their problems.

Understanding Your Audience

Design professionals must develop a presentation that resonates with the audience, and to do that, they must understand that audience. Of course, designers have a tremendous advantage if a client has hired them previously, or if they have been courting the client for a period prior to the selection process. In such a case, the designers seeking the project will have a sense of the personalities, preferences, and dynamics of the selection committee. In other cases, designers need to know everything there is to know about the project. But it is not enough to know about the proposed project. It is also necessary to understand the concerns of each member of the committee, and these concerns may differ from individual to individual. Ideally, designers should understand every angle and must play to each concern. They should also consider the style of the client, so that they may mirror that style to a certain extent. A bunch of suits pitching to some dot-com executives in jeans doesn't telegraph chemistry. On the other hand, the presentation will not work if the professionals giving it come across as blatantly phony. Presenters will be most comfortable (and persuasive) just being themselves.

Preparing for the Presentation

To get ready for a presentation, it is good practice to invite all that can contribute—even if they may not actually attend the presentation—to a strategy session. The session should start with a data dump—everything everyone knows about this client and this project. Next, the session should devote time to determining the overall message of the presentation. The team should worry about delivery style and visuals only *after* it has decided on the message. The advertising firm of Hill and Knowlton used to call this message the SOCO—the *single overriding communications objective*. What is the one thing that the presentation team wants the client to remember about the designer and the firm? Everything the presenters say must support this overall message. The team must figure out what the client does not need to be told. Remember, no one can retain more than three or four key ideas. Some presentations (lectures, for instance) are informational and happen in a logical and sequential order. Sales presentations are motivational, intended to persuade the audience. The order of topics and time allocated to each are determined by the issues of the audience.

In determining the media and tools, the presenters must consider the message, the audience, the room, and the cost (versus the resulting commission). Experts say that visual aids can raise the effectiveness of a speech some 40 percent. Visual aids must support your message and will *never* take its place. Presenters may choose to use presentation boards, simple photographs, electronic media such as PowerPoint, videos (on their own or embedded in a PowerPoint show), or models. Less is more, so presenters should not feel compelled to use visuals all the time. These aids should be used only when they add value to the message or to the designer's and firm's image.

The presenters should consider as well the quality of their visuals. They should be sure that their visuals remain uncluttered. If they use only bulleted topics and simple graphics, they allow the audience to concentrate on them and their topic. If they use graphics and color, they can draw the audience's eyes to their most important points. Bigger is definitely better. If the audience can't see it, the point will be lost.

For all presenters, rehearsals are *mandatory*. Preparing for presentations involves three key elements: coaching, team-building, and motivation. Rehearsals are to benefit the entire team, so they should allow enough time for the entire group to rehearse and for individuals to receive coaching. The first go-around is strategic, as each presenter determines what he or she will say and receives the concurrence of the group. In the next round, the presenters should determine timeframes for their portion of the presentation and do one or more timed rehearsals, offering comments at the end. These comments should be in the form of constructive, not destructive, criticism. And the presenters should not forget to rehearse questions and answers. If presenters have the answers to the toughest questions worked out, they will enter the presentation with more confidence.

Delivering the Presentation

Style alone never sells a job. However, presenters' physical skills do have a profound effect upon their message. Presenters communicate a great deal about themselves and their abilities with verbal and physical skills (including body language), and interaction with your tools and visuals communicates a great deal about you and your abilities.

Presenters can benefit from close attention to verbalization. Speakers must be seen as experts; they should avoid words and phrases like, "I think," "perhaps," or "maybe." If they sound insecure or unsure, why should clients believe them? They should also be conversational and should avoid talking like an interior designer or architect, in technical terms and flowery descriptions. Presenters should also be candid in order to demonstrate that they are aware of the client's concerns and conflicts. Actual delivery is important as well. Presenters should speak slowly—much slower than their normal rate of speech. They should talk loudly enough that the people in the back of the room can hear them (speakers always sound louder to themselves than they do to their audience). If they increase volume, their inflection and energy will increase, too. Voice, pacing, tone, and volume should generally match the words presenters are speaking. Presenters should *not* rely on notes; notes only serve to diminish the design professional's aura of expertise.

Body language can provide additional—potentially negative—information. Speakers should not fold their arms, as that move is considered to be hostile and aggressive move. Similarly, they should not put their hands in their pockets—it telegraphs nervousness and distracts the audience, especially if the speakers have change in their pockets. Clasping the hands is another way of saying, "What shall I do now?" Presenters should avoid that gesture and other types of fidgeting.

Presenters can also use their bodies to create an immediate positive impression. They should move quickly and with enthusiasm as they approach the stage/lectern/front of the room. Their gestures should be about the same as their gestures when they are having a normal conversation with friends. If their gestures feel fake, they will look fake. Presenters should alternate between body movement and no movement at all, and underscore their words with their facial expressions. For the best effect on the audience, body positioning is important. Presenters should always face the audience; they should never turn their back or talk to the projection screen. Normally, presenters (and their shoulders) should be at a forty-five-degree angle to the room. This positioning establishes a nonthreatening stance and opens the presenter's body to the screen when it is necessary to gesture or move.

To get the message across, presenters need to make visual connections with the audience. They should establish eye contact with one person for the duration of a sentence, or while they explain a concept. Presenters should not feel that they have to look at every audience member at any given moment; if they try to maintain too much eye contact around the room, their eyes will be all over the place, and they'll look frantic. They should simply look at one person at a time. This "connected" approach will allow speakers to really see someone, and to get some visual feedback. When presenters are not speaking, they should pay attention to the speaker, in order to focus the attention of the audience.

Presenters can work not only with their physical cues but also with their dress to make clients feel comfortable. They should dress appropriately, considering the client. Presenters will benefit if they find out what the majority of the audience is likely to wear, and dress just a bit nicer. By all means, presenters should wear comfortable clothes. If speakers are pulling at their pants or wincing because their shoes are too tight, they will be distracted (as will their audience). Designers should not hesitate to use "color psychology" to their advantage. Dark colors have more authority, power, and control. Bright colors get attention.

To make these physical considerations work in the context of the whole presentation, the presenters should set the room up in advance. They can mark the light switches they intend to use. They should know the location of electrical outlets. If possible, presenters can arrange the seating in a semi-circle to focus and contain the energy of the audience. Throughout the presentation, presenters should keep the lights on. Bright lights increase the energy in the room and make the audience and the speakers more alert.

If the speakers plan to use a computer during the presentation, he or she should master it in advance. Under the intense pressure of an interview is an incredibly poor time to try out any new technology. Speakers should make sure that they do not waste time serving the technology; the technology they use must serve them and their audience. Above all, presenters should remember that they themselves are the most powerful visuals.

Speakers send the strongest message when their words, body language, and tools all support each other. Ultimately, it is up to the presenters to make clients feel comfortable with their team's material and style. As presenters, their main task is to engage their audience's attention and keep it focused on their message. The audience will forgive a stumble or two, but they will not forgive a boring performance.

After the presentation, presenters should always get a debriefing, win or lose. They will benefit if they learn why they succeeded or where they made mistakes. Presenters should think of debriefing as research. They will get the most out of the process if they use open-ended (but not leading) questions. Presenters should develop a format for sharing what they have learned with the team, and debrief humanely.

Proposal Preparation

Usually, design professionals will be asked to make a proposal in conjunction with their presentation, or shortly thereafter. The primary purpose of the proposal is to delineate the designer's services and present the proposed fee for these services. A proposal may become the basis of a formal agreement (contract), or it may serve as the agreement itself. Firms sometimes specify that fees that are over a certain amount require a formal agreement rather than a proposal form of agreement.

Designers should keep in mind that the proposal is distinct from the process leading up to it. The qualifications and presentation are persuasive, promotional exercises, while the proposal is a legal document. While designers are still in a selling mode, they should be fully prepared to actually do everything they say they will do. There are three basic parts of a proposal: the scope of the project, the scope of services, and professional fees. A proposal may also contain sections relating to schedule, team, and work plan. It is a smart move to initiate this document, rather than to respond to an owner's contract, so that the designer can establish the framework for negotiation.

Identifying the Scope of Services

The *scope of services* is the defining element of the proposal and should be written with great care. It should be preceded with text that clearly describes the scope of the project, so there is a common understanding between owner and designer. The scope of services is usually divided among *basic services*, which are covered under the designer's base fee, and *additional services*, which the client may add as options. If designers are working with an owner's agreement as a base document, they should make sure that the client has not shifted services that they normally consider additional to basic services. Sometimes it is advisable to list items that are not covered in the usual scope of services, to reduce the possibility of future misunderstandings, but for the most part, the proposal should be a positive document.

Identifying Compensation

Professional fees are the second key part of the proposal, and perhaps the most agonizing part of its preparation. Designers can make use of definite strategies for presenting their fee. If the owner is considering several firms, the designer will want to present the fee so that the owner can make an apples-to-apples comparison. This comparison is usually easiest when designers keep the basic services simple and in conformance to industry standards. If designers include certain services in their basic service that most other firms do not, their fee is likely to be higher. Fees can be presented on a per-square-foot or other unit basis; on an hourly basis, as a single lump sum; or as a percentage of the construction cost (although this is more common in architectural proposals). The proposal should clarify the terms of payment, by time period or phase. It should protect the design firm against unreasonable withholding of fees and give the firm recourse when payment is delayed. Later, in an attachment or in the formal agreement, designers can cover more negative provisions, such as limiting the time to contest invoices, dictating the amount of interest charged on late payments, and for adjustments to the fee if the project is delayed or put on hold.

Negotiating the Terms

Once the client has selected the designer, the client and design firm are in a mutual love-fest. Neither wants to destroy that harmony with a nasty negotiation process. However, the negotiation of satisfactory terms is critical to the success of the project and, ultimately, to the financial health of the design firm. Ideally, if the designer's (or the client's) proposal is fairly reasonable and the fee acceptable, there will be no confrontation. But if there are issues to be addressed, designers have an opportunity to use the negotiation as a forum to communicate the project process. An experienced client already knows that the project process is not a straight path, but the inexperienced client needs to be educated about potential risks in the process. Most owners expect designers to approach negotiations with the same level of professionalism and analysis that they will exhibit on their project. Like the presentation, the negotiation is another demonstration of how the design professional will work. The designer's goal in negotiations is mutual understanding and an equitable agreement. To get there, designers should prioritize issues and get help when they need it, from their attorney or their insurance carrier.

Formalizing the Agreement

Once signed and dated, the proposal may serve as the agreement, often augmented with additional terms. It may serve as the basis for a formal agreement, customized by the firm or the client, or as offered by a professional organization. The American Institute of Architects' B-101 (2007) form can be used for interiors as well as architecture, and AIA's B-171ID is written specifically for interiors projects. Whatever the form, it formalizes the project terms and the relationship. Launching a new collaboration or continuing an existing one should be a celebratory occasion. Design professionals are advised to take the time to acknowledge it with their clients as a key step in building a solid platform for the creative process.

14

Financial Management

BY GARY WHEELER

Introduction

Design professions have struggled between the art and business of design for decades. As artists, we naturally focus on the aesthetic and design-driven aspects of our talent. As members of the profession, we have made great strides in the past ten to fifteen years in focusing on our clients business needs through a deep understanding, of not only the physical aspects of their projects, but also the underlying business goals and objectives. In today's global economy, we must have a foundation of good business practices. To thrive in the current climate, we must view the environments or products we design as the strategic and financially sound representation of business goals while, at the same time, applying such best practices to the internal management of our own firms, projects, and initiatives.

By definition, financial management is the measure of how well linked all the components of our business are (i.e., what we do, what it costs to do it, and how profitable these actions are). According to *Webster's New World Dictionary*, the definition of financial is *1. money resources, income, etc. 2. the science of managing money*, and the definition of management is *1. managing or being managed; control, direction, etc. 2. the persons managing a business, institution, etc*. Regardless of whether one works for a large design or architectural organization or in a one-person firm, the same basic practices and principles apply.

First, we need a business plan—what we are trying to accomplish within a given practice must be tied to our financial resources and goals. Strategic planning teaches us to review the world around us, to assess our impact on our business environment, and to plan to accomplish our goals and objectives. Therefore, financial management is not just the reporting of results but is rather integral to practice management and success.

Financial management is necessary for two very simple reasons: first, because we want to do our very best work, and second, because we need to financially support our practice. Responsible financial management will provide and maintain the opportunity to do consistently more challenging work (i.e., it will keep you in business).

Fundamental Principles of Financial Management

INCOME OR "PAYMENT FOR SERVICES"

To have a clear understanding of the fundamentals of financial management, we need to define the following terms:

- Gross Income—total compensation for all services and product
- Sale—award of a commission upon which income can be earned
- Net Income—total compensation less
  - Vendors cost—products and services
  - Consultants
  - Out of pocket non-reimbursed expenses
- Earned Income
  - Net Income recognized as a result of delivering a portion or all of the product or service
- Profit
  - Earned Income less all cost of service and expenses

The fundamentals for management and profitability are the same for contract or residential design practices. Both need to be based on the value of services and the time it takes to deliver and manage these services. Remember, all you have to "sell" is your talent and time.

PRACTICE EXPENSES OR "COST OF SERVICES"

One of the biggest issues in many design firms is the disconnect between income and expenses. Since time is money, many design firms *give away* the only asset they have: their time. This is an area in which many residential designers underestimate their value. If you are compensated solely through the sale of product (i.e., furniture, accessories, materials), the time you invest in research, selection, acquisition, installation, and handholding is easily lost. If you do not track this time, you will most likely give away more than you receive.

In a contract practice, the tracking of time to deliver a project is easier, mechanically. Getting staff to fill out their time cards accurately and in a timely manner is the key to efficiently earning revenue, issuing invoices, and speeding payment for services.

Once you understand the various areas of expenses, setting up a tracking system is relatively easy. Your accountant will be able to assist you in establishing these systems. The cost of services can be generally grouped into three categories.

- Cost of labor—*generally variable*

  ○ Direct salaries or hourly wages

  ○ Customary and statutory benefits such as social security, vacation, health benefits, etc.

- Cost of operations—*generally fixed*

  ○ Rent

  ○ Phone

  ○ Technology

  ○ Lights

  ○ Heating

  ○ Taxes

- Cost of sales and marketing—*generally variable and nonbillable*

  ○ Cost of winning work (although you might decide to go after something you stand a small chance of winning, pitching costs need to be managed properly if you are not to go seriously out of pocket)

  ○ Staff support

  ○ Brochures

  ○ Advertising

  ○ Business development

  ○ Client entertainment

  ○ Public relations

Financial management is the balance between income and expenses.

FIXED VS. VARIABLE EXPENSES

The following two areas of expense are the foundation for financial planning. Certain items are nondiscretionary, such as rent, phone, lights, heating, and taxes. You must pay these items to stay in business. Others are discretionary, such as advertising and photography. While advertising may help you position your firm within your target market, it is not required for you to operate your firm.

Fixed expenses are long-term, slower to change, and less controllable on a day-to-day basis. They include such items as a lease for office space or equipment. Generally, these fixed expenses require a commitment of five to ten years. Taxes on your lease, while generally stable, can change depending on the economic climate of the city and state in which you practice.

Variable expenses are short-term and more controllable. They are generally the focus of most financial management approaches and tools because of this element of control. Items like advertising, reproduction, photography, and salaries are all items we can manipulate on a short-term basis.

Financial Management and Control

There are two basic ways of tracking income and expenses.

- Accrual accounting—net business value. This process accounts for all assets and liabilities.
  - ○ Assets
    - - Fixed assets—furniture, computers, etc.
    - - Nonfixed assets—accounts receivable, value of uncompleted contracts
  - ○ Liabilities
    - - Fixed liabilities—long-term commitments for example: bank loans, leases, etc.
    - - Nonfixed liabilities—consultant/vendor cost, accounts payable

The accrual value is the net amount remaining after you have collected everything due you and paid everything you owe.

- Cash Accounting—operating worth
  - ○ Business value excluding fixed assets and liabilities

The cash accounting process shows you the value of your company at any given snapshot in time. If you have done the work but not been paid, there is no value on the books. Therefore, your bank will look very closely at how you manage your billings.

- It is possible to have a positive accrual value and a negative cash value.

○ For example—the cost of office furniture is accrued by spreading its cost by depreciating its value over time, but you have to have all the cash up front to buy it.

Financial Management Structure

The financial management structure of your company will depend on your business philosophy, type and size of practice, and legal description.

RESIDENTIAL

The residential interior design practice is generally composed of single practitioners or firms of twelve or fewer employees. If you are in a primarily residential practice, there are several ways you can receive compensation for your services. The traditional way has been through the sale of furniture and accessories. Usually, these items are purchased from a wholesale source with a service charge ranging from 20 to 33⅓ percent applied to cover overhead and administrative cost. Depending on the complexity and rarity of the service or products, the percentage of service charge can be considerably higher at 100 to 200 percent. However, in the past few years, many manufacturers have opened their showrooms to the public or established retail outlets. This was a business decision necessary for them to survive. It has also led the residential design community to rethink their compensation structure. Today we find most firms charging an hourly fee and either arranging the acquisition of product through a third-party supplier (dealer) or selling the product to their clients with a service charge. In addition, the retail market has been greatly expanded by savvy marketing and excellent products from such companies as Crate&Barrel, Conran, and IKEA. Although consumers can now buy well-designed products without a designer assisting them, they still need the designer's *talents* to coordinate their home environment into more than pieces of furniture from a sales floor.

More and more residential designers are acting as consultants, requiring an hourly arrangement because of the changing nature of their practices. In many markets, designers are part of a team consulting on such areas as kitchens and bathrooms or other remodeling, and they require time to coordinate with the project architect, contractor, or design-build team.

It appears that the trend towards an hourly or value-based compensation structure is similar to the contract practice. This is an easier way of being compensated for services but will require a major shift in the residential practice throughout North America. Most of Europe already practices this way. The interior designer or architect designs the space and specifies the furniture. The client then buys these items directly from the manufacturer or through a service provider selected by the designer.

CONTRACT

The other major segment of the design industry is the contract design practice. These practices tend to be larger and are composed of firms that have twenty to 200 employees. Often, these firms are divisions of architectural firms or are stand alone interiors practices that often partner with architectural firms. Much like the residential practice, the standalone contract design firm usually has one senior leadership team—or principals—within the practice that are the standard bearers for the design direction of the firm. These practices can focus on corporate, financial services, institutional, healthcare, retail, hospitality, and education, just to name a few. What is common among all of these practice groups is the way most of them receive compensation through an hourly based structure.

Generally, these practices charge an hourly fee based upon a commodity compensation structure of cost per square foot. During the last decade or so, contact design services have come under great pressure by the real estate community, resulting in tighter profit margins. At the same time, clients are not only expecting more service but also better quality of services at a faster turnaround time. Increased client expectations, coupled with higher salaries and expanded benefits, have resulted in a reevaluation of the compensation philosophy of the contract practice. As we shift from a "project-based" practice to a "relationship"-based practice, the value of the service is becoming more important than the time it takes to produce it. Having borrowed from the financial consulting firms, who discovered some time ago that the impact one has on a business is more valuable/important than the time it took you to evaluate that business, more and more design firms are "consulting" with their clients long before there is a project. Assisting clients in the evaluation of existing real estate and strategy development to support the client's expansion or retraction goals are just two examples of consulting services.

Most contract projects are broken down into several phases starting with pre-design services, such as programming, and ending with construction administration, client move-in, and post-occupancy evaluation. Each of these phases requires certain talents and expertise to execute. Through tracking time and productivity, firms are able to establish benchmarks for developing fees on new projects. By learning from past projects, one can more accurately develop a marketing and fee strategy for new projects. In addition, through the use of sophisticated software such as Microsoft Project, one can analyze and project the time it will take to do a project, and also the labor cost. This enables the team to then monitor their time to efficiently deliver the project and ensure the financial viability of the practice.

Many design firms have at least one key leader that is a doer/seller. In other words, the key marketing person is also the one leading the project delivery effort. In a small practice, the process of selling and doing can be easier to control. One gets a project, does the project, and then searches for another project. While this process can lead to times of being very busy and others that are slow, the small practice can generally anticipate these shifts in the workload. However, for the larger practice, the ups and downs cause problems with cash flow and staff allocation. Today, many offices are diversifying into multidisciplinary practice areas to make sure that when one practice area is slow, another is busy. Diversification in the firm's project scale and expertise can alleviate the surges and lags in workload. Depth of expertise and leadership focus are key to this diversification.

Other practices have full-time, dedicated marketing staff that focus solely on developing project leads and client relationships. Others use a combination of business development staff and administrative support staff, working with senior marketing staff (usually principals) that are experts in their given program area, such as interior design. This format usually exists in a large firm where staff resources are sufficient enough to support such an organizational strategy.

A great deal of contract design work is based upon responding to requests for proposals (RFP) and requests for qualifications (RFQ), which often requires extensive resources of time and documentation to properly prepare these responses. The proposal can often be the first and only opportunity one has to get in front of prospective clients. Without focused and appropriate proposals your one chance to make an impact can be lost before you are even in the game.

Your marketing approach should be developed on the basis of your target market and the maturity of your service offerings. Generally, marketing cost range between 8 and 10 percent of your overall budget. If you are entering a new market area where you have little or no reputation or experience, marketing costs can be considerably higher. Your approach to entering a new market can vary depending on your reputation and knowledge. By using research, writing papers, speaking at public forums where potential clients or partners may be in attendance, and publishing your findings, you can build a strong professional reputation that will enable you to broaden your product offerings. Through a targeted publishing strategy, it is possible to reach the decisionmakers in the area upon which you wish to focus; however, each area is unique and a scattergun approach to PR and publishing will not serve you well.

Whether you are compensated in mark-up on product, hourly rate, or a cost per square foot, the bottom line is that your talent and the time you take to develop your ideas are the key to your success. For sound financial planning, it is necessary to accurately track the time you spend to service your clients. Without this data, you cannot manage the resources necessary to successfully run your business.

Financial Management Tools

Alice: *Would you tell me please, which way to go from here?*

Cheshire Cat: *That depends a good deal on where you want to go.*

Alice: *I don't much care where.*

Cheshire Cat: *Then it doesn't matter which way to go.*

THROUGH THE LOOKING-GLASS—*Lewis Carroll, 1872*

If you do not know where you want to go, how can you possibly get there? We all struggle with this issue. In today's fast-changing business environment, not only are we under pressure to adapt, but our clients are also constantly reevaluating their professional and personal lives. To help us try and get a handle on where we are going, there are some tools such as strategic planning we can use to guide us.

"When you come to a fork in the Road, take it."—*Yogi Berra*

STRATEGIC PLANNING

Strategic planning is the lead effort in business organization planning and growth. It sets the stage for change, provides a framework for everyday decisionmaking, and guides an organization into the future. It helps an organization decide which fork in the road to take. The strategic planning process was used by many of the nation's top corporations in the past, but has gained new status through the use of scenario building. Strategic planning enables us to look at multiple options for the future, and therefore, to be prepared to proactively react to the world around us.

In its most basic form, strategic planning is a process that involves analysis of the world around us—not just the design world—by investigating the current trends. What is happening now . . . and what will happen in the future?

- Economically

- Technologically

- Politically

• Culturally . . . Socially and Demographically

• Environmentally

By taking this global view, we can then focus on how these areas may impact the design profession. An example is the government and private sector initiatives undertaken by the United States Green Buildings Council (USGBC). The USGBC's initiatives have a direct impact on the products and services we can provide our clients.

> Strategic planning *is "the process by which the guiding members of an organization envision its future and develop the necessary procedures and operations to achieve that future . . . the plan that helps an organization create its future."*
>
> —*L. Goodstein, T. Nolan, J. W. Pfeiffer*

Once the environmental scan is complete, we can focus the issue of "where are we?" Through an internal evaluation process known as a SWOT (Strengths, Weaknesses, Opportunities, and Threats) Analysis we can evaluate the impact of our clients' changing needs. First, we focus on the strengths and weaknesses of our firms: What differentiates us from our competitors? In which fundamental areas are we strong or weak? This requires the leadership to be open and honest in their internal evaluation of current staff, financial standing, design abilities, personality issues, etc. This first analysis focuses on what is generally under our control.

Next, we look at the opportunities and threats for the future. These items are often not in our control. Issues such as legislation, the global economy, and political change are not directly in our personal control. However, we must be prepared to react to both the positive and negative aspects of changes in these areas. Quite often, an opportunity can also be a threat and vice versa. If there is an opportunity you do not address, it may come back to haunt you.

When the external and internal analysis is complete you can develop a strategy for "where you want to go." By establishing goals (broad description of a nonmeasurable or time-sensitive aim) and objectives (measurable outcome derived from a goal), we can set the course for our business and financial planning. Strategic plans are generally a three- to five-year look at where we want to go. These plans are supported with detailed plans for the current year outlining what needs to be done to achieve the larger goals.

Develop Alternatives—Scenario Planning

Creatively develop and explore alternatives that move the organization toward achieving its vision and mission. This is the fun part . . . it's essentially brainstorming.

Decide on the Goals and Objectives.
Goals and objectives are intended accomplishments, designed to resolve a critical issue, and/or improve the execution of key operations or responsibilities.

Decide on the Strategies.
A strategy is a statement of how an objective will be achieved through the allocation of human and financial resources. It frequently specifies a time frame for accomplishment.

Decide on the Performance Indicators.
A performance indicator is an observable measure or attribute, which reflects how well an organization is implementing or accomplishing its strategies in support of an objective. How will we have succeeded?

Upon completion of a strategic plan, the year's business plan can be developed. Resources both human and financial are assigned on the basis of the priorities established in the strategic plan. Therefore, the combination of strategic planning and the development of the business plan are the road map for meeting your company's long-term goals. The fundamental principals of financial management all come into play during this process. The foundation for a successful practice has now been established. Now, implement the plan. Make it Happen!

Financial management requires sound business planning. By knowing where you want to go, understanding the business climate that impacts your area of expertise, and developing sound management tools, you will be able to properly plan and manage the business of design.

15

Goals of Project Management

BY KATHY ROGERS

Introduction: What is Project Management?

Design professionals see themselves as good managers. To succeed, designers must manage time, staff, their own needs, and clients' expectations; they must allocate resources, motivate, guide, communicate, and learn. When designers are accomplished at managing a business, a professional life, and the complex bases of knowledge they must master, "project management" may seem to be business as usual, but on a larger scale. Yet this approach discounts the complexities of project management and may lead design professionals to involve themselves in a set of responsibilities that will ask too much of them if they are not prepared. Project management is the act of leading a group of people through a process to achieve a goal. Successful project management requires that the design professional employ leadership skills, management skills, professional and industry knowledge, and practical experience. It is also critical that the designer who acts as a project manager understands people and what motivates him or her. The project manager role is based on good communication, listening skills, and good people skills, including respect, trust, and patience.

Project management is also a discipline, one that requires a special and broad skill set. Design professionals can benefit from understanding project management as a set of interrelated responsibilities. This chapter will first identify the key components of the project management task, then go on to detail the responsibilities that the project manager must undertake and the factors that contribute to (and detract from) successful project management.

The Key Components of Project Management

THE PEOPLE

Ideally, the group of people involved in the project becomes a team working together. The team includes, at a minimum, in-house design firm staff and the client. It is also likely to include specialty consultants and, as the project progresses, contractors and vendors. The project manager must therefore understand the relationship of the work of each group to each other group and to the accomplishment of the total project. Everyone, whether directly or indirectly, looks to the project manager to guide the effort. A successful project manager has developed the skills to work with many different kinds of people and to orchestrate those individuals into a strong, cohesive team working toward shared goals.

The in-house staff encompasses not only design professionals, programmers, interior designers, architects, and engineers, but also firm management, administrative support, accounting staff, and technology (information systems) support staff. The client may include representatives from different levels or different business units, departments, or agencies within the client organization.

It is most common for the team to include specialty consultants whose expertise does not reside within the design firm. Examples of such expertise include lighting, acoustic, audiovisual, security, food service, and information technology design. Depending either on the resources of the design firm or the way the team has been put together for a specific client project, another design or consulting firm may provide basic design services such as mechanical, electrical, plumbing and fire protection engineering, and building code consulting. It is increasingly common for the team to include relocation consultants whose responsibility it is to plan and manage every aspect of the client's move to their new facility. Design firms frequently form associations or joint ventures for the purpose of providing all or most of the services required for a specific client project.

Teams sometimes include the real estate brokers responsible for acquisition of space, either through lease or purchase. When a client engages a broker to provide oversight, the client relies on the broker to protect the client's interests. Brokers frequently offer oversight services such as selection of the design firm(s), project scheduling, and cost management. These oversight services are in addition to the traditional project management responsibilities in these areas provided by the design firm.

No matter what its size at the inception of the project, the team will expand over the course of the project. The team's size will depend largely on the size and complexity of the project. At a minimum, the team will grow to

include the general contractor and his subcontractors; the furniture manufacturers and dealers; and the information systems cabling and hardware vendors.
It may also include vendors from specialty areas, such as audiovisual, food
service, sound-masking, and security vendors.

Depending on the size of the project, the number of people in each of
these groups can vary from a few to a large number. Each group is made up
of individuals with differing experience, attitude, goals, approaches, and personalities. Some of the groups will be managed directly by the project manager in order to accomplish the work of the project. Even though the project
manager will not directly manage the work of other groups, these groups will
rely on the project manager as an interface between themselves and others. If
each group is to perform well, the project manager must coordinate all efforts.

THE PROCESS

The project process encompasses the phases of the design effort discussed in
chapter 2, from pre-design services through contract administration. The
project manager is responsible for leading the team through the process by
establishing that process and guiding team members through every step. As the
project begins, the project manager must establish the infrastructure within
which the team will be able to execute each phase of work until the project
is successfully completed. This infrastructure includes all of the supporting
processes of establishing scopes of work, contracts, work plans, quality standards, communication protocols, documentation methods, fee budgets, project
schedules, project budgets, etc.

Once this infrastructure has been created, the project manager must guide
the team through the phases of work within the context of a defined scope of
services, contractual agreements, staff hours and fee projections, quality standards, communication and documentation methodologies, and an approved
project schedule and budget. While it is critical that the project manager continually monitor the progress of the project against this context, monitoring is
not enough; effective project management is a proactive rather than passive
activity. The project manager must actively guide and coordinate the team
effort if the team is to successfully move through each phase of work and meet
quality, time, and cost objectives.

THE PROJECT MANAGER

The project manager is the team's orchestra leader, using his or her baton to
direct the different groups of people at the right time through many tasks and
activities, to achieve the goals of the project. If project managers want individual team members' efforts to create a whole, they must make sure that these

efforts are made within a framework that takes into account knowledge relevant to each component of work and how each component creates a total project. This coordination effort is key to the success of every project. In order to be successful, a project manager must have good technical knowledge and understand people.

The project manager's technical knowledge comes from experience. Experience begins with design education and expands when design professionals work in the profession performing or participating in the execution of components of project work. A project manager would find it difficult to understand how a project is made up of individual components of work without the experience of performing the components and seeing firsthand how they come together. This includes both the design and business sides, such as scopes of work, contracts, fee projections, staff hour projections, etc.

The most successful project managers understand people not only as team members, but also as individuals. These project managers have learned not only that the whole of a team is greater than the sum of its individual parts, but also that all individual team members must be valued if they are to contribute successfully to the team. In order to get a group of people to work as a team, the project manager must have developed good people skills and communication skills. The project manager can best ensure the success of the individual, the team, and the project by creating an atmosphere of cooperation, teamwork, and individual responsibility through leadership and empowerment.

Objectives Common to All Design Projects

The objectives of every project are as varied as the clients and design firms who come together to execute the project. At the most basic level, however, the objectives for every client and design firm are:

For the Client:
- A project delivered within established time and cost parameters
- A project that meets organizational, functional, operational, and business goals
- A project that supports and enhances the lives and work of the clients' employees or residents
- A project delivered by a team who understands the client, who listens and responds to the client, and who uses their professional knowledge to guide the client through difficult and unfamiliar decisions
- A project that supports the professional goals of the individual client members

For the Design Firm:

- A project that meets the financial goals of the design firm

- A project that utilizes the resources of the firm

- A project that challenges the staff and allows them to grow professionally

- A project that the firm will be proud of—a good example of their work

- A project that satisfies and hopefully delights the client

- A project that promotes a relationship between client and design firm

The project manager is responsible to understand the objectives of each group, to structure a project process that supports these objectives, and to guide the team through the process. A project manager's success can be measured by whether the client is happy at the end of the project; whether the design team feels professionally fulfilled by the process and the project; and whether the project is a financial success for both the client and the design firm.

A Happy Client

A happy client is the best client. Every client deserves to feel good at the completion of his or her project. The design firm typically benefits, too, from a satisfied client, either through additional work and a long relationship with the client or via reference with new clients. The project manager is the primary client contact and has the major responsibility for keeping the client happy. Successful project managers understand that happy clients believe that the project manager should listen well and communicate clearly and regularly and work to satisfy or exceed clients' expectations for the project.

A happy client believes that he or she is being heard. The project manager fosters this belief first and foremost with good listening and communication skills. It is imperative that the design firm, led by the project manager, hears and understands what the client is saying. The project manager must ask questions so that the design firm can understand the real concerns and issues being expressed by the client. The best way to do this is to develop good communication with the client. Good communication includes understanding the client's communication style, frequent communication, and the use of tools for documenting all communication. A happy client typically believes that he or she is being heard and has a part in directing the work of the design team.

In addition, a happy client feels that the project process, which may be unfamiliar, at least at the start of the project, is comprehensible and does not add additional stress to his or her life. Frequently, the client representative has been asked to take on the responsibility for the project in addition to normal job responsibilities. Whether the project is an additional task or the main job responsibility for the individual, projects are fraught with stress—deadlines, decisions, construction problems, etc. The project process should not in itself create additional stress. If the client can count on the project manager to lead him or her clearly and calmly through the myriad of decisions, issues, and problems, the client will indeed be a happy client.

Furthermore, a happy client feels that the work of the design firm is meeting the established expectations and objectives of the client. Very frequently, clients have not worked with a design firm and have not experienced the design process. For the design professional, each project offers new opportunities for the design firm to deliver a project that exceeds expectations and delights the client. For the client, it is critical that the process is working toward meeting his or her established objectives on this project. Frequently, a client will not realize until the end of the process, typically when the space comes on line, that the work of the team truly exceeds the expectations and objectives.

Finally, a happy client believes that quality, as defined by each client, has been achieved. Quality may pertain to the overall design of a new facility, to the materials specified, to the building systems engineering, to practical details, to the absence of errors, to the perceived value of the facility against the cost, or to all of these. The project manager cannot achieve quality without establishing processes and procedures within the design firm and with the client/design firm team. The project manager is responsible to establish and enforce these processes and procedures. Even though this responsibility requires a rigor that is difficult in the heat of delivering a project, especially when project schedules are tight, that rigor costs the design firm little compared to what would happen if the processes were not monitored and enforced.

A Professionally Fulfilled Design Team

The project manager is responsible to provide opportunities for professional fulfillment for his or her staff. Project managers can easily become so focused on serving the client—sometimes at all costs—that they overlook the professional fulfillment of the design team. If the individuals on the design team are not challenged, given the opportunity to produce quality work and to grow professionally, the immediate project may suffer, but the design firm will suffer in the long term. It is increasingly difficult to find and retain staff, due to the shortage of professional staff and the economic stability the country is experiencing. The work of a design firm is nothing more than the work of individuals. All of the firm's credentials, standards, and procedures are nothing if the corporate memory walks out the door. To retain valuable staff, the project manager must perform a difficult balancing act—balancing the client and project requirements with the individual requirements of his staff. The project manager must have an astuteness and attitude, borne of experience, about what motivates and inspires people. The client can only benefit from the leadership of a project manager who achieves this balance.

A FINANCIALLY SUCCESSFUL PROJECT FOR THE CLIENT AND THE DESIGN FIRM

If a project is to succeed for the client, it must be a financial success, i.e., it must meet established budgets. It is equally important that the project be a financial success for the design firm. Design practices are businesses. No design practice can exist long-term if its products—the services it sells—are not financially successful. The project manager, more than any other individual on the client/design team, holds the key to the financial success of the project for both the client and the design firm.

Competition is typically fierce for design projects and as a result professional service fees remain highly competitive. Fee negotiations between clients and design firms are typically tough negotiations. Clients do want to work with firms that are financially sound. Most clients realize that it is reasonable to expect to pay a fair price for design services. Their problems grow exponentially when a design firm incurs financial difficulties while delivering their project.

Once a fee has been established, it takes a skilled project manager, utilizing a variety of tools, to guide a project through the entire process and achieve financial success. As will be discussed later, the process begins with planning the project and establishing expectations, and continues through the project with ongoing monitoring of hours spent against progress on the project. If every project proceeded per the initial project plan, it would be relatively easy to monitor the expenditure of fee. Rarely does a project proceed that easily. A project manager must have the skill and flexibility to also manage change over the course of the work and still achieve financial success.

For the client, he or she will develop budgets and manage the delivery of design services and products to those budgets. For the design firm, he or she will establish the number of hours required for each component of work and manage the design team to deliver the work for those hours. Change, whether due to scope or schedule change or any number of other variables, must be monitored because it impacts the financial success of the project for both the client and the design firm. Good planning, communications skills, an in-depth understanding of the total design process, and proactive management skills are the keys to financial success.

Responsibilities of the Project Manager

The project manager touches every aspect of the project, from marketing the project to closing out the last details of the project. Project managers are typically identified during the marketing of the project, when the design firm makes initial contact with the client, by responding to a request for proposal and/or presenting qualifications and a project approach to the client. The project manager is almost always a significant player in these pre-project efforts. The project manager is also typically the last person from the design firm to have contact with the client. After the project is complete, the client has occupied its new facility, and the rest of the design team has moved on to other projects, the project manager will still represent the design firm to close out remaining contractual, financial, and administrative issues.

Project management responsibilities fall into eight broad categories:

1 Understand the Client

2 Document Project Goals

3 Develop a Project Work Plan

4 Establish Communication and Documentation Protocols

5 Establish Project Budgets

6 Maintain Client Relations

7 Lead the Project

8 Manage Change

Understand the Client

In order to complete a successful project, the design team must first understand its client. It must understand its client's objectives—as an organization and as the individuals who they will work with daily on the project. The design team needs to understand their client's expectations, perceptions, and biases about the project; how they make decisions; their organizational and individual values; and what will make the organization and individual successful. Projects are increasingly complex and frequently involve multiple client groups. The project manager must implement procedures that enhance the team's capacity to fully understand the clients' and the firm's conflicting objectives, requirements, expectations, and values. These procedures must encourage listening, the exchange of information, and self-knowledge.

The project manager must lead the design team to recognize that they bring their own expectations, perceptions, biases, and individual and firm values to the project. It is important to sort through the differences and similarities between the client's values and the firm's and team members' values. Frequently this sorting happens during the process of selecting the design firm. It is very common for clients to select a design firm they perceive to share values and expectations about the project at hand. When this occurs, it can create a very positive and comfortable working relationship from the start of the project, a natural "fit."

Whether or not this sort of fit occurs during the selection process, it is critical for the project manager, as the leader and integrator of the effort, to create the conditions of listening and responding in which the sense of fit can develop. The project manager must listen carefully to the client and help the design team understand their client. It is incumbent on the project manager to help the design team find ways to tailor its approach to the project to best serve its client. The success of the project depends on the ability of the client and design firm to work together.

Once a design firm has been selected, the best opportunity to begin to understand the client occurs during the dialogue associated with documenting project goals and developing or refining the scope of services and schedule for the project. In this stage, the design firm and the client must address many issues if they are to develop a clear scope of services and project schedule. This conversation offers a wonderful opportunity for the project manager and design team to get to know their client. The astute project manager asks questions and listens to and observes the client throughout this process, then shares his or her understanding with the design team.

Document Project Goals

It is easy for a design team or a client to get caught up in a project in such a way that the original goals are forgotten, and when this happens there is usually a day of reckoning when everyone is reminded of the original goals. However, such a situation can be avoided if the project manager focuses the team by involving it in documenting project goals. The client's goals for the project should be clearly documented before the design team begins work. The project manager should initiate this documentation on the basis of his or her understanding of the client, and share it with the design team.

The team will find that it is very worthwhile to discuss how it feels it can achieve the client's goals through its work on the project. The discussion should include project approach, budgetary and schedule parameters, and design objectives. This exercise provides an opportunity for the team to begin to work together and typically results in parallel sets of goals for the effort both of the design team and the individual. It is positive for the team and individuals to see each new project as an opportunity for growth. The client can only benefit from this attitude.

Once the team has documented the project goals (those of the client, the design team, and the individual on the team), the project manager can use them as a benchmark to be referred to throughout the course of work on the project. The project manager should ask the team to review the goals at key points during the work on the project—typically at the beginning or end of a major phase of work. Such benchmarking will help reorient the team.

Just because project goals are documented does not mean that they cannot change during the course of a project. There are many reasons a client's goals for a project can change. Once the project manager senses that the goals are changing, it is critical to discuss the change with the client; assess the impact on the project; address any scope, schedule, and contractual issues; document the change; and share it with the design team. They cannot be held accountable to deliver a project that meets a client's goals if they are not made aware of them.

Develop a Project Work Plan

The most critical phase of any project is planning the work. The work plan establishes the scope of work, including detailed lists of tasks, activities and deliverables, the schedule for the work, and the professional service fees associated with accomplishing the work. It is the basis for all contracts with the client and consultants. It establishes the base line for monitoring the progress of the work—the completion of tasks, activities, and deliverables within a specific timeframe and expenditure of staff hours. If a work plan is developed, the likelihood of having a successful project increases dramatically. Without a plan the team may get lucky, but as the number of complex issues associated with design projects has increases, it becomes increasingly risky to work without a clear plan.

The work plan is a road map for everyone on the team to follow. If the project manager monitors it throughout the course of work on the project, any deviations from the work plan will be known immediately. The project manager then has the opportunity to make the necessary adjustments to get the project back on track, or make modifications to the work plan. Such modifications may be as simple as a fine-tuning of the work plan without contractual, schedule, or budgetary adjustments. If significant changes have occurred, it may be necessary to re-examine the project scope, schedule, and fees, which may mean contractual modifications.

As important as it is to develop the work plan tool, it is equally important to strike the right balance between an underdeveloped and an overdeveloped work plan. If the work plan is not fully developed, it will fall short of being a useful tool against which the progress on the project can be monitored. If it is overdeveloped, it will become so cumbersome that it will either be ignored or the project manager will spend so much time managing the work plan itself that there will be no time for him or her to lead the project.

A work plan is typically initiated during the marketing effort associated with the project, responding to an RFP, or presenting the design firm's approach to the project during a marketing interview or presentation. Once the firm has been selected for a project, the project manager should begin to develop a detailed work plan, with participation from key project team members and in communication with the client. This process provides the opportunity for understanding and buy-in by both parties.

There are seven key components to a work plan, which the project manager must establish before the team starts substantive work on the project:

1 Scope of Work

2 Tasks, Activities, and Deliverables

3 Contracts with the Client and Consultants

4 Design Team

5 Project Schedule

6 Internal Project Budget

7 Administrative Procedures

Scope of Work

The scope of work must be clearly defined or refined together by the client, project manager, key members of the design team, and consultants. This process builds solid working relationships and provides the basis for the contract between the client and the design firm and consultant firms.

Essentially, the scope of work describes what is to be done—what the project is. All project parameters and requirements should be reviewed. Project parameters include the client's goals for the project, the design firm's project goals, the phases of work necessary to deliver the project, the deliverables associated with each phase of work, the overall project budget, and schedule expectations.

At the center of this discussion is the question of overall level of design for the project. While the broad phases of work may be the same for a relatively straightforward project and one that is more complex or "high-end," the scope of work for the two projects will be quite different. This discussion should address aesthetics, level of design detail, material selections, maintenance requirements, and environmental concerns. It should also address issues such as the requirement for flexibility in the design to accommodate future change, start-up and long-term operating costs, and the impact of anticipated future business plans on the design of the facility. If all project parameters and requirements can be discussed, everyone can start on the same foot.

A client's availability and decision-making process may impact the project, in time, money, or relations. It is important to discuss these topics so that everyone has the same expectations as the project moves forward. Some clients are unaware of the amount of their time a project may require, and their unavailability may slow down the project. Some clients are unable to devote time to the project except for key decisions, and rely heavily on the experience of the design firm they have selected to produce the project. Some clients have lengthy review processes by multiple parties for decisions and approvals, which require time and extensive presentation materials.

Tasks, Activities, and Deliverables

Once all of the project parameters and requirements have been discussed and documented, the next step is to develop a detailed list of the tasks, activities, and deliverables necessary to fulfill the scope of work.

At various points in the project, the tasks and activities result in products, or deliverables, that document a component of work. In order for the team to begin work on the project, it must be broken down into components of work that combine and build upon each other to produce the desired project. In order for the project manager to be able to build a project with detailed tasks and activities, some of which are sequential and some of which are parallel and sequential, the project manager must have the right kind of project experience. He or she must have been a part of similar efforts, either as a team member or as a leader. The more detailed the list of tasks, activities, and deliverables, the easier it will be for the team to execute the project. The structure of their work is in place. The project manager has thought through each component of work and how it interfaces with other components of work. The team has their roadmap and is free to focus its creative energy on the work itself.

The list should be used to select or finalize the design team or consultants on the basis of the skills required for each component of work, and to determine the number of staff hours required to produce the project—and thus, the fees for the project. Even though normative data exists for fees per square foot for interior design services, the best way to calculate professional service fees and explain the fees to the client is to show how the fees are based on staff hours for each task, activity, and deliverable. It is a mistake to enter into a contract with a client until this step is complete.

If, when calculated, the fee is too high, the project manager can make reductions by adjusting the tasks, activities, and deliverables. Ultimately, it may be necessary for the project manager and client to review the list together if there is a serious disparity between the number of staff hours required for the tasks, activities, and deliverables for the scope of work and the fee the client has in mind. This is the time, before a contractual agreement has been signed, to come to agreement on the detailed work and the cost associated with it. Either the design firm may need to alter their approach to the project, or the client may need to rethink the fees they anticipated for the scope of work.

Contracts with Client and Consultants

Once the client, design firm, and consultants are in agreement about the scope of work and detailed tasks, activities, and deliverables, contractual agreements should be finalized so that all parties understand their baseline agreement. Contracts legally bind the client, design firm, and consultants together. The contract should document all agreements that address expectations, scope of work, and the plan for executing the work. The firmer the understanding and agreement on these issues between all parties, the less likelihood there is of misunderstandings during the course of the project. The contract is a legally binding document, but it should also be viewed as a tool, to be referred to over the course of the project when questions about scope or methodology arise. It is the baseline understanding between client, design firm, and consultant firms. If conditions or expectations change during the course of the project, the contract can and should be modified to reflect changes to the baseline.

Design Team

Design projects are a team effort. The best teams function like a well-oiled machine, with each part working in the right way and at the right time with the other parts. The project manager's role will be easier and the opportunity for a successful project greater if this level of performance can be achieved. It will also be a more rewarding project for all involved.

The first step in structuring the design team is to select the right number of individuals with the right skills and experience for the work. Ideally, the individuals will also have the right attitude and motivation for the project. The project manager will probably work with the management of the design firm or discipline leadership, depending on the organization of the firm, to establish the team. The size of the design team, and the number of hours of work required of each member of the team, is directly proportional to the magnitude of the overall effort and the timeframe in which the work is to be completed. It will take a smaller team a longer period of time (than it would a larger team) to produce a large project.

Establishing the size of the design team is a balancing act. Too few people can extend the schedule, necessitate overtime work, and possibly impact the quality of the project. Too many people can cause inefficiencies, make it difficult to manage the project to an agreed upon number of staff hours and fee, and possibly also impact the quality of the work.

Once the team is selected, it is the project manager's responsibility to document the organizational structure of the team, including team members from consultant firms. Everyone associated with the project should have a clear understanding of who the team members are and what their respective responsibilities.

The individual team members, their role and responsibilities, and the organizational structure of the design team should be shared with the client. The design team, in turn, should understand the client's organizational structure and representatives for the project.

Project Schedule

Once the detailed tasks, activities, deliverables, and design team have been established, the project manager can develop a project schedule. The project schedule is a tool. At the beginning of the project it is used to graphically show how the work will be accomplished over time for both the client and the design team. It can be used to fine-tune the project approach in order to achieve the client's schedule parameters. It can also help determine staffing resources required for the project. As the project moves forward, progress on the project should be monitored regularly against the project schedule.

The project schedule simply overlays the tasks and activities on a calendar of days, weeks, or months, depending on the level of detail of task or activity. The tasks and activities are assigned a duration of time on the basis of the amount of work and number of people producing the work. They are also laid out in the sequence that the work must be accomplished. The schedule will typically show deliverables and key decision points, meetings, or presentations as milestones.

Project managers must determine how detailed the schedule should be for each team and each project. Project schedules can be as simple as a schedule that shows the five or six major phases of work or as complex as a schedule that is hundreds of lines long, showing many tasks and activities within each phase of work. A large, complex project typically requires a rather detailed project schedule that assists both the client and design team in managing the work and monitoring the progress on the project.

As changes occur to the goals, the scope, the tasks, the activities and deliverables, or the design team, the schedule should be revised to reflect these changes. A project schedule is essentially a diagram of the work. It shows tasks that may be performed on parallel tracks of work and tasks that cannot start until all or part of another task is completed. Interdependent tasks form the critical path for the project. Before the project manager can change the completion date of the project, he or she must adjust the tasks that form the critical path in some way. For example, in order to complete the project earlier, the project manager may be able to apply additional staff resources to specific tasks on the critical path. Sometimes, the contract and negotiated fees can accommodate such changes. Other times, the contact and negotiated fees will also require adjustment.

Internal Project Budget

The contract between the client and the design firm may structure the design firm's compensation in a variety of ways: as a lump sum fee; as a fee per project square foot; as a fee as a percentage of construction; as a not-to-exceed fee based on approved tasks, activities, and deliverables; or at hourly rates for professional services. No matter how the firm will be paid by the client, the project manager should establish an internal budget for the project based on number of staff hours per phase of work, task or activity, at the appropriate salary costs. Once this budget is established, it will provide a key tool for the project manager to measure progress on the project.

The approach to and methodology for establishing internal project budgets varies widely from firm to firm. It is the most important tool for monitoring the progress of the work and, ultimately, the financial success of the project. Still, no matter what the firm, the internal project budget generally contains several components. It identifies all design firm labor costs, reimbursable direct project costs, non-reimbursable direct costs, overhead and profit, consultant costs, and costs associated with any special services.

Labor costs are simply the compilation of all salary costs for the staff assigned to the project. Labor costs are based on individual salaries plus direct personal expenses (DPE)—costs associated with the employment of people including benefits such as vacations, holidays, health insurance, pensions, etc. In order to preserve confidentiality, many firms address average labor costs by category or discipline.

Direct costs are the costs that are incurred in the execution of the work and include those associated with travel, reproduction, printing, photographs, postage, telephone and fax, etc. These costs may be either reimbursable or non-reimbursable, depending on the contract with the client.

Firm overhead and profit are calculated in many different ways. The internal project budget must account for overhead and profit, however they are computed in the design firm.

Consultant costs fall into the same categories as those of the design firm. Fortunately, the project manager for the design firm typically need only manage and monitor the overall consultant fee. The project manager for the consultant firm has the same responsibilities as the design firm project manager to manage their internal project budget.

Most project managers have learned, and some design firms insist, that a portion of the design fee be set aside as a management reserve. This reserve is intended to be used to cover work, which takes longer to produce than planned and is usually at the sole discretion of the project manager to use. Ten percent of the fee is typical management reserve.

Administrative Procedures

In addition to establishing internal financial budgets, it falls to the project manager to set up all project procedures, files, and records for the project. It is important to the design firm that procedures are followed and records are maintained by the design team during the course of work on the project to insure that all contractual obligations are met. These records also become important historical data for future business decisions and marketing efforts.

Some firms require a project procedures manual as a part of starting every new project. The manual provides the team with project information such as client and team directories, organizational charts, and schedules. It also establishes the framework for all communication protocols and documentation procedures and formats for the project.

The project files should include the marketing materials for the project, the documented project goals, the project scope, the work plan, the schedule, the internal project budget, and all project contracts, amendments, and additional service documentation. All project correspondence, drawing files, reports, surveys, and other project documentation should be added to the files over the course of work on the project. It is important to organize both paper and electronic files.

As tedious as these housekeeping duties are, it is important that they be addressed at the beginning of the project. Once the project is underway, there will be no time to address these administrative responsibilities. The files and recordkeeping may be sloppy, and the team will not enjoy the advantage of being able to move through the project work within a framework of established administrative rules and procedures.

Establish Communication and Documentation Protocols

Good communication is essential to the success of the project. The project manager is typically the primary contact between the client and the design team and consultants. In this capacity, the project manager establishes the way that information is transmitted among all parties. It is his or her responsibility to see that information is transmitted in a timely manner and that it is fully documented. Once a project is underway, this alone can be a full-time job. Even though other key members of the design team and consultant firms may develop communication channels with the client, it is essential that the project manager be the primary contact, so that he or she can remain directly connected to the project, constantly monitor the progress of the project, and insure that all goals are being met.

A record of the many conversations that lead to decisions concerning the project, and the decisions themselves, is an essential part of the historical data of the project. Much of the communication on a project is verbal—telephone conversations, voicemail messages, in-house design team meetings, project team meetings with the client, and formal client presentations. It is in these conversations and meetings that decisions are made that set the direction for the project. It is difficult for either the client or design team to look back and remember every decision, or the reasons for those decisions. A paper trail produced throughout the course of work on the project can mitigate a lot of anxiety on the part of the client and design team. This is especially true when questions about work based on earlier decisions arise. The best way to respond to such questions is to be able to refer to documentation of those decisions that is a part of the project record and that was distributed to everyone on the team.

Most firms have standard formats for all project documentation. The documentation for conversations and meetings should include:

- Telephone logs that document conversations containing project data or decisions. E-mail is a good way to document telephone conversations.

- Meeting agendas that are distributed in advance of a meeting and that notify participants of the topics to be discussed or presented at the meeting.

- Meeting notes that document the discussion, decisions, and issues from the meeting.

- Action item reports, which are frequently attached to meeting notes and identify and track outstanding issues and the party responsible for addressing or resolving the issue.

At the beginning of the project, the project manager should establish a distribution list for these documents. He or she will need to update the list throughout the course of work on the project as the number of parties involved increases. Documentation of conversations and meetings should be distributed in a timely manner. Telephone logs should be distributed immediately if information relevant to the immediate work has been addressed. Meeting notes and action item reports should be distributed for review no later than a week after the meeting or presentation.

Other kinds of project documentation, which are important parts of the project data, include:

- Letters, which are typically used for more formal communication.

- Memorandum, which are more commonly used to communicate project information.

- Transmittals, which should accompany every submission to the client or consultant firm as a record of the submittal.

- E-mail, which is commonly used to communicate a wide range of project information. It has become the preferred method of written communication with clients and consultant firms because of the speed with which information can be communicated.

- Monthly status reports, which summarize all activities and issues and update the project schedule for the client.

The project manager will initiate much of this communication and documentation. It is his or her responsibility to see that all team members communicate and document in the same way. All project correspondence and documentation should be added to the project files.

Establish Project Budgets

The project manager is the responsible for seeing that client budgets for the project are established and updated at agreed-upon points in the development of the project. The design firm typically has responsibility for establishing and maintaining budgets for construction and furnishings. It is increasingly common for the design firm to be asked to oversee as well the budgets for furniture inventories, audiovisual equipment, security systems, food service equipment, information systems, and relocation costs. The project manager must arrange for budgets to be developed, and he or she must also monitor and update them and communicate regularly to the client regarding them.

Some budgets are typically developed in-house, when the skills are available. Cost estimators typically develop construction budgets in-house. If these skills do not reside in-house, it is advisable to retain a cost-estimating firm as a consultant to the project. If a general contractor has been retained in the early phases of work either through negotiation or as a part of a design-build process, the general contractor will be the best source for construction budget information. Furnishings budgets are also typically developed in-house. Interior designers or furnishings specialists can work with furniture manufacturers and dealers to develop furniture budgets.

Budgets for the furniture inventories, audiovisual equipment, security systems, food service equipment, information systems, and relocation costs are best developed by the consultant firms or vendors who specialize in these areas. Consulting services should be structured to include cost estimates. Vendors will provide cost estimates either for a fee or as a part of their services associated with selling the equipment.

The project manager is ultimately the keeper of all project budgets. It is his or her responsibility to establish the budgets and see that they are updated per the approved scope of work. If the project manager senses a change in the project or a decision that will impact costs, it is his or her responsibility to advise the client of this potential impact on costs immediately. The client may elect to add an additional budget update to the scope of work if the impact of the change or decision is serious enough.

The client's checkbook pays the project costs, and the client has every right to be fully informed about the costs of their project throughout the design of the project. The project manager must assume responsibility for making sure that the entire design team knows that when clients are presented with options they should be informed of any cost differences associated with each option. No client likes to be surprised at the cost of a design they have approved. Costs that are too high can cause difficulty for the client within their own organization. They certainly can cause bad feelings between the client and the design firm, whereas costs that are low may be received very positively by the client. They may also be perceived to represent a missed opportunity for a better project. If the client feels that they have choices, are given cost information about each choice, and are given good reliable budget information regularly through the course of the project, they will develop trust in the design firm. Without trust, the relationship between the client and design firm will be strained.

Maintain Client Relations

Everyone on the design team bears a responsibility to develop a good working relationship with the client, but the project manager is primarily responsible for tailoring the project's management to the client's needs and for including the client in the design team.

Maintaining a good relationship with a client is a continuous effort that requires dedication, sensitivity, patience, and good listening and communication skills. It also takes understanding that it is necessary to modify project management style with every client. The project manager should make every effort to understand how the client likes to receive information, how decisions are made, the client's communication style, their management style, their time availability, and the level of formality they wish to maintain in their relationship with the design firm. With this knowledge, the project manager can tailor the way the project is managed to the client.

It is also an important part of maintaining client relations to make sure the client understands his obligations in the development of the project. The client will be responsible for providing information, arranging access to existing facilities, setting up meetings, making decisions, etc. The project manager can help the client fulfill these obligations by advising the client as early as possible of upcoming tasks or decisions. It is important to give the client timeframes for all activities or decisions that require their time and/or coordination with other members of the client organization. Clients who have never participated in design projects are usually grateful to the project manager who guides them through the process. All clients like to feel that they are being treated respectfully and that the project manager recognizes the value of their time.

It is important for the project manager to be forthright in discussing problems with the client. Unfortunately, it is unlikely that everything will go smoothly on a project and that there will be no rough bumps along the way. Since people create projects and people are not perfect, there will be mistakes, misunderstandings, communication problems, documentation problems, and other problems generated by the team doing the work. The client should feel comfortable raising concerns about the project, the work, or the team with the project manager. These conversations should be handled in as professional and calm a way as possible. The client should always feel that the project manager is there to support them in the good times and the rough times.

Lead the Project

Even though the project manager position includes plenty of behind-the-scenes responsibilities, the role is not a passive, behind-the-scenes one. The project manager must actively lead the project. He or she is the orchestra leader, the captain of the ship, the coach, the mentor, the negotiator, the moderator, the voice of reason, and the figure of authority.

Controlling the team's work and leading the team are two very different approaches. Certainly, in order to be successful in this role, the project manager must be knowledgeable about every aspect of the project and how the parts come together. The project manager must continually monitor the work. The team looks to the project manager to guide them. This does not mean, however, that the project manager does all of the work or makes every decision. It is the project manager's responsibility to support the team in the delivery of their work within the infrastructure, which he or she has established.

The client, too, looks to the project manager to be knowledgeable about every component of the project and also to delegate authority properly. To meet this expectation, the project manager must actively lead project meetings and communication with the client. Because client's organizations are not dissimilar in structure to that of the design firm, most clients also expect the project manager to lead rather than do the work of the project team. Clients are astute in this area. They want to do business with leaders.

Manage Change

Change has become the norm during the delivery of nearly every design project. Even though project schedules are shorter than in the past, client organizations and businesses continue to change so fast that it is rare to complete a project without experiencing a change to the work. Change can occur at any point in the design process and frequently even during construction. The project manager must monitor requests for change and establish a dialog with the client about how such changes impact design fees.

Clients expect to pay for changes. The project manager must address the changes with the client as soon as they are known and work with the client to develop an agreement on how the cost of the changes will be addressed. It is almost impossible for everyone—the client and the design firm—to accurately and fairly address changes at the end of a project. No one will remember the details and it will be difficult to reach agreement on costs. The design firm may not be able to recoup the cost of work already delivered. The client may refuse to pay because they don't remember the details or because their resources have been expended. They may feel pressured to pay for work, the depth and impact of which they no longer understand. Not only could the design firm realize a financial loss on the work, but also a good client/design firm relationship may be impacted.

The project manager should always look for ways to accommodate change to the project with the least impact to the project budget, schedule, and fees. Work sequence may need to be altered or parts of the project moved ahead while the components of work impacted by the change are revised. There are many creative ways to keep a project moving and to mitigate the impact of change on the schedule and budget. Looking after the client's interests is one of the project manager's responsibilities. A proactive approach like this on behalf of the client will strengthen the relationship between the client and design firm and raise the level of trust the client holds for the project manager and the design firm.

Conclusion: Variables Affecting Success

There are many components that contribute to the success of a project manager. Other than performing the responsibilities as described above, there are a few variables—some within the project manger's control, others not—that can have an impact upon the success of the project manager. They include:

- **Listening, Hearing, and Communication Skills.** Listening and hearing are different. Understand the difference and practice each accordingly.

- **Personality Conflicts.** In dealing with people, personalities are a big factor, and sometimes there are conflicts. If so, address the issue, and if it can't be corrected, take action. This includes replacing a member of the design team—even the project manager.

- **Client Trust.** Without client trust, the project will be difficult for everyone—client, project manager, and design team. Work hard to earn clients' trust.

- **Design Team Experience.** If the design team does not have the experience to do the project, it will be difficult to deliver the project the client expects and will put a huge burden on the project manager. Structure design teams carefully to achieve a balance between experienced and inexperienced team members.

- **Design Firm Support.** The design firm must support the project manager in the delivery of projects with staff resources, timely financial performance information, and appropriate technology. If the design firm has not put its own infrastructure in place, it cannot expect the project manager to be successful in his or her work.

Project management is a pivotal role in the business of design. It is as creative and challenging a role as the individual makes it. Project managers have tremendous opportunities not only to influence projects, but also to lead clients and design teams.

16

Managing the Client Relationship

by Frederick J. Schmidt, Joseph T. Connell, and Gina A. Berndt

Other chapters in this book focus in detail on the rationales and mechanics of professional practices—the day-to-day steps involved in managing a career in interior design, from making sound choices about education to specialization to business development to working on a project. In each of them, design professionals will find themselves reading often about a central character, "the client," and they will find it easy to imagine who clients might be, what they are like, what their needs might be. Designers think that they must know how to handle clients and their relationships with them; they do it every day, and firms have institutionalized, in varied ways, many aspects of relating to clients. Yet if client relationships are so easy and natural, why is it that bad client relationships develop, that clients do not return, and that often, good client relationships may seem to depend on personality, "fit," or chance?

Designers may not think of themselves primarily as people who, like other professionals, are in the business of managing relationships. They manage ideas, vision, space, and their relationships with peoples' needs; in its best moments, their work is an art form. Yet relationship management is an art form as well, and one that designers would do well to study—and master. When designers know how to assess just who the client is, just what the client's needs are, and just how well they have been satisfied by design services, they will be designers who can sustain a business that delivers meaningful results for human beings. This chapter will look first at the "ideal" client relationship, from both the client's view and the designer's view, in terms of a feature important to both parties: total satisfaction. It will then go on to discuss how designers can manage the client relationship to best ensure that the client has a quality experience of total satisfaction. Finally, it will introduce a method designers can use to measure whether they have indeed provided total satisfaction, and how they can adjust to better provide it in future client relationships.

The Ideal Relationship

THE CLIENT'S VIEW

From the client's perspective, what is the "ideal interior designer?" Each client has unique goals, constraints and expectations, so there may be as many definitions of "ideal" as there are clients themselves. Yet there are at least three core attributes that define a client's aspirations for an effective service relationship:

- **Understanding.** Clients are human beings who want to be heard and understood. They want to work with service providers—designers—who listen to what they say, receptively, empathetically, and actively. They want designers to take their ideas into account, and they want responsive answers to their questions.

- **Value.** At its most basic level, the relationship between client and designer represents a business transaction where service is rendered and payment is made. As the buyer, the client is practically obligated to seek a fiscally responsible solution—a fair price, a good deal, or an outcome that serves the organization's business needs within budget.

- **Success.** Ultimately, clients want results: not just a designer with a good reputation, an impressive client list and a host of awards, but a designer whose solution and behavior reflects a true understanding of this client's needs and motivations. Ultimately, clients want to know that the outcome the designer delivers is exactly what they need to achieve their business objectives. They want the designer to help them succeed.

In all these areas, clients desire complete fulfillment. They want more than a little value, a bit of understanding, or a hint of success; they want *total satisfaction*. And they will reward the designer for it. For example, three Harvard Business School professors researched why certain service organizations excel. In their book *The Service Profit Chain,* they revealed that customers who gave Xerox a rating of five on customer satisfaction surveys were six times more likely to repurchase a Xerox product than those who gave the company only a four (on a five-point scale). Thus, "it was quickly concluded that fours were relatively meaningless," and Xerox management set the company's sights on achieving total satisfaction as a means of sustaining and gaining business.[1]

In other words, "satisfied" is a minimum standard, and it makes no guarantee for the designer's continued success. Authors Benjamin Schneider and David E. Bowen, drawing on the Harvard research noted above, assert that "businesses must strive for 100 percent, or total, customer satisfaction and even *delight* to achieve the kind of loyalty they desire."[2] Knowing the importance of total customer satisfaction, service providers may view their customers in a new light. (See diagram.) Some customers are so satisfied they become "apostles" for the provider—spreading the word about the product or service to other potential customers. An effective cadre of apostles can generate tremendous value for an organization at virtually no cost. Thus, service providers are wise to invest in converting "near-apostles" to "apostles." The other end of

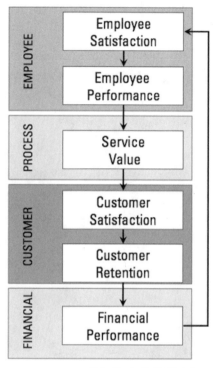

"The Service Profit Chain"

the spectrum warrants attention as well. There we find the "terrorists," whose dissatisfaction is so great that they also spread the word, professing their bad experience with the service provider to as many listeners as possible.[3]

THE DESIGNER'S VIEW

To be confident that clients will come back again and again, an interior designer must ensure that clients are delighted with the services and solutions delivered. Such relationships are "ideal" for the designer because they contribute to the long-term viability of the designer's business through increased client retention and profitability.

Satisfying the client is the designer's job, and achieving total satisfaction is largely within the designer's control as service provider. However, this is much more easily attained with clients who are more able and willing to "engage" the project process.

The truth is, not every organization needs or is prepared for the support of a professional designer. Organizations that *are* in the best position to engage design professionals have defined a specific business problem and are prepared to put forth the resources to reach a solution. These organizations recognize

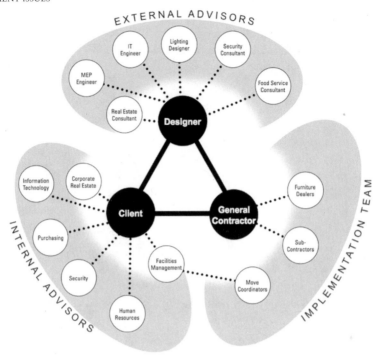

Adaptation of "The Service Value Chain"

that the design of a workspace is a full-time job, even for the client, and they are ready and willing to apply their will, people, time, and resources to make decisions and advance the project process.

At an even grander scale, there are concepts embedded in the design process that go beyond the simple exchange of interior design services for payment. The interior designer's broader altruistic mission is to create environments that meet human needs and support human activities. The most mutually gratifying relationships may be with clients who respect and share this mission and are willing to embrace the process of creating the built environment. And, as might be expected, the most rewarding relationships include an atmosphere of mutual respect. As the designer respects the client's business needs, the client respects the designer's potential to make a creative contribution to the client's business.

The Project Circle

The client/interior designer relationship is not a simple experience between two parties. Rather, it is an integral piece of a larger business collaboration involving a number of organizations represented by the Project Circle. The Project Circle depicts a key feature of design projects: inside it is the client, a unit made up of competing interests, and surrounding the client are a web of players all with their own professional interests and their own role to play in providing a quality experience for the client.

Inside the Client

Within the client organization alone, there are several groups and individuals that represent "interest groups" for which the designer must provide an integrated and workable quality experience.

- **Sponsor.** The sponsor is "the client" personified. Generally speaking, he or she is the client's most senior person involved in the project and is a member of (or reports to) senior management. In turn, everyone working on the project—both within and outside the client organization—must satisfy the sponsor. The sponsor represents the client organization's business vision, builds the internal business case, and secures and manages funding for the project.

- **Client Project Manager.** The client project manager generally comes from either a corporate real estate or a facilities management department. He or she is involved in the project's details and participates in ongoing work with the interior designer and other service providers. He or she is concerned with critical decisions and operational matters, such as space allocation, project scheduling, and adherence to fee and construction budgets. The client project manager also serves as a central point for communication within the client organization.

- **Human Resources.** The client's human resources staff may be involved in a project from a communication standpoint. They may relay information to the design team, providing details about the organization's practices, structure, headcount projections, policies, culture, and employee behaviors—factors that define the client's needs and therefore the design response. They may also communicate with the workforce, helping the organization to manage change. For example, when a move is necessary, the human resources team often works closely with the facilities manager to facilitate the transition for employees and business groups, informing them of new schedules and fostering a cooperative environment.

- **Information Systems and Telecommunications.** The technology requirements are one of the most critical challenges faced by the project team because they are very costly and integral to nearly all business today. Representatives from the client's technology departments can speak for current and anticipated requirements, enabling the project team to design an infrastructure that will support present and future plans.

- **Users.** The users are the people who ultimately will occupy or use the designed environment. Depending on the facility, the users may be internal or external to the client organization—employees, customers, recruits, vendors. In addition to their desires and preferences, these users depend (albeit unknowingly) on a design solution that allows for their personal safety and health.

Each of these interest groups may claim to be entirely distinct from the rest, and each may assert that its priorities should take precedence over the rest. For example, an individual department may declare that its unique activities call for a deviation from the standard floor plan to achieve an efficient work process. The project manager, on the other hand, may hold fast to standardized space and/or amenity allocation to help reduce management costs, consolidate suppliers and buying power, maintain equity among various users, or perform other defensible strategies that may serve a larger objective.

Who resolves this conflict between efficiency and cost savings? Occasionally the client team is led by an authority figure who defines the priorities and makes such decisions. But more often than not, projects are complicated by a variety of points of view, and the designer is left to reconcile the conflicts. The designer's challenge, then, is to:

- Integrate all the interests to achieve a workable compromise. Each constituency must feel "embraced" and assured that the designer has made reasonable efforts to accommodate all points of view.

- Understand whose interests must be served for the project to meet the client's business objectives. Rarely can a design solution satisfy every desire of every individual or group. By identifying the client's larger business goals and realities, the designer can make fact-based decisions about the inevitable tradeoffs.

Outside the Client

As if the client's internal structure didn't hold enough challenge and complexity, an even more intricate organization develops outside the client's walls . . . a virtual team of service providers who are all part of the project delivery mechanism. The interior designer must operate effectively as a part of this team throughout the entire project process. A host of additional players around the Project Circle bring both support and challenges to the designer:

- **External project manager.** The project manager, sometimes known as "program manager" or "owner's representative," is a third party hired by the client to ensure that all phases of the work proceed as planned. In this capacity, the project manager may be in a position to serve as advocate for or monitor of the interior designer and allied team members.

- **Real estate consultant.** From the interior designer's perspective, the real estate consultant is both customer and service partner—customer, because the consultant sometimes acts as advisor to the client, and partner, because both designer and consultant attempt to develop and manage a solution that meets the client's business objectives. The designer's work reflects on the real estate consultant's success, and vice versa.

- **Manufacturers.** Manufacturers want designers to use their products (carpet, lighting, furniture, and the like) in the client's space. Generally, the client seeks product recommendations from the interior designer. Therefore, the manufacturer will feel compelled to make its most favorable impression on either the designer or the client. Yet, manufacturers can provide a wealth of information to assist both the client and the designer.

- **Builder/contractor.** The builder/contractor uses the interior designer's plans as a framework for constructing the client's environment. Thus, the designer's input influences the builder/contractor's output. Conversely, the builder/contractor's execution may be seen as an indicator of the designer's effectiveness.

- **Other consultants.** The client or other project participants may enlist the support of other expert consultants for particular and usually highly technical areas such as mechanical, electrical, plumbing, acoustics, audio/visual systems, food service, lighting, security systems, fire protection, and structural engineering.

If designers can effectively collaborate with everyone around the Project Circle, they can help build future business because new assignments can come through any of these channels. Yet the designer's loyalties and focus must remain on the client and the project process. If the designer makes each decision with the client's interests in mind—not with an eye on pleasing other players—then the designer will gain a reputation for integrity. Members of the Project Circle who respect professional, responsible behavior likely will become future advocates for the designer.

Accepting Accountability for the Project Circle

Because the activities of all players in the Project Circle are so closely intertwined and contingent on one another, it can be difficult for the client to know where to assign responsibility for breakdowns or praise for accomplishments. From the client's perspective, all the players collectively hold account-ability for attaining the project's goals. A wise strategy for the interior designer (and for all players, for that matter) is to think and act as the client's representative in all relationships. This can also be described as assuming a "steward-ship" or "advocacy" role for the client.

Any appearance of preference could make the designer appear biased, calling the designer's recommendations into question. The designer is a pro-fessional working to achieve the client's total satisfaction, not to gain other service providers' approval. Certainly, no one wants to burn bridges with other service providers. But even a hint that a designer acts outside the client's interest can destroy the current relationship and put an everlasting tarnish on the designer's reputation.

Handling the Complexity of the Project Circle

As the Project Circle illustrates, virtually any commercial interior design project involves a complex web of players both inside and outside the client organization. And no single player—not even the client—can be completely responsible for the project experience because so many factors are beyond one party's immediate control. Yet because anything that happens throughout the entire experience reflects on the designer, the interior designer is in a unique position of *perceived accountability*. For example, members of the interior design team do not physically build the space, hire subcontractors, order materials or arrange for and monitor jobsite safety, nor can they control unpredictable occurrences such as labor strikes or so-called acts of God. Yet the client's facility manager may look to the interior designer to provide guidance and delivery on the expectation of a safe journey in the creation, construction, and occupancy of a new facility.

The interior designer's challenge, then, is to *act responsibly without having total responsibility*.

In the following ways, the designer must work to make accountability fea-sible and to influence the entire project experience without being truly liable for others in the Project Circle:

- Be vigilant in reporting. Although the designer may not create the work schedule for all parties involved in a project, the designer likely will assemble a project timeline for the client by drawing upon input from many sources. The designer is not author of the schedule, but rather the reporter. Yet if problems arise in the timeline, the designer may be implicated by mere association in any inaccuracies. The designer must be attentive and proactive in reviewing the details that come in from all parties, to make certain that the schedule represents the best and realistic estimates of those who are responsible for the activities.

- Probe for details. Particularly in the early stages of a project, the client (and to some extent even the designer) may be content to deal with vague information. Although the client may not want to be bothered with minutiae, engineers and contractors live in a world of facts, where details help them make safe judgments. The designer can influence a positive project experience for all parties by serving as a detail-minded strategist:

  (1) Educating the client about the value of detailed specifications so all providers can make fact-based decisions.

  (2) Alerting the client that the need for details will come—and when.

  (3) Helping the client assemble details that are meaningful to the other players in the Project Circle.

- Manage information. Even the smallest projects involve volumes of information. Regardless of project size, the interior designer must exercise careful judgment in handling all specifications and data. The designer's task is to get the appropriate information at the appropriate time from the appropriate source. Then, they must deliver it in a suitable format to the appropriate users when and where they need it.

In a now-famous interview with Charles Eames in 1972, interviewer Madame L. Amic asked if Eames had ever compromised. He replied, "No, but I have willingly accepted constraints." A thorough understanding of relevant constraints and details shapes the attributes of a design solution. Vigilance in understanding the need creates a more intelligent response—one that may solve more problems than are presented by the client or are apparent upon engagement or preliminary review.

This thorough understanding does not mean that designers step outside their field of expertise, just that they understand how their field works in connection with other fields contributing to the project. None of the actions described above will take the designer outside of the scope of the designer's responsibility. Yet actions such as these will allow the designer to exert an appropriate measure of influence on the project process as a whole.

Just Designer and Client

It is difficult to conceive of the interior designer's relationship with a client in isolation from the rest of the Project Circle; the relationships are numerous and intertwined. However, if it is important to recognize the complex web of players involved in an overall project, it is just as important to understand the client/designer relationship. The interior designer may have limited control over the experience of the Project Circle as a whole, but the interior design team members have complete responsibility for the client's experience with their own service and outcomes.

In fact, the way a designer manages a client relationship has a sizable impact on how the client will evaluate the designer's contribution to the business situation. This section of the chapter describes how interior designers can work to achieve total client satisfaction through effective business practices: building and supporting the core team, communicating effectively, and becoming a business consultant.

BUILD SUPPORT AND THE CORE TEAM

Generally, the client expects to deal with a consistent team of a few talented, capable individuals who are attuned to the client's business challenges, goals, and constraints. Typically, the design team might include a director, project manager, senior designer, project designer, technical manager, and studio support staff.

But the client and design team members also need to know that appropriate extra resources and talent are available when needed. For example, the project may call for the knowledge of an expert in programming, lighting, or technical integration. The design team needs to know how and when to enlist support from such experts; and the client needs to know upfront that this additional assistance may be required, as well as how, if at all, specialized resources may affect project costs.

COMMUNICATE FOR EFFECTIVENESS

During predictable times of project routine and when unexpected or possibly difficult situations arise, effective communication is the strongest bridge between client and service provider. Successful communication occurs when both parties' messages are received and understood as intended. Good communication does not rule out the possibility of disagreements, but it does open the door to constructive discussion about the best course of action for meeting the client's business objectives. Designers can better ensure that clients will feel satisfied if they use the following strategies to encourage familiarity with procedures, clarity, and a heightened flow of information between individuals.

USE STANDARD COMMUNICATION TOOLS

Designers can accomplish some communication according to "formula," that is, where the designer follows a standardized, familiar format for project status reports, scheduled meetings, contracts, and so forth. For the designer, such tools simplify the work of preparing communications, and thus they preserve time in which the designer can develop thoughtful, creative content that will address the client's business needs. For the client, standard communication tools lend a helpful measure of predictability. Once clients are acclimated to a standard report format, for example, they will know exactly where to find the information they need—and the designer will have created a positive experience in which the client feels knowledgeable and in control.

SPEAK IN TERMS CLIENTS CAN UNDERSTAND

The process and profession of design often utilize a vocabulary unfamiliar to "outsiders." To communicate effectively, designers must avoid jargon or a professional lexicon that makes it hard for clients to understand. If this seems obvious, compare the following statements made by client and design team to express the same process.

- Client: "First, select the architecture, then design the system, then program."
- Design team: "First, develop the program, then design from the program, then build the architecture."

In this case, the client is a multinational consulting firm with roots in information technology and systems development. Imagine how such transposition of terms and sequences could hinder a successful project launch.

In addition to creating confusion, "foreign language" can alienate the client from the designer and the design process. Moreover, a person's self-esteem can be bruised if he or she feels less knowledgeable about a subject—particularly if the subject is discussed in apparent code. Commonly, these subjects include:

- Highly technical or detailed issues of electronics or machinery
- Building codes
- USGBC LEED rating systems
- Detailed knowledge of the furniture industry
- Color
- Spatial attributes
- Elements and principles of design (rhythm, balance, proportion, mass, form, etc.).

Designers provide a terrific service when they carefully guide clients and all project participants along the project path in areas where individuals may be uncomfortable or unable to express their views.

Build Trust through One-to-One Relationships

Despite the value of standardized communications, designers and clients share much knowledge and information in situations that are not necessarily prescribed by the project process: frequent phone calls, short conversations during meeting breaks, an exchange of thoughts during an elevator or cab ride. These unplanned encounters, when designers and client interact one-on-one, can be effective ways to learn from one another, and they may serve as the building blocks for interpersonal relationships that outlast a single project and result in a long-term association between client and interior designer.

Such one-to-one relationships need not arise solely for the sake of project efficiency, but also out of common interests or sheer interpersonal chemistry. So it is important to cultivate an atmosphere where rapport can build between individuals on both sides of the project. Primarily, this atmosphere requires that designers see team members unrestricted by job titles and work responsibilities. The designer must recognize where natural fits occur and allow those relationships to form.

Ask Good Questions at the Right Time

One of the most important skills in client management is the ability to ask excellent questions. The designer must draw out the client's desires in terms that are specific enough for the designer to deliver a solution that does not merely meet expectations, but totally satisfies.

Listen

Reaching a true understanding of what the client wants can feel like an exercise in mind reading, but it is really an exercise in effective listening. The designer must be invested in listening for answers—both to the questions that have been asked (as described above), and to those that have not.

Respond

The designer's ultimate response to the client will be the end product: the designed environment. But the client must sense a designer's responsiveness long before the project is completed. In fact, some clients expect a response from the designer daily, or even more often, during critical phases of the project. The following precepts demonstrate "responsiveness" in action:

- Keep the client informed. The client has a right to know what is happening. Regular status reports and meetings may be sufficient under normal circumstances. If a special issue or problem arises, the designer may need to offer updates via phone or e-mail, or even an impromptu meeting.

- Be available. The client is paying to be able to talk with the designer, whenever they want, during working hours. So the designer must be accessible. If the designer needs to be inaccessible for a short period, he or she should leave detailed information with the person who answers the phone, on voicemail, and, if possible, as an automatic response to e-mail. This way, clients will know not to anticipate an immediate response and/or whom to contact in the designer's absence.

- Be prompt. The designer should deliver standardized communications according to schedule (such as the second day after weekly meetings or on the first of the month). If the client asks for information off-cycle, the designer must provide it promptly. A design firm may have standards for appropriate response times, such as returning phone calls and e-mail messages within one business day. Even if a designer doesn't have the answer, he or she should return the call to indicate that someone is working on it.

- Keep promises. If the designer promises a report or answer by Monday, the client must receive it by Monday. If the designer promises to get back to the client on a special issue, it must not be allowed to slip through the cracks.

- Don't just react—anticipate. Responding does not necessarily mean reacting to a client's request, question, or concern; in fact, some of the most responsive actions are those that anticipate the client's need.

GET THE PICTURE

Much of the interior designer's work produces outcomes that are visual. The client pays the designer to create something that looks "right." Although the client defines "right," the interior design team must understand and translate that definition into a physical solution that lives up to the client's vision. To reach such an understanding, the designer must ask effective questions (as described above). Additionally, the designer and the client must share a "visual vocabulary" so that the design team understands the aesthetic perceptions the client puts behind such terms as "global," "first-class," "collegial," "warm," "modern," "high-tech," "nice but not too nice," and "colorful."

BE EFFICIENT

In years past, getting information to and from the client added days—and even weeks—to the design process. The mere act of sending drawings for review, even with express delivery service, could take a day or more for a client cross-country. But current technology and alternate business practices allow clients and designers to use information immediately. For instance, electronic media technology allows both designers and clients to transmit information without delay. Internet or Web-based tools allow designers to post drawings electronically for immediate review by a client, who can offer quick feedback by e-mail or conference call. Designers who avail themselves of such technologies can trim time off the overall project schedule, or at least conserve time for more value-added activities.

Technology is not the only way to achieve greater efficiency in communication. Innovative changes in work process also can accelerate work routines. An alternative to the traditional "go-away-and-work" model is the charrette process. Charrettes are workshops that involve the client's decision-makers and our designers working and collaborating directly to achieve quick, immediate results.

Be a Business Consultant

Interior design for corporate and professional services clients is the strategic exercise of design principles to satisfy business objectives. As such, the people who work in corporate interior design must be not only creative but also business-minded. Designers must understand the business problem as deeply as they understand the design problem. Thus, the members of an interior design team are business consultants in the eyes of their clients and must live up to the rising expectations for this breed of service provider. This section continues to emphasize the drive for total client satisfaction, and describes several consulting tactics interior design professionals can use to advance their client relationships.

Define Goals and Constraints

Thinking like a business consultant means knowing what the client hopes to achieve, then developing a strategy for reaching that end. Thus, when meeting with a client regarding a new project, the designer's first order of business is to learn where the client wants to go. What will make the project a success in the client's eyes? This is the designer's first opportunity to ask effective questions, as described above. In particular, some of the most critical questions, as a new project begins, are about goals and constraints:

- **Goals.** What does the client want? What is the organization's business mission? By what criteria does the client measure success? What does the client envision in terms of outcome? Who must the client satisfy? What message should this facility project? Learning about the client's goals will help the designer understand what the interior design solution needs to accomplish.

- **Constraints.** What are the client's limits? What potential "inhibitors" might stand in the way of achieving or framing the client's goals? The designer's questions should drive at customary constraints such as budget, timeframe, and design standards, as well as less expected issues such as density targets (square feet per person), national purchasing contracts, and reuse of existing assets.

Doubtless, the client's goals and constraints may present numerous contradictions. The designer must reconcile these contradictions and define a solution that achieves the appropriate balance between considerations.

PROVIDE THE EXPERT OPINION

As insightful and educated as the clients may be, they are not responsible for understanding the many interior design possibilities for the spaces they manage. Their time and attention are occupied by a host of other issues. So they hire interior designers to provide them with excellent ideas, solutions, and service.

Notice that last word: "service." It is not "servitude." Accepting an interior design assignment does not place the designer in bondage to the client's beliefs. As business consultants, designers have a professional obligation to educate and guide the client. Any proposed solutions must reflect the designer's best assessment of how to reach the client's business goals. Although designers should take the client's preferences into account, they need not propose a mere regurgitation of those preferences. The clients deserve educated advice, not just "yes."

Yet, the client is not obligated to take the designer's advice. In fact, it is the client's prerogative to make a decision that the designer deems "wrong." If the client insists on a direction different from the one the designer prefers, the designer must respect and support that decision (unless, of course, the direction violates local codes or the designer's code of ethics). The best the designer can do is educate the client on the benefits of investing in the proposed solution and make clear the consequences of the client's decision.

MAKE APPROPRIATE PROMISES

Because the designer is considered an expert, the client will rely heavily on the designer's word. So the designer must be clear about what he or she can and cannot promise (recognizing once again that the complexity of the Project Circle leaves so many factors beyond the designer's immediate control). For example, a designer can promise a delivery date for drawings, but cannot guarantee a firm date for completion of construction. A designer can provide a statement of probable cost, but cannot define a precise budget without qualified bids from the marketplace.

Avoid and Resolve Conflicts

Most conflicts in client relationships arise from "misses"—misunderstandings, miscommunications, miscalculations, missed deadlines. While these misses can occur on either side of the relationship, any problem can be construed as a negative reflection on the interior designer ("You should have warned us," "You should have anticipated this," "You should have known what I meant."). Thus, the designer must take strategic and proactive steps to avoid conflict and resolve disputes should they arise. The designer must always remember to think of the relationship with the client is a business relationship, and to document it carefully.

For example, designers must ground their aesthetic recommendations on a business-based rationale. If clients are to believe in and support the designer's ideas, they need evidence that the recommendations are sound. Sufficient grounds for a client to spend thousands to millions of dollars to implement a design solution do not include gut instinct, intuition or a sense of art. Therefore, when presenting ideas, the designer must provide more substantiation than a mere "trust me." For example, in making lighting recommendations, the designer can educate the client that 30 percent of electric costs are spent on lighting and show how a proposed lighting solution may actually save at the bottom line. This way, even if conflicts do arise, they likely can be discussed in terms of logic, reason, and business realities. When designers rely on such a business-based rationale, they can avoid arguments on subjective matters of taste, which are decidedly more difficult to reconcile.

Another useful strategy is to make documentation a discipline. By keeping a record of decisions and communication between interior design team and client, the designer creates an information source of value to both parties and the entire design team. Particularly when a discrepancy arises, the designer will have ready access to the facts needed to resolve the issue quickly and with minimal disruption to the project. In addition to the expected documentation such as contracts, proposals, drawings, correspondence, schedules, and cost estimates, designers' files should grow as they add e-mail messages and notes from meetings and phone conversations. If possible, designers should take advantage of electronic storage, whether on individual workstations, shared networks, or project Web sites, to make it easy for team members to locate, retrieve, and share documentation.

Transform Clients into Apostles

The interior designer is in business not just to satisfy its clients' objectives, but also to accomplish his or her own business vision. Fortunately, one follows the other. In the best of relationships, designer and client become "patrons" for one another. A patron is a person chosen, named or honored as a special guardian, protector, or supporter. As the designer guards, protects, and supports the client's business initiatives through design, the client will support and advance the designer and his or her reputation.

As we have seen, when clients are totally satisfied, they are far more likely to rehire the designer. The result is not a mere project relationship, but an enduring account-based relationship, where the client becomes an "apostle" and returns again and again for the designer's trusted expertise and support.

But there is more. As mentioned earlier in this chapter, apostles are not just loyal, but so satisfied they will recommend a service to others.[4] Thus, as satisfied customers become apostles, the designer gains not just long-lasting accounts, but new relationships as well.

RECOGNIZE HUMAN NEEDS

For all its bottom-line concerns, business is still a human endeavor. Designers may speak in terms of "clients," "organizations," and "enterprises," but they deal on a day-to-day basis with human individuals. And success, or total client satisfaction, depends on the general contentment (or even delight) of these human beings. Therefore, the interior designer as business consultant must take action to make personal connections with these people, treating them with the genuine respect and care they crave.

Schneider and Bowen suggest that human needs are so important that when a service provider fails to gratify them, customers can feel outrage, and conversely, when the service provider succeeds for customers, this success can generate exceptional delight. Borrowing concepts from psychology, philosophy and personality theory, they maintain that businesses can make or break the client's experience according to three basic human needs: security, justice, and self-esteem.[5] The designer who violates trust in these areas faces great difficulty to "change the resulting outrage to satisfaction, much less delight." Threats to a person's physical or financial security are particularly difficult to overcome. A challenge to justice or fairness amounts to violation of trust, which also is hard to rise above.

Suffice it to say that designers must seek to understand the client's human concerns. One person may worry about making a safe journey from old to new space. Another may have anxieties about individual job security. Still another may experience stress under intense workloads that interfere with his or her quality of life. Although the designer may not be able to mitigate such issues through design work, a designer's willingness to hear and understand personal challenges may provide the client with a sense of relief. Also, the designer may build a friendship that not only strengthens the client relationship, but also enriches the designer personally.

Measurement

By and large, interior designers have measured quality by relying on intuition or only the most basic measurements to evaluate the success of their work. A designer might track the number of clients who answer "yes" to questions such as, "Would you hire us again?" or, "Would you give us a positive reference?" Perhaps the nearest the interior design industry has come to a scientific evaluation method is the Post-Occupancy Evaluation (POE). Typically, the POE is conducted six to twelve months after occupants move into a designed environment. The objective is to assess how people are functioning in the space. Ideally, the same population would have participated in a baseline evaluation to see how they measured the prior environment before the interior design project began.

Such measures of quality can't help designers to ask whether their practices really do the job. Even with comparative data, so many factors may have changed during a move that survey respondents may be unable to isolate their feelings for the design of the facility; their opinions may be influenced by longer commutes, changes in child-care routine, difficulty finding a parking place, or new phone or computer systems—factors outside the interior designer's control. In addition, such measurements are purely historic: they define a level of acceptance at a moment in time.

Most important, these measures do not convey *how we are doing*. They cannot help improve performance during the process. If these traditional attitudes toward measuring client satisfaction are ineffective, and total client satisfaction is the goal, then how will we know when we've achieved it? Is there a reliable way to track and measure the client's satisfaction? Yes. This section describes a system that designers can use to measure their success according to client-defined criteria.

Process/Outcome Measurement System

The alternative to traditional methods of measuring the client's satisfaction with the interior designer's work is a method for measuring the value of services in light of client requirements. In this client-based method, "quality" has a unique definition for each assignment because every client has a range of goals that in combination make their project unlike any other. The interior designer's role is to understand those goals and deliver an appropriate solution in response to each client objective. This method is notable because it separates the client's *encounter* with the designer from the ultimate *artifact* produced by the project. That is, the method evaluates client satisfaction in two distinct areas: the *process* of the interior designer's work and the *outcome* of that work.

Not coincidentally, we will discuss process first. Clients who express satisfaction with the process generally also express satisfaction with the outcome. A positive project experience predisposes the client to a positive feeling about the outcome, whereas a negative project experience will bias a client toward negative feelings for the end result.

Measuring Quality of Process—The Journey

The *process* is the experience of the client and others involved in the project as they move toward completion of the designed environment. If the current environment is Point A and the new environment is Point B, then process measures are the vector connecting the two points.

The process can be viewed in two categories: delivery and experience. *Delivery* measures are typical measures used as part of any project management process—variables such as fee compliance, schedule compliance, and resource allocation. *Experience* is more intangible and focuses on the client's relationship with the interior designer—the designer's communication, knowledge, empathy, timeliness, and so on.

Experience. Customers expect good experiences, and they deserve them. The project team's responsibility is not only to solve problems but also to take the client through the journey of solving the problem, making it a collaborative exercise. An interior designer's future economic growth lies in the value of the experiences he or she provides to clients; goods and services are not enough. The journey is as important as the destination. A client's experience through the project process plays a pivotal role in the client's overall satisfaction with a project. Many experiences are characterized in "moments of truth"—such as when a consultant surprises the client with an immediate response or, conversely, fails to return a phone call. Experiences can play a negative role and decompose the client's perception of the interior designer in a very short time, regardless of how talented a project team is or how good the solution is.

Delivery. Given the complexity of the Project Circle—with its web of relationships, alliances, partners, contractors, and subcontractors—many extraneous factors contribute to and influence an interior designer's service delivery. Even with a designer's best intentions, sometimes projects cannot be completed on time or within budget.

However, customers expect results, delivered on time and within or under budget. And the minimum expected from the interior designer is compliance with approved, well-communicated and formalized schedules, budgets, timelines, and deliverables. These delivery-focused aspects of the project process are understandably of concern to clients who want to achieve bottom-line results.

Measuring Quality of Outcome—The Destination

The outcome is the completion of the designed environment, and it can be seen from both a *physical* and a *behavioral* perspective. Naturally, an interior design project will change the physical space in functional and environmental terms. And such physical changes can profoundly influence the overall behavior of the organization and its culture, image, and effectiveness. While interior designers can make a clear and tangible impact on the physical outcome, the behavioral outcomes are, arguably, more critical to the client organization.

Physical Outcome. The physical elements of a space are perhaps the most beloved by interior designers because they are the elements designers can influence directly. Any interior design project includes a planning or programming phase where the client's specific requirements are captured, quantified, and approved. The requirements may include head count projections, cost information, spatial layout information, and equipment information.

Behavioral Outcome. Interior designers don't simply design a physical environment in a vacuum; they create a space within the context of the client and its business and behavioral objectives. Environments designed to reinforce business objectives are a strategic means of facilitating the achievement of business objectives. Whether the client aims to achieve worker collaboration, improve recruitment, or raise employee satisfaction, the designed space plays a role—either as reinforcement or as detriment.

The System in Practice

Even when using a client-defined approach to measurement, in which the client defines "quality," the interior designer bears the responsibility of tracking, measuring, and acting on results. Implementing a measurement system may be a challenge for interior designers who have never used a formal evaluation method, but the process is not difficult:

1 Expectations—Before the project begins, members of the client team meet to identify their expectations.

2 Qualifications—During the project and often at completion of each project phase, the design team uses the expectations document (described above) to remain focused on meeting the client's explicit goals and objectives. The interior designer and client work together to make any mid-course corrections that may be necessary.

3 Evaluation—At the close of the project, members of the client team share their perceptions to evaluate how well their expectations were met.

4 Action—After evaluation is complete, the interior designer dissem-inates the results of the client's assessment among design team mem-bers and prepares a plan for acting on the feedback.

The measurement system outlined here is a framework, and interior designers or design groups will need to customize it to align with their own business objectives. No matter how the process is customized, designers must use the ultimate process with the following basic guidelines in mind:

- Integrate measurement with the project process

- Administer by a disinterested and unbiased party; project owners must not measure their own work

- Communicate so all members of the firm can embrace and easily understand the process

- Use to enrich the entire organization, not just a few individuals or even individual project teams; share knowledge gained from the process throughout the organization so all can learn from each project.

The benefits of the process/outcome measurement system are at least three-fold:

1 The mere fact that a designer measures satisfaction, as well as the scientific means the designer uses, will raise the client's perception of the designer's value. That is, the fact that a designer asks for feed-back may be even more important than the suggestions the client makes. Moreover, any ongoing quality process is likely to improve ongoing client relationships.

2 The designer will be in a constant process of discovery to identify flaws in the work product and project process. This process will equip the designer to take immediate steps to solve problems in cur-rent projects. And, perhaps even more important, the designer will know where to make process improvements that will benefit proj-ects and clients in the future.

3 The designer can substantiate his or her value with tangible meas-ures of performance linked to business strategy and can communi-cate these measures to clients, prospective clients, and counterparts.

Conclusion

If designers and clients carefully attend to and nurture client relationships, they both gain immediate and long-term benefits, such as:

- Diligent relationship management is likely to produce a positive experience for all parties involved in the project at hand, and there is great value in that intangible sense of pleasure and accomplishment. In design firms, for instance, an individual designer's sense of personal satisfaction adds value because a satisfied employee translates to low employee turnover.

- Experiences that not only satisfy but also delight the client engender a sense of loyalty that keeps the client coming back for more. Because it is easier and less costly to develop business with current clients than to find new ones, the designer benefits financially.

- In the ultimate client relationship, a delightful experience—or a series of them—converts the client to an apostle: an uninhibited, credible, no-cost marketer for the designer. In addition, apostles contribute to a firm's long-term viability because they bolster the designer's reputation and attract new customers, not to mention contributing their own continued business.

Even though relationship management may not be the designer's craft, it certainly is an art form worthy of study—and mastery—by designers who are serious about creating a sustained, lucrative business that delivers meaningful results and meets human needs or, better yet, creates human delight.

ENDNOTES

1. James L. Heskett, W. Earl Sasser and Leonard A. Schlesinger, The Service Profit Chain (New York: The Free Press, 1997) 81.

2. Benjamin Schneider and David E. Bowen, "Understanding Customer Delight and Outrage," Sloan Management Review, Fall 1999, 35.

3. James L. Heskett, W. Earl Sasser and Leonard A. Schlesinger, The Service Profit Chain (New York: The Free Press, 1997) 86–87.

4. James L. Heskett, W. Earl Sasser and Leonard A. Schlesinger, The Service Profit Chain (New York: The Free Press, 1997) 84–85.

5. Benjamin Schneider and David E. Bowen, "Understanding Customer Delight and Outrage," Sloan Management Review, Fall 1999, 38.

Contributor Bios

Pamela Anderson-Brulé

PAMELA ANDERSON-BRULÉ is a founder of Anderson Brulé Architects, Inc. Her studies in business management and expertise in facilitating clients through pre-project planning and visioning augment her drive to create buildings that reflect the culture and passion of their inhabitants.

Gina A. Berndt

GINA BERNDT is a principal of Perkins + Will. Gina has a Bachelor of Fine Arts degree in interior design from Northern Illinois University and has studied architecture and urban planning at the University of Copenhagen. She is a member of the American Society of Interior Designers, has received certification by The National Council on Interior Design Qualification, and is a LEED AP.

Thomas Lambert Boeman

TOM BOEMAN, AIA, LEED AP Principal, is a registered architect with over eighteen years of professional experience and has been with Powell/ Kleinschmidt since 1987. As a senior project architect, his primary responsibility is to ensure that the completed project meets established goals and project requirements and manages "P/K Excellence" in implementing standards, policies, and procedures to insure quality throughout all phases of P/K work.

Stuart Cohen

MR. COHEN, AIA, is a partner in the firm of Stuart Cohen & Julie Hacker Architects, specializing in custom residential projects. He was a full professor of architecture at the University of Illinois, Chicago, where he taught architectural design. Mr. Cohen has authored numerous articles on architecture and served as a corresponding editor for *Progressive Architecture* magazine.

Cindy Coleman

Editor CINDY COLEMAN is an associate professor in the department of Architecture, Interior Architecture, and Design Objects at the School of the Art Institute of Chicago and a partner in the design and communication firm Frankel + Coleman. Coleman is a contributing editor for both *Interior Design* magazine and *Chicago Architect* magazine.

Joseph T. Connell

JOE CONNELL is a principal of Perkins + Will. Joe holds a Bachelor of Science degree in interior design from Southern Illinois University. He is a member of the International Interior Design Association, is certified by the National Council on Interior Design Qualification, is a LEED AP, and was elected an ad hoc reviewer for the *Journal of Interior Design*.

Orlando Diaz-Azcuy

Cuban-born ORLANDO DIAZ AZCUY is one of America's most respected and awarded designers for elegant, disciplined, and intelligent work of innovative economy. He was among the first in his profession to be inducted into the industry's prestigious hall of fame, sponsored by *Interior Design* magazine.

Ed Friedrichs

ED FRIEDRICHS, FAIA, FIIDA, joined Gensler in 1969, opened the firm's Los Angeles office in 1976, and was appointed president in 1995, guiding Gensler's transition to a seamless platform for global delivery. Ed formed Friedrichs Group in 2003 to pursue his interest in guiding the development of high-performance organizations and places.

Beth Harmon-Vaughan

BETH HARMON-VAUGHAN, FIIDA, LEED AP, is a recognized Phoenix-based practice leader in the field of design with more than twenty years' experience. Beth is sought by end-users, design professionals, and academics for her synthesis of practice, research, education, and public service. Beth is a principal in the Phoenix office of Gensler, a global architecture, interior design, and planning firm.

Barry B. LePatner, Esq.

BARRY B. LEPATNER, ESQ., is the founder of the New York City-based law firm LePatner & Associates, LLP. For three decades, he has been prominent as an advisor on business and legal issues affecting the real estate, design, and construction industries. He is head of a law firm that has grown to become widely recognized as one of the nation's leading advisors to corporate and institutional clients, real estate owners, and design professionals.

Eva Maddox

EVA MADDOX is a pioneer in the development of brand strategy and communications through design. As founder of Eva Maddox Branded Environments, her research-based design approach identifies and integrates a client's "DNA" into tangible experiences. As principal and leader of the Perkins & Will's Branded Environments group, her solutions focus on alternative learning processes, restorative and green spaces, and the integration of community and cultural interpretations within corporate, education, and healthcare environments.

Derrell Parker, FIIDA

DERRELL PARKER, FIIDA, is partner and interior design studio principal with Parker Scaggiari in Las Vegas, NV. Derrell is a Professional Member of the International Interior Design Association and is a member of the College of Fellows of the Association. He served as the vice president of GRA for IIDA and he is currently serving as International President of IIDA. Derrell was the 2004 national president for the National Council for Interior Design Qualification, NCIDQ.

Lisbeth Quebe, FSMPS

LISBETH QUEBE led the marketing programs of two major international design practices and shared her knowledge through numerous clinics, speeches, books, and articles. She was inducted into the first class of Fellows of the Society of Marketing Professional Services and, in 1995, was awarded SMPS's highest accolade: the National Marketing Achievement Award.

Kathy Rogers

KATHY ROGERS has thirty-three years of experience in the interior design profession. She has worked with The Stubbins Group in Boston, Gensler & Associates in Denver and Salt Lake City, HOK in St. Louis, and Jacobs in St. Louis and Washington, D.C. In addition to serving as project manager for large corporate and government projects, she headed Interiors Groups at HOK and Jacobs Facilities in St. Louis.

Frederick J. Schmidt

FREDERICK SCHMIDT is a principal of Perkins + Will and holds both a Bachelor's and a Master's of Architecture from Kansas State University, where he earned his graduate degree in environment-behavior research. He is a member of the International Interior Design Association, the International Facility Management Association, and the Environmental Design Research Association and is a LEED AP.

Gregory T. Switzer, AIA, NCARB

GREGORY T. SWITZER is the managing principal/chief executive and founder of SWITZER Architecture, founded in 2003. SWITZER Architecture is a full-service architectural practice whose services include architecture, planning, and interior architecture. He received his Bachelor's degree in architecture from Pratt Institute in Brooklyn, New York, and a Bachelor's of Interior Design from Louisiana State University. He was also a research fellow at Cornell University.

Robert T. Sutter, AIA, NCARB

ROBERT SUTTER is an architect with more than twenty-eight years' experience in commercial interior alterations and architectural projects. His New York-based firm, RTSPCPinnacle, specializes in designs for domestic and international projects. Mr. Sutter attended the Cooper Union and Pratt Institute, is licensed in fifteen states, and is a member of the International Code Council (ICC). Over his tenure in the profession, he previously served as president of The Switzer Group, was the American Management Association's interior design course leader, and held various notable design and facility management positions.

Sharon Turner

SHARON TURNER is a principal for workplace consulting and interior design for international design firm Swanke Hayden Connell Architects. She specializes in advising end-user clients, global organizations, and developers on space and workplace strategies to enhance business performance. She joined SHCA in 1995 to develop workplace consulting as an integrated service within the firm, and became a principal in 2001. She has served as an awards chairman for the British Council for Offices and speaks frequently on the international debate about effective space use, workplace effectiveness, and design.

Gary Wheeler

GARY E. WHEELER, FASID, FIIDA, is a renowned professional with more than thirty years' design experience. Wheeler is recognized internationally for his strategic leadership in workplace design and his advocacy for integrated design solutions. In 2004, he joined Gensler as the European director of interior design, and in 2009, he established WHEELER KANIK, a new agency focusing on strategic business objectives specializing in the corporate, financial, media, and educational sectors.

Index

A
Ackerman, James, 29
The Act. *See* Americans with
   Disabilities Act
"Action Office," 8
ADA. *See* Americans with
   Disabilities Act
ADA Accessibility Guidelines for
   Buildings and Facilities
   (ADAAG), 130
ADAAG. *See* ADA Accessibility
   Guidelines for Buildings and
   Facilities
Adam, Robert, 1
Adaptation of "The Service Value
   Chain" (diagram), 220
Affiliated Artists, 1
AGCA, 135, 152, 154
AHJ. *See* Authority Having
   Jurisdiction
AIA. *See* American Institute of
   Architects
AIA Interior Design Accord,
   34–35
AID. *See* American Institute of
   Interior Designers
Albers, Josef, 5
Allen, Davis, 7, 17
American Institute of Architects
   (AIA), 17, 19, 26–27, 60, 65,
   66, 135, 152, 154, 157, 173
   B-101 (2007) form of, 183
   B-171ID of, 184
American Institute of Interior
   Designers (AID), 49, 52
American Society for Healthcare
   Engineering (ASHE), 168,
   173
American Society of Interior
   Designers (ASID), 18, 34, 36,
   38, 48, 49, 52, 53, 59, 66,
   135, 152, 154, 157, 173
Americans with Disabilities Act
   (ADA), 43, 57, 134. *See also*
   architectural barriers
   architectural barriers for, 73–74
   new construction/alterations
   for, 75
   non-compliance penalties for,
   75–76
   overview of, 72–73
   Title III of, 72–75
   Titles I–IV of, 72

Amic, Madame L., 225
*Analysis Of The Interior Design
   Profession*, 42–43, 55
Anderson-Brulé, Pamela, 93–101
architectural barriers
   "readily achievable" factors for,
   73–74
   removal of, 74
Architectural Digest, 14, 169
Architectural Record, 26
Architectural Works Copyright
   Protection Act, 68
architecture, 109, 131
   four traditions of, 29
   interior design v., 17–18,
   26–27, 59–60
   licensing of, 17–18
   process, 94–95
   professional history of, 28–29
   surveyors v., 29
arts and crafts movement, 1–2, 5
asbestos, 70–71
ASHE. *See* American Society for
   Healthcare Engineering
ASID. *See* American Society of
   Interior Designers
ASPA. *See* Association of
   Specialized and Professional
   Accreditors
assembly line, 3–5, 8, 25
Association of Specialized and
   Professional Accreditors
   (ASPA), 49
AT&T, 4
Authority Having Jurisdiction
   (AHJ)
   advance planning for, 130
   building/fire departments as,
   129
   conflicting requirements of,
   130
   levels of alteration for, 131
   occupancy classification for,
   130–131
   permit application for,
   131–132
   permit considerations for, 132
   revenue source of, 130,
   131–132
   special inspectors/inspections
   by, 132–133
automobile insurance, 151

B
Baldwin, Billy, 6
bandwidth, 24–25, 28
   furniture/manufacturing on,
   24–25
   for interior designers, 24–25
Barnard, Chester, 4
Bauhaus (building house), 2,
   5–7
   fascism on, 6
   furniture, 12
   members of, 5–6
Bayer, Herbert, 5
Bell, Alexander Graham, 3
Berndt, Gina A., 217–238
Berra, Yogi, 192
Bertoia, Harry, 9
bidding process. *See also*
   construction documents
   bid evaluation spreadsheets in,
   143–146
   bid opening/compliance in,
   143
   bid set preparation for,
   133–134, 147
   construction documents for,
   133–135
   contract award in, 146
   contractor pre-qualification for,
   135
   RFP preparation in, 135–142,
   147
   walk-through/clarifications for,
   143
BIM (Building Information
   Modeling), 123–124
   advantages of, 125–126
   parametric model of, 125
Boeman, Tom, 117–127
Bowen, David E., 219, 233
Bramante, 29
Brand, Stewart, 25–26
branding, 7, 159
   in market management,
   161–162
   positioning/maintaining, 162
   third-party endorsement, 162
Braungart, Michael, 15
Breuer, Marcel, 5, 6
Brown, Jerry, 18
Brunelleschi, 28
building designers, registered, 19

building ecology, 22
buildings
  construction changes in, 42
  six components of, 25
  time-layered perspective of,
    25–26, 27
business, corporate, 42
  campus, 10
  globalization for, 12–13
  headquarters of, 5
  hierarchy of, 3–5, 9, 12
  Japanese competition for, 12
business development, 158–159,
    185–186, 191, 194. See also
    cold-calling; networking;
    sales presentations
  cold-calling for, 174–175
  lead-finding, 172–173
  market research for, 171–172
  networking for, 173–174
  prospect qualifying for,
    175–176
  qualification packages for,
    176–178
  relationship building for, 176
  sales presentations for, 178

C
CADD (Computer Aided Design
    and Drafting), 123–124, 126
  basic applications of, 124
  object-oriented, 124–125
carpel tunnel syndrome, 13
Carroll, Lewis, 192
CBS headquarters, 10
"Certified Interior Designer"
    (title), 59
Chagall, Marc, 6
Chase Manhattan Bank, 7, 160
CHEA. See Council for Higher
    Education Accreditation
CIDA. See Council for Interior
    Design Accreditation
Civil Rights Act, 1964, Title VII,
    72
client agreements, provisions for,
    66–68
client organization
  conflicts in, 222
  designer's challenges in, 222
  interest groups in, 221–222
client relationship management,
    105, 169–171, 176, 198,
    202–203, 217–238. See also
    client organization;
    client/designer team; meas-
    urement of satisfaction;
    Project Circle
  benefits of, 237–238

client advocacy in, 224
client attributes for ideal, 218
designer, 226–233
  designer's ideal, 219–220
  dissatisfaction with, 219
  ideal, 217–220
  immediate/long-term benefits
    of, 237–238
  measuring method for, 218,
    234–237
  mutual respect in, 220
  total satisfaction for, 199–200,
    206–207, 213–216, 217,
    218–219
client-designer collaboration, for
    cost estimates, 65–66
client/designer team
  appropriate promises with, 231
  avoid/resolve conflicts in, 232
  business-minded, 230
  clients into apostles by,
    232–233
  design team expectations by,
    226
  effective communication
    between, 226
  efficiency for, 229–230
  expert opinions for, 231
  goals/constraints for, 230–231
  human need recognition in,
    233
  listen/response by, 228–229
  one-on-one, 228
  standard communication tools
    for, 226–227
  timely questions for, 228
  understandable terms for, 227
  visual vocabulary for, 229
client-manufacturer collaboration,
    13–14
Codman, Ogden, Jr., 2
Cohen, Stuart, 109–115
Cohen & Hacker Architects,
    111–113
cold-calling
  contact record form for,
    174–175
  target, 174
Coleman, Cindy, 1–16
communications, 158–159, 179
  client/designer, 226–227
  contractor, 148–149
  market, 167–171
  project manager, 202–203,
    211–214
competency, 30–31
Comprehensive Storage System, 9
computer technology, 2, 13,
    110–111, 123–127

confidentiality, 30
conflict of interest, 30
Connell, Joseph T., 217–238
Conran, 189
consonance, 25
construction documents, 114–115
  detail list example for, 133–134
  page-specific notes for,
    134–135
consulting role, 22–23, 85, 91,
    107, 189–190, 207
  accommodations strategies in,
    88
  fees for, 88
  pre-design feasibility studies in,
    88–89
contract administration, 190. See
    also Authority Having
    Jurisdiction (AHJ); bidding
    process; contractor selection
  bidding process of, 133–147
  buildout management in,
    152–154
  contractor selection in,
    147–152
  permit process of, 129–133
  special attention items for,
    154–155
contract documents. See also
    working drawings
  "specifications" in, 117
  working drawings in, 117–127
contractor, licensed, 131, 223
  pre-qualification for, 135
  selection of, 147–152
contractor selection
  communication/customer
    service in, 148–149
  dispute resolution in, 151–152
  experience/viability in, 149
  expertise in, 147–148
  insurance/licensing, 150–151
  lowest price for, 150
  references for, 149–150
  summary of, 152
contractual liability claim, 62–63
Copyright Act, 68
copyright laws, 68–69
  four author rights in, 69
  patent v., 68
  registration for, 69
CoreNet Global, 173
cost estimate liability, 64–66
  client collaboration for, 65–66
  provision for, 65–66
cost estimating firm, 212–213
cost of services, 88, 209–210. See
    also fees
  three categories of, 187

cost-per-square-foot, 190, 192,
206
Council for Higher Education
Accreditation (CHEA), 49
Council for Interior Design
Accreditation (CIDA), 37,
38–39, 47–51
accreditation process of, 49, 51
contact information for, 55
history of, 49–51
Council of Delegates, 41, 52–53
Coxe, Weld, 159–160
The Coxe Group, 159
Crate&Barrel, 189
cross-functional teams, 4, 96

D

The Decoration of Houses
(Wharton, Codman), 2
Dell, 25
Deming, W. Edwards, 12
design, 2, 12
in four dimensions, 25–26
"recognition of need," 8
schematic, 103–107
social/environmental, 15, 57
"technician who cares," 19–20
design development, 109–115.
See also drawings, computer/
freehand; schematic design
architects for, 109
construction drawing phase in,
114–115
drawing to scale/full-size,
113–114
elevation drawings in, 113–114
interior/exterior, 109–110
main spaces models in,
111–112
presenting materials in,
112–113
steps in, 115
working drawings in, 111
design/build, 25
Diaz, Orlando, 103–107
Dictionary (Johnson), 29
document ownership, 66
drawings, computer/freehand,
110–111
Drucker, Peter, 10, 23, 24
Duffy, Frank, 25

E

Eames, Charles, 225
furniture, 8–9
Eames, Ray, furniture, 8–9
earned income, term of, 186
Edison, Thomas, 3
Eiffel Tower, 4

Einstein, Albert, 6
engineering, 21, 28, 131
FP, 88, 91 ·
MEP, 86, 88, 91
Environmental Protection Agency
(EPA), 70
EPA. *See* Environmental
Protection Agency
ergonomics, 4, 13, 21
*Excellence by Design: Transforming
Workplace and Work Practice*
(Horgen, Joroff, Porter,
Schon), 94–95

F

Facilities Design and Management,
169
fees, 201, 209. *See also* cost-per-
square-foot; product mark-
up; rate, hourly
consulting, 88
financial management,
189–192
project initiative, 87
sales, 182–183
Feingold, Ronald B., Esq., 57–77
The Fifth Discipline (Senge), 28
financial management, 185. *See
also* cost of services;
income/expenses tracking;
strategic planning
business plan for, 185–186, 194
compensation structure for,
189–192
cost of services in, 186–187
fixed v. variable expenses in,
187–188
fundamental principles of, 186
income/expenses tracking in,
188–189
strategic planning for, 192–194
Finished Library Shown in
Sketch-1 (Cohen, Hacker),
113
Florida Board of Architecture &
Interior Design, 59–60
Follett, Mary Parker, 4
Ford, Henry, 3, 25
Ford Foundation, 114
Ford Motor Company, 4, 5
Foundation for Interior Design
Education and Research
(FIDER), 49, 50. *See also*
Council for Interior Design
Accreditation (CIDA)
Fowler, John, 6
Frick, Henry Clay, 2
Friedrichs, Edward C., 17–32
furniture, 13–14, 24–25

"Action Office," 8
bandwidth for, 24
Bauhaus, 12
Eames, 8–9, 225
manufacturers research on, 8
"systems," 8
technological/physiological, 13

G

General Electric, 10
general liability insurance, 151
Gensler, Arthur, 9, 17
Gensler, Inc., 9–10, 23, 32
Girard, Alexander, 9
globalization, 23, 192–193
for business, 12–13
for interior design, 13–14
in market management, 160–161
Goodstein, L., 193
Gore, Al, 15
Grant, Margo, 23
Gropius, Walter, 5, 6
gross income, term of, 186
Guggenheim Bilbao, 159

H

Hacker, Julie, 111–113
Hampton, Mark, 14
Harbour, Antony, 22
Harmon-Vaughan, Beth, 47–55
Harvard Business School, 4, 8
Xerox study of, 218–219
Hawthorne experiments. *See*
Western Electric Hawthorne
Works
Hayden Planetarium, 159
health issues, 13, 31, 35, 36, 38,
42–43, 44–45, 59, 118, 130
of "building-related illness,"
69–71
designer liability for, 71–72
of sick-building syndrome,
70–71
Herbert, Terence, 6
Herman Miller, Inc., 8, 9
Hill and Knowlton, 179
Hitchcock, John Russell, 7
Hitler, Adolf, 6
How Buildings Learn (Brand), 25
human relations movement,
4–5, 8
Hawthorne experiments of, 4

I

IBD. *See* Institute of Business
Designers
ICC. *See* International Code
Council
idea-driven firms, 159–160

IDEC. *See* Interior Design
    Educators Council
IDEP. *See* The Interior Design
    Experience Program
IDS Center, 113
IFI. *See* International Federation
    of Interior Architects/
    Interior Designers
IFMA. *See* International Facility
    Management Association
IIT. *See* Illinois Institute of
    Technology
IKEA, 189
Illinois Institute of Technology
    (IIT), 6, 8
income/expenses tracking
    accrual accounting for,
        188–189
    cash accounting for, 188–189
Industrial Revolution, 1, 3
Information Age, 3, 15–16
information economy, 10
    "knowledge worker" of, 25
Institute of British Architects, 29
Institute of Business Designers
    (IBD), 34, 157
insurance, 57–58, 150–151
interdisciplinary teams, 27–28
interior decoration, 2, 60
    celebrity, 6–7
    interior design v., 17–18
    magazines of, 6–7, 14
interior design, 15–16, 110, 199,
    224–225. *See also* client
    relationship management;
    client/designer team
    advocacy for, 36–37
    altruistic mission of, 220
    architecture v., 17–18, 26–27,
        59–60
    bandwidth for, 24–25
    client advocacy by, 224
    client organization for,
        221–222
    client relationship with,
        219–220, 226–233
    coalitions for, 35, 38
    collaboration in, 20, 24–25,
        65–66
    consultants, 189–190
    contract, 6, 9, 11, 186–187,
        190–192
    corporate, 2, 7–11, 17
    diverse experience for, 39–40, 48
    education of, 21–22, 38–39,
        47–51
    ethical issues of, 29–30, 43–44
    examinations for, 40–41,
        47–48, 51–54

    expertise/scale diversification
        for, 191
    globalization issues for, 13, 14
    health issue liability for, 71–72
    health/safety knowledge base
        for, 43–45
    history of, 1–16
    interior decoration v., 17–18
    legal exposure for, 57–58
    legislation history of, 33–35
    licensing of, 17–19, 26–27,
        33–35, 58–61
    multitasking of, 48
    pre-design services in, 85–92
    project team for, 4, 44
    residential, 2, 3, 11–12, 14, 186,
        189
    sealing power for, 37–38, 59
    service confusion of, 11–12
    by SOM, 7, 17
    strategic consulting for, 22–23
    sustainable design for, 31–32
    title/practical acts for, 34–36
    workplace impact by, 22–23
Interior Design, 169
Interior Design Educators
    Council (IDEC), 38, 48, 49,
    52
The Interior Design Experience
    Program (IDEP), 40,
    54–55
Interior Design Model Language,
    37–38
Interior Designers of Canada, 48,
    52, 53
Interiors, 169
International Code Council
    (ICC), 130, 131
    A117.1 guideline of, 130
International Council of
    Shopping Centers, 168
International Facility
    Management Association
    (IFMA), 173
International Federation of
    Interior Architects/Interior
    Designers (IFI), 53
International Interior Design
    Association (IIDA), 18, 36,
    38, 48, 52, 53, 157, 173
International Society of Interior
    Designers (ISID), 34
international style, 7
*The International Style: Architecture
    Since 1922* (Johnson,
    Hitchcock), 7
ISID. *See* International Society
    of Interior Designers
Ivy, Robert, 26

J
Japan, 12
Jefferson, Thomas, 1, 29
Johnson, Philip, 7, 113
Johnson, Samuel, 29
Johnson Wax Company, 6

K
Kandinsky, Wassily, 5
Klee, Paul, 5
Knoll, Florence, 7
Knoll, Hans, 7
Knoll Associates, 7
Knoll International, 9
Knoll Planning Unit, 7, 8

L
"the law of situation," 4
Leadership in Energy and
    Environmental Design
    (LEED), 15, 125–126
LeCorbusier, 114
LEED. *See* Leadership in Energy
    and Environmental Design
legal issues. *See also* Americans
    with Disabilities Act (ADA);
    client agreements; copyright
    laws; liability insurance;
    Request for Proposal (RFP)
    ADA, 72–76
    client agreement, 66–68
    contract negotiation, 76–77
    copyright, 68–69
    designer exposure in, 57–58
    document ownership, 66
    health/safety, 69–72
    liability/contract protection as,
        62–66
    licensing, 58–61
    of proposals, 61–62
legislation issues
    of advocacy, 36–37
    of coalitions, 38
    for current practice, 41–43
    of education, 38–39
    of ethics, 43
    of examinations, 40–41
    of experience, 39–40
    history of, 33–35
    model language for, 37–38
    of practice acts v. title acts,
        35–36
    of regulatory boards, 41
LePatner, Barry B., Esq., 57–77
liability insurance, 57–58
Liberty of London, 1
Library Perspective Sketch
    (Cohen, Hacker), 111
licensing, professional

of architects, 17–18
of interior design, 17–19,
26–27, 33–35, 58–61
legalities for, 58–61
Maister's traits for, 19–20
by NCIDQ, 53–54
political component to, 19
life safety, 30, 33, 35, 36, 38,
44–45, 59, 118, 130, 131
knowledge base for, 43–45
Lockheed Martin Building, 31

M
Maddox, Eva, 79–83
Maister, David, 159–160
professionalism by, 19–20
"technician who cares" by,
19–20
malpractice/professional
negligence, 63
"management by objectives," 10
manufacturing, 189, 223
bandwidth on, 24–25
client collaboration with,
13–14
furniture, 8
research, 14
Marino, Peter, 14
market communications
audiences for, 167–168
brochures/website/exhibits/ad
for, 168–170
client relationships for, 170–171
client trade press/print media
for, 169
projects/curriculum
vitae/teaching for, 169–170
market management, 167–172,
187–188, 191. *See also*
branding; market communi-
cations; market plan
branding for, 161–162
company practice models for,
159–160
connections/visibility in, 157
differentiation message for, 161
idea/service/product values for,
159–160
market plan/budget in,
163–167
resources for, 158
specialization/globalization in,
160–161
strategic planning for, 162–163
three components of, 158–159
market plan
audit in, 164
basic components of, 163–164
budget for, 166, 170

goal setting in, 165
implementation of, 167
outlook development in,
164–165
result measurement for, 167
tools/resources for, 166
Marshall Field, 4
mass customization, 25
mass production, 9
Massachusetts Institute of
Technology, School of
Architecture, 94–95
Mayo, Elton, 4
McClelland, Nancy, 3
McDonough, William, 15
McMillen, Eleanor, 3
McMillen, Inc., 3
McNair, Malcolm P., 8
measurement of satisfaction, 218.
See also process/outcome
measurement system
client-based, 234
POE for, 234
process/outcome, 234–237
Memphis group, 12
Michelangelo, 28
Microsoft Project, 190
MIPIM, 168
Modern Healthcare, 169
Moholy-Nagy, Laszlo, 5
Morris, William, 1
multidisciplinary practice areas,
191
Murray, Chris, 23
Museum of Modern Art, 7

N
NAIOP. *See* National Association
of Industrial and Office
Properties
National Association of Industrial
and Office Properties
(NAIOP), 173
National Council for Interior
Design Qualification
(NCIDQ), 20–21, 34,
37, 38, 40–41, 47–48,
51–54
certification/licensure/record
maintenance by, 53–54
contact information for, 55
history of, 52–53
National Fire Protection
Association (NFPA), 130
National Legislative Coalition of
Interior Design (NLCID),
34
National Society of Interior
Designers (NSID), 49, 52

NCIDQ. *See* National Council
for Interior Design
Qualification
Nelson, George, 9
net income, term of, 186
networking, 158
information from, 173
rules of, 174
New York Times, 169
NFPA. *See* National Fire
Protection Association
NLCID. *See* National Legislative
Coalition of Interior Design
NMB Headquarters, 31
Noguchi, Isamu, 9
Nolan, T., 193
NSID. *See* National Society of
Interior Designers

O
Occupational Safety and Health
Administration (OSHA), 70
open office, 10, 42
organization, learning, 12
organizational behavior, 8
organizations, nature of, 8
OSHA. *See* Occupational Safety
and Health Administration

P
Parish, Sister, 14
Parker, Derrell, 33–45
Pepsi-Cola, 7
Perkins & Will Branded
Environments, 79
Perkins & Will Eva Maddox
Branded Environments
Design Process Project
Phases. *See* Scope of Service
Matrix
permit processor, 131
Permitting Statute for Interior
Design, 34
Pfeiffer, J.W., 193
POE. *See* Post-Occupancy
Evaluation
Post-Occupancy Evaluation
(POE), 234
pre-design services, 190. *See also*
consulting role; project
initiation phase; strategic
facilities planning
consultants for, 91
objectives/measures for, 89
real estate professional in,
90–91
strategy development process
of, 89–90
three ways of, 85

pre-lease service. *See* strategic
facilities planning
Probst, Robert, 8
"process architecture," 94–95
facilitation methods in, 95
process/outcome measurement
system
behavioral outcome measures
in, 236
benefits of, 237
guidelines for, 237
implementing, 236–237
physical outcome measures in,
236
process delivery measures in,
235
process experience measures in,
235
product driven firms, 160
product mark-up, 189, 192
profit, term of, 186
programming, 93–101, 103–105,
190. *See also* systems analysis
for change, 93
cultural development in, 97–98
process design/development in,
94–95
reconciliation for, 101
space program elements in,
98–100
systems analysis for, 95–97
tools for, 100–101
traditional, 94–95
Project Circle, 220–226. *See also*
client organization
accountability for, 223–224
designer detail probing in, 225
designer information
management in, 225
designer reporting in, 224–225
inside client, 221–222
outside client, 222–223
project initiation phase, 85–87
checklist for, 86
fees for, 87
space program in, 86
project management. *See also*
project manager
client objectives for, 198
design firm objectives for, 199
financially successful, 201
fulfilled design team for,
200–201
happy client for, 199–200, 206,
207, 213–216
interrelated responsibilities of,
195–216
manager for, 197–198, 202–205
process of, 197

team of, 196–197, 205,
207–208
project manager, 197–198,
222–223. *See also* work plan
change managed by, 215–216
client communication/
understanding by, 202–203,
213–214
communication/documentation
protocols by, 211–212
eight responsibilities of, 202
project budgets by, 212–213
project goals documented by,
203–204
project procedures manual/files
for, 210
success for, 216
team leading by, 214–215
work plan by, 204–205
"project-based" practice, 190

Q
"quality circles," 12
Quebe, Lisbeth, 157–184

R
rate, hourly, 189–190, 192, 206–207
relational database, 100
"relationship"-based practice, 190
Request for Proposal (RFP), 145,
176, 191, 205
for bid process, 135–142, 147
examples of, 137–142
legal ramifications of, 61–62
preparation elements for,
135–136
rules for submitting, 62
Request for Qualifications
(RFQ), 191
qualification statement for,
176–177
"Supplemental Information"
section for, 177–178
Request of Information (RFI),
176
RFI. *See* Request of Information
RFP. *See* Request for Proposal
RFQ. *See* Request for
Qualifications
Robsjohn-Gibbings, 6
Roche, Kevin, 114
Rocky Mountain Institute, 31, 32
Roethlisberger, Fritz, 4
Rogers, Kathy, 195–216

S
Saarinen, Eliel, 7, 9
sales presentations, 205. *See also*
sales proposal agreement

audience understanding for,
178
delivery of, 180–182
media/tools for, 179
preparation for, 178–179
rehearsals for, 179
three part proposals of,
182–184
two objectives of, 178
sales proposal agreement
formalization of, 183–184
negotiation in, 183
professional fees in, 182–183
scope of services in, 182
sales/marketing, cost of, 191
San José Martin Luther King Jr.
Library, 95
Sangallo, Antonio, the Younger,
29
scheduling liability
language for, 63–64
precautions for, 64
schematic design
aesthetics/functionality in,
106–107
client identity in, 105
conflict resolution in, 105
consultants for, 107
creativity in, 104, 107
economic/time for, 106
programming for, 104–105
from single mind, 103–104
space quantity/distribution in,
105–106
visual presentation of, 104
Schmidt, Frederick J., 217–238
Schneider, Benjamin, 219, 233
Schoenberg, Arnold, 6
scientific management, 3, 23
criticism of, 4–5
Scope of Service Matrix, 80–83
scope of services, designer's, 182
Perkins & Will Branded
Environments, 79–83
Seagram Building, 10
Senge, Peter, 28
"The Service Profit Chain"
(diagram), 219
The Service Profit Chain
(Schneider, Bowen),
218–219
service-driven firms, 160
settings, 21, 27
changes in, 25, 32
cultural impact on, 22
virtual, 24–25
Simon, Herbert A., 8
single overriding communications
objective (SOCO), 179

Skidmore, Owings & Merrill
(SOM), 7, 17
SMPS. *See* Society of Marketing
Professional Services
Society of Marketing Professional
Services (SMPS), 157
SOCO. *See* single overriding
communications objective
SOM. *See* Skidmore, Owings &
Merrill
Space and Organization Research
Group (SPORG), 94
space-planning services, 9–11
speculative office building, 10–11,
13
SPORG. *See* Space and
Organization Research
Group
The Steelcase Corporate
Development Center, 8
Stickley, Gustav, 1
strategic consulting, 22–23
strategic facilities planning, 85
stand alone commission for,
88
typical building appraisal
checklist for, 87
strategic planning, 185
alternatives/scenario planning
for, 193
goals/objectives for, 194
for market management,
162–163
performance indicators for, 194
strategies decisions in, 194
SWOT for, 193
surveyors, architects v., 29
sustainability, 25
interior design with, 31–32
Sutter, Robert, 129–155
Switzer, Gregory T., 129–155
SWOT Analysis (Strengths,
Weaknesses, Opportunities,
and Threats)
goals/objectives in, 193
internal/external analysis in,
193
systems analysis, 5, 8
cross-functional teams for, 4, 96
external factors/drivers for, 97
logistical issues for, 97
work-flow analysis/live-flow
analysis for, 96

T
Taylor, Frederick W., 3, 4, 15, 23
technological innovation, 24
technology, 22
Third Reich, 6
Through The Looking-Glass
(Carroll), 192
Tiffany, 1
Tile Layout for New Arts &
Crafts Fireplace (Cohen,
Hacker), 112
time, tracking of, 186–187, 190
time-layered perspective, 27
on buildings, 25–26
"total quality management"
(TQM), 12
TQM. *See* "total quality
management"
Turner, Sharon, 85–92
Twelve Standards of Excellence
for the Interior Design
Profession, 38–39

U
ULI. *See* Urban Land Institute
Union Carbide, 7
United States Green Building
Council, U.S. (USGBC), 15,
193
United States v. Ellerbe Becket,
Inc., 76
Urban Land Institute (ULI), 168,
173
user advocacy, 30
USGBC. *See* Green Building
Council, U.S.

V
van der Rohe, Mies, 5–9, 12, 114
Vitruvius, 28
Voysey, Charles, 1

W
Walmart, 160
Wanamaker's Inc., 3
Webster's Dictionary, 20
Webster's New World Dictionary,
185
West Bend Mutual Insurance
Headquarters, 31
Western Electric Hawthorne
Works, 4
Wharton, Edith, 2

Wheeler, Gary, 185–194
White, Stanford, 3
Wiener Werkstratte, 2, 5
de Wolfe, Elsie, 2, 41–42
work plan
administrative procedures for,
210
client/consultants contracts in,
207
design team for, 207–208
internal project budget for,
209–210
monitoring, 204
schedule for, 208–209
scope of work for, 205–206
tasks/activities/deliverables in,
206–207
underdeveloped/
overdeveloped, 204–205
working drawings, 111. *See also*
BIM (Building Information
Modeling); CADD
(Computer Aided Design
and Drafting)
code/regulation conformance
in, 118
computer applications for,
123–127
design intent communicated
by, 118
efficiency/cost-effectiveness in,
123
essential content in, 118–119
organizational uniformity in,
127
PDF files for, 126
qualities of, 121–123
software considerations for,
126–127
staff production of, 127
structure of, 119
workman's compensation
insurance, 151
workplace, 3–4
changes in, 22–23
consonance in, 25
designers impact on, 22–23
locus/mode of, 23
social dislocation for, 13
Wright, Frank Lloyd, 1, 6

X
Xerox, 218–219

Books from Allworth Press

Allworth Press is an imprint of Allworth Communications, Inc. Selected titles are listed below.

Marketing Interior Design
by Lloyd Princeton (6 × 9, 224 pages, paperback, $24.95)

Starting Your Career as an Interior Designer
by Robert K. Hale and Thomas L. Williams (6 × 9, 240 pages, paperback, $24.95)

Interior Design Clients: The Designer's Guide to Building and Keeping a Great Clientele
by Thomas L. Williams (6 × 9, 256 pages, paperback, $24.95)

Challenges of Interior Design: Professional Values and Opportunities
by Mary V. Knackstedt (6 × 9, 272 pages, paperback, $24.95)

How to Start and Operate Your Own Design Firm: A Guide for Interior Designers and Architects
by Albert W. Rubeling (6 × 9, 256 pages, paperback, $24.95)

The Interior Designer's Guide to Pricing, Estimating, and Budgeting
by Theo Stephan Williams (6 × 9, 240 pages, paperback, $19.95)

Business and Legal Forms for Interior Designers
by Tad Crawford and Eva Doman Bruck (8½ × 11, 208 pages, paperback, $29.95)

Design Thinking: Integrating Innovation, Customer Experience, and Brand Value
edited by Thomas Lockwood (6 × 9, 304 pages, paperback, $24.95)

Building Design Strategy: Using Design to Achieve Key Business Objectives
by Thomas Lockwood and Thomas Walton (6 × 9, 256 pages, paperback, $24.95)

The Graphic Design Business Book
by Tad Crawford (6 × 9, 256 pages, paperback, $24.95)

The Graphic Designer's Guide to Clients: How to Make Clients Happy and Do Great Work
by Ellen Shapiro (6 × 9, 256 pages, paperback, $19.95)

Creating the Perfect Design Brief: How to Manage Design for Strategic Advantage
by Peter L. Phillips (6 × 9, 224 pages, paperback, $19.95)

Designers Don't Read
by Austin Howe (5½ × 8½, 224 pages, paperback, $24.95)

Designing Logos: The Process of Creating Logos That Endure
by Jack Gernsheimer (8½ × 10, 224 pages, paperback, $35.00)

To request a free catalog or order books by credit card, call 1-800-491-2808. To see our complete catalog on the World Wide Web, or to order online, please visit ***www.allworth.com***.